FROM THE
TRACK

Other books by Barry and Alan Wood

Off the Track

At the Track

FROM THE TRACK

MORE RACING STORIES
INCLUDING SCAMS, SCANDALS, RING-INS AND ROGUES

BARRY & ALAN WOOD

The Five Mile Press

The Five Mile Press Pty Ltd
1 Centre Road, Scoresby
Victoria 3179 Australia
www.fivemile.com.au

Part of the Bonnier Publishing Group
www.bonnierpublishing.com

First published 2014

Printed in Australia at Griffin Press.
Only wood grown from sustainable regrowth forests is used in
the manufacture of paper found in this book.

Page design and typesetting by Shaun Jury
Typeset in Newzald 11.5/15
Cover design by Luke Causby
Cover illustrations: iStock
Cartoons by Brian Doyle

National Library of Australia Cataloguing-in-Publication entry
    Wood, Barry, author.
    From the track : more racing stories including scams, scandals
    ring-ins and rogues / Barry and Alan Wood.
    9781760060718 (paperback)
    Horse racing–Anecdotes.
    Race horses–Anecdotes.
    Horse trainers–Anecdotes.
    Wood, Alan, author.
    798.4

To Darren Wood (20.10.1968–3.10.2008)
He would have added so much to the landscape and love of
our lives if he were with us to share all of this today.
The authors will donate a percentage from the sales
of this book to **beyondblue.**

HONOURABLE MENTION
To our wives, Sandra and Beth, and our children and
grandchildren, for without whom we would never enjoy
the warmth that we call 'home'.

FOREWORD

Although my knowledge of the turf is miniscule, Barry and I share a 30-year track history. We ran parallel courses in the graphic arts, Barry in his screen-printing business, me cartooning commercially for our many clients. We've slogged down some very heavy tracks together, making our occasional wins all the more enjoyable when cracking open the bubbly or, in our case, flipping the tops off a few coldies!

It's surprising then, that we've never found time to combine what skills we have on a project of our own … the pressures of business I guess. So, when Barry and Alan's mate casually suggested that they put their incredible collection of fascinating facts into books, I jumped at the chance to illustrate them.

But even more importantly than that, it gave the three of us a priceless opportunity to dedicate the books to the memory of Barry and Sandra's son Darren, he of the mile-wide grin and wit, who could defuse the tension and put his finger on the cause of any technical problem in seconds with a joke.

Perhaps in another 30 years Barry and Alan's three books of racing stories and trivia will be appreciated for what they are, extremely valuable reference material on the other side of racing, the FUN side.

As Darren would have said, "Supaaaaaah!"

Brian Doyle

CONTENTS

INTRODUCTION

There are many ways of describing what has happened to us since August 2009, but really we would need too many words to sum up what we have been involved in. It is all about working outside of your comfort zone and being willing, no matter what age, to accept truthfully that old dogs can in fact be taught new tricks.

We have learnt that one single detour may turn out to take you to a place never before experienced – and sometimes never expected. We liken our journey to climbing a tree: as you choose a different branch to explore, the possibilities and opportunities that are presented seem endless.

We started to climb our tree back in 2009, and it has been a revelation to us to experience the new growth and to follow the different branches that have educated us in roles in which we were never trained. We are not authors, not serious storytellers, but maybe we have found that niche where the reader enjoys simple and unabashed nostalgia. It may be that some of the stories we have told resonate in the minds of those readers who can remember some of the players and those readers who at some stage have become emotionally involved in these tales.

Yes, it was our dear mate Rolf Westin who uttered those words, 'Gee, Baz, you should write a book.' It was because of Rolf's comment that Barry and I made the journey, sometimes out of step, sometimes stumbling, but always having the support of the other to steady the ship and steer it in the right direction. That direction took us to the islands of *Off the Track* and *At the Track,* and lo and behold, we now enjoy another stopover, on the island called *From the Track.*

So here we stand in the wheelhouse of the good ship *Opportunity* and we look back at some lessons learnt. We have learnt to really listen to advice, heed what the experts say and, most importantly, never take anything for granted.

Our families have been our rocks and our greatest supporters; those who have been there understand that it takes a unit of people to create an environment where a writer can selfishly indulge in what he enjoys. We have always had great support from those in our homes and our hearts.

We are forever indebted to the professional and personal team at the Five Mile Press, who have been very important members of the crew on our journey over the last five years.

We liken our three books to a horse race: *Off the Track* – off to a great start; *At the Track* – steady in running; and *From the Track* – home with a brilliant finish.

Oh, and just one other thing. Towards the end of 2013, we were sitting back, reflecting on our achievements over the last few years, when we had a light bulb moment, another bright idea.

Because Her Majesty Queen Elizabeth II has such a love for the thoroughbred – whether it be racing them or breeding them – we thought, 'Why don't we send Her Majesty copies of our first two books, *Off the Track* and *At the Track*?'

It seemed a bit audacious but we followed protocol and we received an email back from the Governor-General's office giving us the green light. It was all systems go. The books were posted and, towards the end of December 2013, much to our surprise, we received a letter from Lady Elton, the Queen's Lady-in-Waiting, on behalf of the Queen. The letter stated that Her Majesty was very touched to receive the books, and she was also interested to learn of our contributions to **beyondblue**, which we make through the sales of our books.

This was the icing on our cake, and, yes, Her Majesty will also be receiving a copy of *From the Track* later this year.

Alan and Barry Wood

Federico Tesio

'The Wizard of Dormello'

Federico Tesio (1869–1954) is considered to be the most successful breeder in the history of thoroughbred racing. His beloved Dormello Stud lies on the banks of Lake Maggiore in Northern Italy.

'A horse gallops with his lungs,
perseveres with his heart
and wins with his character.'

CHAPTER 1

Australia
and Its Neighbours

Who's that new jockey bloke?
... gee, he looks familiar

One of Australia's most famous characters in the 1920s and 1930s was the legendary punter Bob 'The Baron' Skelton. *The Sydney Morning Herald* named him as 'one of the greatest and gamest punters the world has seen'. Just like fellow legendary punters Eric Connolly and Rupert 'Rufe' Naylor, Skelton was always on the lookout for an edge to beat the bookies – any way that was legal, of course.

One day at the old Kensington pony racecourse in Sydney, Bob came up with an ingenious plan to once again relieve the bookies of their money. He had a horse entered in a race that was to be ridden by a jockey by the name of John Nugent, a name unfamiliar to course patrons.

When betting on the race began, the horse opened at quite lengthy odds – and with that, the Baron let loose. By the time he left the bookies' ring, the horse had shortened into favouritism. If it were to win, Bob would win a fortune and the bookies would be left 'holding the bag', so to speak.

The horse, with Nugent on board, won brilliantly. However, it was soon discovered that the jockey bore a remarkable resemblance to one of the top riders of the day, Mick Hayes.

All hell broke loose and the bookies were in an uproar. They demanded that the stewards open an inquiry immediately. They did so, and they invited both 'Nugent' and Skelton back to the Stewards Room for a 'please explain'.

Once everyone was seated, jockey John Nugent produced an official document stating that the day before the race, he had legally changed his name by deed poll from Mick Hayes to John Nugent.

It was all legal, and it left the stewards with only one option: 'Weight's right. All clear!'

For a small fee, John Nugent changed his name back to Mick Hayes the following week. Yes, it was just another trick up the sleeve of Bob 'The Baron' Skelton.

In the sporting pages of the *Sydney Morning Herald* on 1 October 1978, journalist Bert Lillye described Bob Skelton as a 'very colourful character'. He recounted that during a strike in Sydney, 'The Baron' had almost staged an entire race meeting with his own horses at the old pony track in Kensington.

Gotta keep the punters happy!

If it wasn't serious, it would have been hilarious

... you have got to be pulling my leg

The 1961 AJC Derby will go down in history as the 'winning' trainer described it: 'the best piece of riding you will ever see.' However, this legendary day also involved the infamous 'jockey leg pull' that gave jockey Mel Schumacher a life disqualification. Yes, this was the day that put Australian racing on the world map – but not for the right reasons.

In the early spring of 1961, Victorian trainer Geoff Murphy engaged leading Sydney rider Mel 'The Shoe' Schumacher to ride the Melbourne colt Blue Era in the AJC Derby in Sydney. (The Derby was held in the spring up until 1977, before being moved to the autumn.) At 24 years old, Schumacher was the golden boy of racing. He had already won a Melbourne Cup, AJC Derby, Epsom Handicap, Australian Cup and Golden Slipper.

The race got under way. Rounding the turn, Blue Era could be seen weaving his way through the field. Over the rise, he moved up on the rails, on the inside of Summer Fair, ridden by Tommy Hill. Both jockeys threw everything at their mounts, and at the finish of their torrid 12-furlong (2400-metre) journey, Blue Era had prevailed by a short half-head from Summer Fair, with King Brian in third place.

Back in the enclosure, Schumacher waved his whip to the cheering crowd of 80,000, but it wasn't long before the jubilation ceased. History was about to be made.

'Protest! Hold all tickets!' Summer Fair's rider, Tommy Hill, had fired in a protest.

When Schumacher was queried by trainer Murphy about the protest, he said, 'No worries, mate. We won't lose it.' However, there was something that he and many of the other jockeys had forgotten about – or maybe they'd not been paying attention when it was announced. Today was the first day a head-on camera was in use at Randwick.

When Hill made the allegation that Schumacher grabbed his right leg just before the finishing line, all Schumacher could say was, 'That's preposterous!' Blue Era had been trained in Melbourne, and this was the first time he had raced clockwise, in the 'reverse' direction. The horse had been on the rails, and Schumacher had switched his whip to his left hand to stop the colt from boring out on Summer Fair.

When questioned by Chief Steward Jack Burke, Hill repeated the claim: 'Oh, he grabbed my leg, Mr Burke.' The stewards were puzzled by Hill's allegation and wondered how Schumacher could have grabbed Hill's right leg while using his whip in his left hand.

It was time for the stewards to run the head-on footage of the race. The film showed that Schumacher had slipped his whip and reins together in his right hand, his left hand darting out and grabbing Hill's leg without missing a beat!

The race was taken off Blue Era, and the stewards invited trainer Geoff Murphy to view the film. Outside, Murphy told journalists, 'We had to lose it. Pity it had to be my horse.'

Schumacher said, 'I couldn't believe it. I couldn't believe they had a camera. You see bike riders do it ... it just happened to be on film and I got caught. What can't speak can't lie.'

Mel 'The Shoe' Schumacher was disqualified for life. The disqualification was later reduced to ten years, and on appeal he served only five-and-a-half years.

What Schumacher did on 30 September 1961 had no doubt been tried many times in the years before what came to be known as 'B.C.' – Before the Camera. Schumacher just happened to be the first jockey to be caught.

In 1967, 'The Shoe' returned to the saddle. In his first race since the disqualification in 1961, he rode a winner for Tommy Smith. At least he wasn't pulling the horse!

A 'ripping' yarn!
... you don't dob on your mates

On 16 October 1941, Hall Stand, ridden by 'Demon' Darby Munro and trained by Bayly Payten, was narrowly beaten by Bangster, ridden by the young jockey Frank 'Paddy' Delaney and trained by Bill Paul.

There had been a huge betting plunge on Munro's mount, Hall Stand. During the race, about six strides before the finishing line, Bangster surged past Hall Stand. That's when Munro didn't hesitate, and reached out and grabbed Delaney to hold him back.

Bangster held on to win. But unknown to both Delaney and Munro, the 'arse' had been ripped out of Delaney's breeches. In those days, stewards didn't have race footage to refer to as they do today, and jockeys never spilled the beans on each other.

Many years later, Frank Delaney recalled the incident and said, 'It was a helluva shock. I was trying to whack his hand, and then my silks tore. The trouble was they belonged to Newcastle trainer Roy Hinton. Believe me, he was not happy.

'Well, Darby fired in a protest as there was only a nose between us, and while in the mounting yard, he noticed the tear in my silks. You should have seen his bloody face – as white as a ghost.'

The protest was dismissed, and Paddy recalled later, 'I didn't give him up; you just did not "dob" in other jockeys in those days – you got square later.' As you would!

Putting the bite into Flight
... Katanga just loved to hate her

We humans for the most part can manage our feelings in the worst of times, but it's also true that we sometimes react with anger or mistrust when certain individuals enter our lives. There are those who just grate on one's person, and we suppose animals feel no differently. For example, when you take your dog for a walk around the streets, there is always that fence where you have to stop so that two barking canines can exchange some spittle and hate with each other. You would swear blind that if your dog could, it would pick off a fence paling and beat the other dog senseless. It is just that simple.

Well, thoroughbred horses are apparently no different. There are some horses that act as the intimidator, and there are some that are singled out and become the victim of intimidation every time they cross paths with the intimidator. Our champion mare Flight is one such example of a horse that was singled out. Before we expose her stalker, let us first take a look at her impeccable record.

Flight was a brown filly born in 1940 at Merridong Stud, New South Wales. She was sired by Royal Step, who was by the great sire Heroic, out of the mare Lambent, bred in New Zealand. During the post-war period, Flight was considered to be one of our greatest mares. She was the highest stakes winner of her time.

The record books show that Flight beat such champions of her time as Bernborough, Shannon and Russia. She raced at the elite level in Australia for five seasons, having 65 starts for 24 wins, 19 seconds and 9 thirds. The mantelpiece of her owner was cluttered with trophies; the most notable were those awarded to her upon winning the WS Cox Plate in successive years, in 1945 and 1946. She also won the LKS Mackinnon Stakes in 1946.

Flight was inducted into the Australian Racing Hall of Fame in 2007, and she has the Group 1 Flight Stakes, run at Randwick Racecourse, named in her honour.

Enter one very cranky stallion, Katanga, a horse that just loved to hate her.

Katanga was an entire that was racing at the same time, although he was not as successful as Flight – and maybe that was his problem.

Generally, his connections thought he was bad and mad, a bit of a 'fruit loop' and unsafe to be around without the proper gear.

Flight showed a real tenacity when racing and no other horse could intimidate her, but Katanga thought he would give it a try on a number of occasions. They were trained in the same area – Flight by Frank Nowland and cranky Katanga by Bayly Payten – so it was inevitable that their paths would cross going to the track or doing track work in the morning, if not in a proper race.

Connections of Katanga said, 'He was always on the lookout for her, no other horse, and you could see him straining his neck to see if she was in the area; if she was nearby, he would try and get to her.'

Punters would flock to the track on a Saturday if they saw that the mighty mare Flight was going to run against 'Cranky Frankie'. They knew that from the time he was on the track, he would be looking for Flight and trying to get close enough to take a bite. Even behind the barriers, the blokes loading Katanga had a hell of a time, as he just wanted to be loaded in the barrier next to Flight so he could do what he wanted to do to her – have a chomp.

Some jockeys said that Katanga was a strong finisher and if he took his mind off chasing and savaging Flight in flight, then he may have beaten her a few more times than he did. As the record stood when both retired, Flight had raced against Katanga a total of eight times, with Flight winning five races and Katanga winning three.

Jack Thompson, who rode Flight on 22 occasions, has the last word:

> Flight was a horse that Katanga couldn't intimidate. If he got close to her he would bare his teeth and flick his tail and turn to look at her and all he wanted to do was bite her, and it wasn't a love bite – it was just hate at first sight.

She was obviously a flight of fancy.

There must be a mistake!
... where is the horse that ran third?

Run over 14 furlongs (2800 metres) at Randwick Racecourse, the 1958 AJC St Leger looked as though it was going to be a two-horse race. The hot favourite was the champion Tulloch, rated at the time as one of the world's greatest three-year-olds.

The only horse given any chance of even remotely giving Tulloch a run for his money was the 1957 Melbourne Cup runner-up, Prince Darius. In their two previous clashes in Melbourne prior to the Sydney Autumn Carnival, Prince Darius had defeated Tulloch in the St George Stakes, over 9 furlongs (1800 metres) at Caulfield, and then finished a nose in front of Tulloch when both horses were defeated by the older Sailor's Guide in the VRC Queen Elizabeth Stakes, over 12 furlongs (2400 metres) at Flemington.

So with that history in mind, both three-year-olds made their way to Sydney for the 'Clash of the Carnival'. Would Prince Darius be able to steal the favourite's moment of glory, in front of a mammoth Sydney crowd?

As the much-anticipated race got underway, no-one could tell what the final result would be: Prince Darius in first place or Tulloch for the win? However, as they entered the final turn into the straight, it became quite apparent that this was a one-horse race.

Tulloch defeated Prince Darius by 20 lengths. And how far behind Prince Darius was the third horse, Pin High? An incredible 1 furlong (200 metres) – believe it or not.

Incredible!

Two days we won't forget
... two track tragedies in 2013

What should have been a great day for the Darwin Turf Club – celebrating the running of the fifty-seventh Darwin Cup – turned into a day that the whole of the racing fraternity of Australia will never forget.

Simone Montgomerie had just been crowned the Northern Territory 2012–13 premiership season's leading rider, with 27 wins, but sadly, on 5 August 2013, she lost her life doing what she loved most, riding in a horse race. The 26-year-old mother of two was riding Riahgrand in race 6, the Wolf Blass Lightning Plate, when she fell and was trampled. She never regained consciousness. The final two races, including the Darwin Cup, were abandoned.

Simone was the daughter of Peter Montgomerie, trainer of On A Jeune, the runner-up to Makybe Diva in the 2005 Melbourne Cup.

Melbourne-Cup-winning jockey Kerrin McAvoy was shattered by Montgomerie's death and said, 'I've never felt so sad and down leaving a racecourse. I knew Simone so well; we did pony clubs together when we were kids.'

Glen Boss, Makybe Diva's triple Melbourne-Cup-winning rider, summed it up best when he said, 'Every single time we go out there and ride in races, we risk our lives. It is the most dangerous land-based job in the world.'

The following day, on Tuesday 6 August, the Darwin Turf Club officially abandoned the 2013 Darwin Cup. The $200,000 prize money was donated to the new Montgomerie Fund, set up by Westpac.

Unfortunately, within a few months, we had another racing tragedy. On 9 November, popular Gympie jockey 45-year-old Desiree Gill, riding Celtic Ambition at Corbauld Park, in Caloundra, Queensland, suffered severe head injuries when both horse and rider crashed to the turf. She never regained consciousness and passed away the following day.

At her funeral service, jockeys Chris Munce, Larry Cassidy, Jim Byrne, Michael Cahill and Damien Browne were among those who formed a guard of honour.

Former top jockey and now Sky Racing commentator Bernadette Cooper marvelled at Desiree's tenacity: 'She had some terrible injuries during her riding career, but kept coming back. She just loved it.'

On Melbourne Cup Day 2012, Desiree had one of her best 'winningest' days, when she rode home four winners and a third at Bundaberg. She also won the 2012–13 Gympie Premiership, riding 27 winners.

Desiree Gill is survived by her trainer husband, Barry Gill, and two sons, Peter and Ryan.

Vale Simone Montgomerie and Desiree Gill.

Archer, winner of the 1861 Melbourne Cup

… never let the truth get in the way of a good story!

Melbourne Cup folklore says that, in 1861, Archer was walked 500 miles (800 km) from Nowra, New South Wales, to Flemington, Victoria, to take part in the first Melbourne Cup. Typical of the New South Wales and Victorian rivalry, he was given a 6/1 chance and took his place in the field behind the 3/1 favourite from Victoria, Mormon, who he eventually defeated by six lengths.

The story has been told and retold – the legend of the horse that walked to Melbourne and beat the best they had to offer, winning the Melbourne Cup and delivering large sums of winning bets into the coffers of his New South Wales connections.

In reality, historical documents relating to the cargo carried aboard the steamship SS *City of Sydney* clearly show that Archer travelled with two of his stablemates, leaving Sydney sometime in September 1861. He never walked to Melbourne from Nowra at all. In 1862, he travelled again by boat back to Melbourne to contest his second Melbourne Cup, in which he duly decimated the field again, beating the luckless Melbourne favourite, Mormon, this time by around eight lengths. His victory in 1861 was in a field of seventeen starters and his second victory in 1862 was in a field of 20 starters.

There you go. It is less about the truth than a good story.

The Great Bookie Robbery of 2013

… they missed it by that much!

'Okay, here they come, put your balaclavas on and remember, I don't want any shots fired. Just grab the money and get out. Ready … NOW!

'What the bloody hell – where's the f***ing money?'

On Saturday 20 July 2013, leading Sydney bookmaker Grant Palmer was with his two brothers and a mate at his residence in Paddington when they were confronted, at gunpoint, by five men wearing balaclavas. They were told to hand over the two bookie bags – supposedly full of cash – and then the masked men took off. But all the home invaders got were a couple of laptop computers. It was definitely not what they expected.

It seems that the robbery of Grant Palmer had been planned for quite some time; it was seemingly well thought out, even to the point that the position where the perpetrators hid was in a black spot that could not be picked up by Palmer's home security system.

Lying in wait to rob the bookies had been a complete waste of time. Most bookies do not take cash home, and their biggest clients are credit clients, who do their settling during the week. These days, cash is left with security personnel at the racetrack.

Yes, they were five 'sophisticated' armed robbers, probably majoring in stuff-ups, who forgot to do their homework. One wonders what princely sum they got for the two laptops.

Okay, boys, next time do your homework!

The underbelly of the racing game
… the stakes are too high for most!

A very unfortunate aspect of our much-loved racing industry is the fact that at times a person can lose the shirt off their back, if they are indeed that way inclined. On the other hand, there are riches for all to strive for, and it's a quest to try to find that 'good one' to back. For some people, regrettably, gambling on horse racing is nothing more than a perverse opportunity to gain something for nothing and to hell with the consequences.

Sometime before midnight on 2 April 1984, a car was torched near Bulli, on the southern coast of New South Wales. Police discovered the burnt remains of horse trainer George Brown. He had also been severely beaten up. Brown was an average horse trainer, trying to make ends meet. He was never going to be known for his training exploits or for a stable of champions; most people would say that he was simply a kind and pleasant bloke who should not have had his life ended in such a shocking way.

The subsequent investigation revealed that on 31 March at Doomben Racecourse in Brisbane, Brown had a filly running by the name of Resley. An ordinary performer, she was heavily backed but ran unplaced. It is believed that George Brown's brutal murder was due to him running the real Resley, and not following instructions to replace her with a better-performing ring-in. It is alleged that the good horse did not run for the bad one because George got cold feet when it came time to swap the horses.

It is fair to speculate that the organisers of this scheme laid their bets on Resley at the appropriate price. When the ring-in did not greet the judge and the ordinary performer ran as her form would suggest, all bets were lost. George Brown obviously ticked off the wrong person.

Brown's murder explains why some of the conspirators in the next big racing scam, the Fine Cotton case, persisted with their scheme even when things started to go wrong and discovery was imminent. As far as the trainer of Fine Cotton, Hayden Haitana, was concerned, persevering with the scheme was certainly justified; after all, he enjoyed fresh air and did not like the confines of what could be a very hot boot of a car.

Haitana said that he was simply told that if he didn't go through with the scam, he would end up just like George Brown. He was quoted in a daily newspaper as saying: 'It is terrible to think that there are some people who are in the midst of these plans, carrying guns and the like around the stables that have been targeted.'

Five months after George Brown's death, on 18 August 1984, at Brisbane's Eagle Farm Racecourse, a horse listed as Fine Cotton very narrowly won a minor race. Fine Cotton's form was very ordinary, and it had deserved its price of 33/1. However, when Bold Personality was 'colour-shampooed' and painted to look like Fine Cotton and then substituted for the lesser horse, the well-credentialed performer went on to win – albeit by the narrowest of margins. The new look Fine Cotton was backed in from 33/1 to 7/2.

This is a story that will probably have no real resolution, but the bold scam began crashing down that day as the jockey led Fine Cotton back to the winner's enclosure. One disgruntled punter couldn't believe his eyes and began to yell out, 'Ring-in! Ring-in!' Pretty soon that call was being echoed by all and sundry in attendance. The conspirators knew the game was up, and they scampered.

The ring-in: it's an unfortunate aspect of our racing history.

Great Melbourne Cup moments
... the triumphs and the tragedy
The triumphs

Carbine – This son of Musket was bred in New Zealand, but after winning his first five races he was purchased by Australian interests. His influence as a racehorse and then as a stallion would put Australia on the world map of thoroughbred racing. Carbine's victory in the 1890 Melbourne Cup saw him lug 10 stone 6 lb (66 kg) to victory, a weight-carrying record that he still holds today. He defeated 39 runners, a record field for the event at that time.

In 1890, the purse of £10,000 made the Cup one of the world's richest races. Carbine had run second in the 1889 Cup despite carrying 10 stone (63.5 kg) and having a split hoof, an injury that continually plagued him throughout his career. A true legend on and off the track, Carbine would in time go to England and sire three generations of Epsom Derby winners.

Comedy King – This English horse was the first imported horse to win the Melbourne Cup. In the 1910 Cup, Comedy King, who had been imported from England as a foal, ran against Trafalgar, one of Australia's favourite horses and winner of 23 races on retirement. The imported horse was a grandson of the great English thoroughbred St. Simon.

Throughout the race, Comedy King was always handy to the lead and after challenging the leaders on the home turn, he swept past them halfway down the straight and looked certain of victory.

The import was travelling strongly, but a roar from the crowd and a quick look told jockey Bill McLachlan that Trafalgar was starting to make his challenge and was storming home out wide, gaining on Comedy King with every giant stride. Comedy King had an impeccable record over Trafalgar: in their previous eight clashes, Trafalgar could never pass him – and the record would continue in the 1910 Melbourne Cup. Comedy King, under the brilliant riding of McLachlan, held off Trafalgar to win by a half-head.

McLachlan enjoyed his second Cup success in as many years, having piloted the three-year-old Prince Foote to victory the previous year. Comedy King went on to become a great sire, and his sons Artilleryman (1919) and King Ingoda (1922) also won the Melbourne Cup.

Windbag – The 1925 Melbourne Cup featured a great line-up, including Windbag, a four-year-old stayer of the highest quality; Spearfelt, the previous year's third placegetter; former Oaks winner Frances Tressady; and the 7/4 favourite, Manfred. Windbag was primed for a Cup victory and started second favourite at 5/1. Standing in the way of victory was the enigmatic and brilliant three-year-old Manfred, who was capable of world-class performances when his mood allowed but was notorious for failing at the start of a race.

The race produced a stirring finale, with Manfred – who had led with a fast pace for most of the race – trying desperately to hold off Windbag's relentless finish. Grinding down his younger rival over the last half furlong in both Australian and race record time, Windbag proved too strong. The Australian Cup winner, Pilliewinkie, fought on doggedly to cross the line in third place.

At stud, Windbag did not sire a Melbourne Cup winner, but he did sire the great miler Chatham. Manfred went on to sire the Melbourne Cup winner The Trump (1937). The unlucky Spearfelt, who finished down the track in the 1925 Cup, made amends the following year by winning the 1926 Cup. He went on to sire another Cup winner, Dark Felt (1943).

The Trump – Foaled in 1932, The Trump stood just fifteen hands high, no bigger than a pit pony. The son of 'mad' Manfred, his behaviour certainly did not take after that of his sire.

After running third in the 1935 Caulfield Guineas, The Trump was made favourite for that year's Caulfield Cup. However, due to leg problems, he did not start. He was pin-fired around his knees, and was gelded before being spelled. (Pin firing was a method of treatment in which either scorching hot or freezing cold bars were applied to a horse's legs to stimulate healing. The treatment was performed while the animal was under sedation, using local anaesthesia.)

In 1937, The Trump showed just how versatile and resilient he could be by winning the Toorak Handicap, the Caulfield Cup and the LKS Mackinnon Stakes, and then finishing the year by winning the Melbourne Cup, giving him his sixth win in succession. Here we had one very tough little racehorse.

Light Fingers – Bart Cummings had three horses prepared for the 1965 Melbourne Cup: Light Fingers, a dour mare; the great free-striding Ziema; and the very consistent horse The Dip. Both Light Fingers and Ziema worked together when doing track work, and during the lead-up races to the Cup, the stable found it hard to separate them and rated their prospects equally. Light Fingers had suffered a setback prior to the running of the Caulfield Cup, however, so the stable leant slightly towards Ziema.

Roy Higgins, the premier Victorian jockey of the time, stuck with his favourite horse, Light Fingers, who he affectionately called Mum. He had all the faith in the world in her, and he recalls how, in track work, if Light Fingers could range up to the free-striding Ziema and get her head within a neck of him, Ziema would always take a peek and inexplicably lose his concentration.

During the Cup, at the 300-metre mark, Ziema was running freely and seemingly with some reserve still in the tank. At the 200-metre point, Light Fingers was under hard riding, clawing at the ground some two lengths away, the only danger to Ziema. Roy Higgins, remembering the trackwork habits of Ziema, threw everything at Light Fingers to see if he could get her just a neck behind Ziema to see if his bad habit would kick into play.

With 100 metres to go and with Light Fingers stretching her neck as far as she could, Ziema had his peek – which was enough for Roy to throw everything at the gallant mare and nail Ziema at the winning post, just like they did at track work.

Gala Supreme – A pedigree horse, a premier trainer and a stable with a winning jockey is a great formula to win the big race, but it's certainly not a prerequisite. Sometimes it is the battlers that take victory, those quiet achievers that toil for years and suddenly burst upon the scene. Gala Supreme's win in the 1973 Melbourne Cup reminded us all that victory in this great race is about the right preparation, a great deal of determination and, always, that little bit of luck.

The last winning stride of the four-year-old gelding Gala Supreme, when he poked his nose between Glengowan and Daneson, gave a well-deserved moment to the 41-year-old jockey – who had at some stage broken nearly every bone in his body. The heart-warming smiles of the connections, and the courteous and modest manner of jockey Frank Reys after his victorious ride on Gala Supreme, is an enduring example of humility on the great stage.

Frank Reys had actually considered retirement before winning the big race, and his acceptance speech remains a special Cup moment. It sums up why the Melbourne Cup is an Australian phenomenon, and how the Cup reaches far into the Australian spirit, amounting to much more than just another race or just another day off.

Kiwi – The 1983 Melbourne Cup will be remembered for the last-to-first victory of the New Zealand horse Kiwi, the incredible ride of the very young Jim Cassidy, and the training feat of Snowy Lupton.

Not having run for a month leading up to the Cup, Kiwi had quite an unusual preparation – and this made him an unknown quantity with the bookies. His trainer, Snowy Lupton, had kept the horse fit, devising a program of training around mustering sheep on his property in New Zealand (yes, this is the kind of story that invokes the colonial spirit!) Kiwi was kept honest in the betting, at 10/1.

Considering he did not have any starts in the month prior to the Cup, it was not surprising that Kiwi raced in a conspicuous last position during the Cup. Even at the 600-metre mark he still sat at the tail of the field. Chiamare led the field clearly down to the

300-metre mark, but was quickly overtaken by Noble Comment and Mr. Jazz.

Kiwi could now be seen weaving and zigzagging his way closer to the rails and taking huge strides, as is the style for Classic stayers. Cassidy piloted him through the pack and at the 150-metre mark, he pulled him wide on the track. In just a few bounds, Kiwi swamped the two leaders to win, racing away from the field. The huge crowd that day roared in surprise, witnesses to what would be regarded as one of the most amazing wins of modern times.

Vintage Crop – The 1993 Melbourne Cup was taken out by a horse brought over from Ireland with the sole purpose of winning the great race. Trained by Dermott Weld, Vintage Crop lost 16 kg travelling to Australia. He had no lead-up events before the great race.

The more favoured English horse, Drum Taps, was the talk of the media, leaving Vintage Crop virtually ignored. Very little was known about Vintage Crop except that he had won that year's Irish St Leger and could handle rain-affected tracks. He was sent out at 16/1. Travelling just better than midfield for most of the race, jockey Michael Kinane made his move at the famous 600-metre mark.

When the big field fanned wide on the turn, some horses were not handling the soft conditions, leaving plenty of space for the Irish contender. At the 350-metre mark, Vintage Crop began to move into the race, and at the 200-metre mark he was looking to challenge the leaders. Reaching the lead about 150 metres out from the winning post, he ran away from the 160/1-outsider Te Akau Nick, trained by Gai Waterhouse, to win by three lengths.

The training feat of Dermott Weld cannot be underestimated. Vintage Crop's victory was the first sign that the Cup's large prize money could attract some of the best international horses. The time had come for Australians to be prepared for more foreign challenges in our big races. Vintage Crop went on to win his second Irish St Leger in 1993. His subsequent third place in the 1995 Melbourne Cup was sensational, considering the trouble he had in the running, and it proved without a shadow of a doubt that his victory in 1993 was no flash in the pan.

Doriemus – Lee Freedman has trained many good horses, including the great Super Impose, Mahogany and Naturalism. He also trained Melbourne Cup winners Tawriffic (1989) and Subzero (1992), and in later years, the champion mare Makybe Diva (2004 and 2005). But as far as Cup winners are concerned, Freedman considered his imported stayer Doriemus his modern-day marvel.

Doriemus's victory at the age of five in the 1995 Melbourne Cup, over the lightly weighted three-year-old VRC Derby winner Nothin' Leica Dane, was a special victory. Subsequent performances in weight-for-age and other major races, including the Caulfield Cup, puts him in an elite group.

In the 1997 Melbourne Cup, Doriemus, at the age of seven, almost stole the show from the all-conquering Might and Power. His late burst and the bob of the heads on the line had many people thinking that he had won his second Cup. Even his jockey, Greg Hall, was confident as he waved his whip in victory after passing the winning post.

The photo showed otherwise, with Might and Power's head being down on the line to deservedly take victory. With a string of Group 1 wins, Doriemus's late arrival to Australian racing showed that age statistics can be broken and that you are never too old to mix it with the very best.

Now, that terrible tragedy!

Dulcify – In the field of the 1979 Melbourne Cup was one of the most exciting horses of the era – and he was the raging favourite. Dulcify was sent out as the 3/1 favourite, after his devastating seven-length win in the WS Cox Plate against Australasia's most elite gallopers just ten days earlier. It was thought that only bad luck would stop him cantering home in the Melbourne Cup.

Dulcify held a position close to the fence and was a little worse than midfield as they swept out of the straight to the back of the course. At this stage, he was travelling easy for his jockey, Brent Thomson, who was waiting to make his move as the field bunched, approaching the 600-metre point. Just behind them was the eventual winner, Hyperno.

Around now, Dulcify seemed to get into trouble, and as the field cornered and started to sprint towards the post, he was clearly lame and showing signs of severe distress. At this point, Brent Thomson dismounted the great horse and took hold of him until the clerk of the course arrived.

Dulcify's injuries were so severe that they were considered beyond any help that the best in the land could offer, and he was immediately euthanised at the track. It was a great loss to Australian racing and to the horse's owners and his trainer, Colin Hayes. Hayes would receive some consolation the following year when his horse Belldale Ball won the great race – but the tragedy of Dulcify somewhat restricted his joy on that first Tuesday in November in 1980.

The famous Cup – full of triumphs, but also tragedy.

The Big Wet and the Melbourne Cup
... it's too wet, I can't see!

In 1976, Kiwi trainer Len Robinson brought his wet-track galloper Van Der Hum to Melbourne for the Spring Carnival. Expat Kiwi jockey Bobby Skelton was engaged to ride the horse throughout the campaign. Skelton was an unfashionable jockey, but he had been riding in Melbourne for quite a few years and pretty well knew his way around the Flemington racecourse.

At his first start in Australia, Van Der Hum won the Herbert Power Handicap at Caulfield. He then ran a great third, behind How Now, in the Caulfield Cup.

Robinson had his horse cherry-ripe for his assault on the Melbourne Cup, and he was now hoping that the unpredictable Melbourne weather would take a turn for the worse come the first Tuesday in November. Why? Well, being son of the renowned wet-track sire Hermes, Van Der Hum was an absolute bolter in the wet.

Len Robinson took all possible precautions to make sure his horse would get to the starting post on Melbourne Cup Day. On the Sunday and Monday night before the Cup, Robinson spent the night in his car, with a shotgun, just outside the horse's stall.

Come the morning of the Melbourne Cup, the city of Melbourne received an absolute deluge during a freak storm. There was so much chaos that all the TABs were out of action until around 1.25pm. Would the races be postponed?

There was a slight break in the weather, and after an inspection of the track, the stewards declared the meeting would go ahead.

By the time the horses got to the starting gates for the Cup, the track was an absolute quagmire, having been churned up by horses in the previous six races. Van Der Hum had been backed for a fortune into favourite, at odds of 9/2; if he won, there would be some very sick bookies, but one very happy trainer. It was now left to the wily veteran jockey Bobby Skelton to play his part.

So heavy was the rain during the race, course patrons had no idea whatsoever what was happening. They had to rely on the racetrack broadcaster to try and do the impossible and differentiate the horses in the field.

At the 200-metre mark, in the doom and gloom, Van Der Hum forged to the front, and at the winning post he was two lengths clear of Gold And Black and Kythera.

At the time of writing, Van Der Hum's 1976 time of 3:34.1 for the 3200-metre race was the slowest since Peter Pan's second Cup win in 1934, at 3:40.5. In fact, Van Der Hum's time was slower than Nalinga's win earlier that day in the Cup Day hurdle, which was won in 3:33.1, also over 3200 metres.

On returning to scale, Bobby Skelton told journalists, 'I have never heard thunder like it or have never seen rain like it before. This is the heaviest track I have ever ridden on in Australia or New Zealand.' He summed it up best by saying, 'It was like driving a car on a dirty wet road, slipping and sliding everywhere, without any windscreen wipers.'

One wonders if Len Robinson, shotgun in his lap on that Sunday and Monday way back in 1976, prayed well into the night for this kind of divine intervention.

If so, he certainly got his wish.

Wonder Women
... they're not comic book heroines!

As the years go by, racegoers are seeing more female jockeys racing than ever before. At one stage, there were only two or three at any race meeting. In 1981, Tasmania's Bev Buckingham was the first female jockey to win a state premiership, when she rode 63 winners. Clare Lindop was the first female jockey to win a mainland premiership, when she won the South Australian premiership in 2005, with 37 winners.

How things have changed. Here is a list of the 2012–13 season's leading female jockeys, including their number of wins in each state's capital city or Tasmania, plus their overall winning position.

- **Melbourne:** Jackie Beriman – 14 wins (20th)
- **Sydney:** Jenny Duggan – 20 wins (17th)
- **Brisbane:** Tegan Harrison – 44 wins (4th)
- **Darwin:** Simone Montgomerie – 27 wins (1st)
- **Perth:** Natasha Faithfull – 10 wins (20th)
- **Adelaide:** Jamie Kah – 42 wins (1st)
- **Tasmania:** Georgie Catania – 29 wins (8th)

Tegan Harrison was Australia's leading female metropolitan winner, with 44 wins. Jamie Kah was Australia's leading female jockey, riding a total of 103 winners. Kacie Connor won the Alice Springs premiership with 29 wins.

Toowoomba apprentice Skye Bogenhuber won her second premiership, with 60 winners. Along the way, she won the feature 2013 double, riding Miss Imagica in the Weetwood Handicap and Bang On in the Toowoomba Cup.

In October 2011, Perfect Punch gave Clare Lindop her 1000th winner, and she became the first female jockey in the southern hemisphere to reach this goal.

Five of the 'fairer sex' have won a total of ten Group 1 races:

- Michelle Payne, 4 wins – 1 with Allez Wonder and 3 on Yosei
- Clare Lindop, 3 wins – 1 with Exalted Time and 2 on Rebel Raider
- Nikita Beriman, 1 win – Tears I Cry
- Kathy O'Hara, 1 win – Ofcourseican
- Laura Stojakovic, 1 win – Miracles Of Life

Sharpen up, boys, the girls are a-coming! In the meantime, the boys have something to cheer about too: Brisbane's Michael Cahill was the leading metropolitan jockey winner in 2012–13, with 86 wins.

Yes, how things have changed!

HEADLINE: Phar Lap to race in America in 1932!
… can he beat America's best?

Newspaper headlines followed Phar Lap – from the shooting attempt in 1930, all the way to his grave.

'Gangsters shoot at Phar Lap!'
Fortunately they missed – but we'll get to that later.

'Phar Lap wins 1930 Melbourne Cup'
In front of 72,000 people, starting at 11/8 ON!

'Phar Lap asked to carry 10 st 10 lb [68 kg] in 1931 Melbourne Cup'
Carbine was given 10 stone 12 lb (69 kg) in 1891, but did not start.

'Phar Lap forces VRC to change rules'
Due to a lack of any real competition for Phar Lap, the Victorian Racing Club (VRC) Committee was forced to alter the conditions of some weight-for-age races to a system of penalties and allowances. Connections were outraged.

'Phar Lap to miss 1931 Melbourne Cup'
'He just cannot win with that weight!'

'Phar Lap ordered to start in 1931 Melbourne Cup'
The VRC Committee told owner Dave Davis and trainer Harry Telford that they would not accept the scratching of Phar Lap. If the horse was scratched, none of Telford's horses would be allowed to run during the entire Melbourne Cup carnival.

'Phar Lap unplaced in Melbourne Cup'
Carrying only 6 stone 12 lb (43.5 kg), which was 3 stone (19 kg) less than Phar Lap carried, White Nose won the Cup at 8/1. Phar Lap finished eighth.

Let us tell you the tale behind the headlines. We'll begin our story before the 1931 Melbourne Cup.

In the months prior to the Cup, one of Phar Lap's part-owners, American Dave Davis, had been approached by the Agua Caliente Racing Club in Mexico, just over the border from the United States. The club was considering staging a race that would be the richest in North American history, with a purse of US$100,000.

Davis kept telling reporters 'Big Red' would not be going to the USA. Phar Lap would see his days out in Australia. However, thanks to the power of the print press, the American public had an appetite for Phar Lap; they had been reading newspaper articles about the amazing 'Wonder from Down Under', including details of his incredible 1930 Melbourne Cup win and his wins prior to the 1931 Melbourne Cup. With $100,000 as stakes, the American newspapers were confident that the hard sell would work, so the papers broke the news: 'Phar Lap, Australia's wonder horse, will arrive in early January to prepare for the Agua Caliente Handicap on 20 March 1932.'

How could a seemingly obscure race club come up with so much money in this era? In the United States in 1930, 1345 banks had closed due to the Great Depression. The Agua Caliente Racing Club was heavily in debt, and it was banking on the Australian attraction. Spokesman 'Big Jim' Crofton decided to get the public campaign calling the horse 'The Red Terror from the Antipodes'. Could the Agua Caliente Racing Club avoid bankruptcy and the government's clutches?

Back in Australia, Dave Davis was advised by the Department of Agriculture that if Phar Lap went to America, he would not be allowed to re-enter Australia.

Prior to the running of the 1931 Melbourne Cup, rumours were starting to surface. Was Phar Lap lame? Was Phar Lap going to be scratched from the Cup? The strongest rumour of all was that if Phar

Lap did indeed run, it would be his last race in Australia. Had his connections booked the sea passage to America already?

Trainer Harry Telford approached Dave Davis about the last rumour and was told, 'No, mate, there is nothing booked. Let's leave it at that, and we'll talk about it after the Cup.'

Harry exploded: 'I am getting sick and tired of your bloody devious schemes. I know you're up to something.'

The Melbourne Cup was run and won by White Nose, defeating Shadow King and with Phar Lap unplaced. Yes, weight will stop a train: the 10 stone 10 lb (68 kg) was too much for the great horse. Dave Davis finally announced that Phar Lap would be heading to America. Australians were shattered.

Phar Lap's trainer, Harry Telford, needed to stay with his wife and child in Australia and continue training. Understanding Harry's predicament, Dave Davis asked if he could take young Tommy Woodcock with him to train Phar Lap for the Agua Caliente race, as Tommy knew the 'nuts and bolts' of the horse. Dave also suggested that he take their vet, Bill Neilsen, too. Dave felt that his normal jockey, Jimmy Pike, was getting a bit long in the tooth, so he decided to take the young jockey Billy Elliott, because he had won a couple of races on Phar Lap.

Leaving the Flemington racecourse after the Cup, trainer Harry Telford told the young strapper Tommy Woodcock to take Phar Lap to the Underbank property, at Bacchus Marsh. He told Woodcock to be ready to leave for America when given the word.

The headlines said it all: 'Phar Lap off to America'. This was it: in for a penny, in for a pound!

In the haste to arrange everything in time for the voyage, Davis forgot one thing: to extend the £8000 insurance policy that covered Phar Lap in Australia. Once the horse was on board the ship, the insurance policy was void. If anything went wrong, there would be no payout.

Davis and his wife arrived in America. They celebrated Christmas Day and Boxing Day at their hotel. They were extremely confident of Phar Lap's ability. However, things were about to take a turn for the worse. Davis received a telephone call at his hotel on 28 December from a reporter who was racing to meet a news deadline and wanted to ask a few quick questions.

And that's when the proverbial hit the fan.

'What! What do you mean that Agua Caliente has gone broke? I was only talking to Jim Crofton on Christmas Eve. There was nothing wrong. He would have told me. Where the goddamn hell did you get that information?'

'I got it from the bankers associated with the club. It's an official statement that says the club has lost $100,000 in the past 26 days of racing. Unfortunately, they are going to suspend operations indefinitely.'

'My God! I've got to get hold of Crofton. My God, this can't be true.'

Rushing to the racecourse, Davis found Jim Crofton in his office nursing a very large bourbon. After a shouting match about what Dave Davis had heard from the reporter, both parties simmered down and Crofton assured Davis that the club would be reopening in January. He said the big handicap race was still on and the prize money remained as discussed previously. But was it the drink talking?

There were rumours circulating that some of last year's winning connections at Agua Caliente had not yet received all their stake money. These rumours worried Dave Davis no end. When he confronted Jim Crofton on the prize money issue, he asked, 'Exactly what is the stake money going to be for this handicap race?'

And Crofton's reply: 'Ah … let me see … with all the finances, etc. … Ah, a guarantee of $50,000. So, don't worry, we'll sort something out.' Dave Davis was furious. This was only half of the original agreement. But he was in America now, and his horse was on its way. They could not back down.

A few days later, weights were announced for the Handicap, and Phar Lap was given 9 stone 3 lb (58.5 kg), a featherweight to what he carried in the Melbourne Cup. Davis was beside himself – 'He'll bolt in.'

SS *Monowai* had an uneventful trip and on 15 January 1932, it berthed at San Francisco, California. Ten inches of snow had fallen overnight and the weather was freezing cold. The plan was to stable Phar Lap near San Francisco's Tanforan Racetrack. In a few days, he would be on his way to Agua Caliente.

Yes, the media played their part: 'Phar Lap, the Wonder Horse' – 'Phar Lap, the Superhorse' – 'The Red Terror from the Antipodes' – 'The Aussie Antelope'. Photographers, reporters, editors, movie stars, politicians, tycoons and the general public: they could not get enough of him. Visiting champion English jockey Steve Donoghue claimed he had never seen a finer specimen of horse anywhere in the world.

At the stables at the Agua Caliente Racetrack, the Aussies were in awe of the 24-hour security patrol, with shotguns, rifles and pistols at the ready.

The Aussie way of hard training had not hurt Phar Lap, and his track times were getting more impressive by the day. Under Tommy Woodcock, he had turned into a ball of muscle.

One morning as Phar Lap was coming off the training track, Woodcock noticed flecks of blood on the horse's stomach. When he lifted a hoof up, it was cracked and bleeding badly. A pebble had lodged between the hoof and shoe – this could be the end of all their dreams.

When a local vet inspected the hoof and was asked whether the horse could race in three weeks, he said, 'This injury could take many weeks to heal. I'll give you one chance in a thousand to be ready for the race.'

How could they keep this from the prying news reporters? Simple: they would tell a white lie.

It was up to Jim Crofton to allay all fears: 'Gentlemen, you haven't seen Phar Lap for a couple of days because he stepped on a stone and bruised his hoof. A mud pack has been placed on his hoof, and it is not expected to hinder his preparation. He will be right in a couple of days.'

Phar Lap's price drifted to 4/1.

After a couple of days it was time to check the damage. The Australian vet Bill Neilsen had cleaned out Phar Lap's hoof and prepared a binding of wax thread. He told Woodcock not to be afraid to walk the horse but not to gallop him.

Together, Woodcock and Phar Lap walked and walked and walked – some days up to 25 miles (40 km).

One reporter published: 'That boy's crazy. The horse is injured and he [Woodcock] just keeps walkin' him as though he is in a marathon. That boy is not right in the head, that's for sure.'

The crack was healing and an elated Bill Neilsen said, 'Just two days, Tommy, and you can canter him.' Two days later, Phar Lap was exercised, but into a few strides – SNAP! The binding gave way, and the horse could not put his foot down. There was a large piece of hoof hanging loose.

Bill Neilsen was distraught, but he just shook his head and said, 'If it wasn't such an important race, I would scratch him right now. Okay, let's see what can be done.'

Neilsen found a blacksmith who could keep his mouth shut and asked him to make a special bar shoe that could be attached over some homemade hardening remedy, keeping pressure on the injured area. He told young Tommy Woodcock not to worry and said that it was their only chance. 'All we can do is hope for the best, son.'

Phar Lap's improvement overnight was enough for them to start walking him again. Just two weeks before the race, Phar Lap had his first hard gallop in front of a large crowd. One clocker could not believe his eyes: 'My God, how good was that. This horse is incredible. You damn Aussies sure do know how to train a horse.'

A week later, noted track clocker Russ Sanders was in awe of the way Phar Lap got over the ground. He said, 'That great leapin' kangaroo covered the last five furlongs as though it was one gigantic leap. Oh, man!'

Many lucrative offers came Dave Davis's way, but he was only interested in talking to a couple of movie moguls from Hollywood and New York. He thought, 'When he wins the Agua Caliente, they will be kicking the door down just to make a movie about him.'

Two days prior to race day, jockey Billy Elliott took a ride in a race so as to get the feel of the track and judge how he might go against the American jockeys. In the past two weeks, Phar Lap had improved so much that many newspaper headlines read 'Phar Lap Unbeatable'. The race was now on.

Race day finally came. With the American style of racing, they do not bring their horse out to the public until a few minutes before post time. However, an hour before the race, Woodcock led Phar Lap around in front of the huge crowd, doing it the way it has always been done in Australia: 'He's huge' – 'He's magnificent' – 'Wow, what a specimen!'

When legged up on Phar Lap and with number 9 on his sleeve, Billy Elliott said, 'Crikey, Tommy, I hope I ride him all right.'

Woodcock reassured Billy: 'Don't worry, mate. Just get him to the outside of the field; he'll run his own race.'

As the horses were heading to the barrier chute, Dave Davis was enjoying the atmosphere in the Roulette Room, but he was certainly starting to feel nervous. Tommy Woodcock and Bill Neilsen stood outside, gripping the handrail in anticipation.

Out of the silence a message came to them above all of the race day noise: 'Cooee! Cooee!' That unforgettable call of the Australian bush echoed through the massive crowd. It was a comforting moment for Tommy and Bill, letting them know that there were other Aussies in the crowd and they were not alone.

The horses were loaded, the starter checked the clock, his flag came down and the course broadcaster announced: 'THEY'RE OFF! The big Aussie, Phar Lap, has jumped well in the Agua Caliente Handicap.'

Coming down the straight for the first time, jockey Billy Elliott manoeuvred Phar Lap to the outside of the field, making sure that the horse would not suffer any interference, and on leaving the straight, dirt and mud were splattered onto the cheering crowd that had gathered at the rails. At the 6 furlong peg, Elliott started to make his move, and with giant strides, Phar Lap began to gather up the race leaders as if they were standing still. Once they entered the straight, it would be all over in seconds – or would it?

At the furlong mark, Phar Lap seemed to falter – 'His hoof's gone!' shouted one of the Aussie contingent – and the American champ Reveille Boy was now putting in a sharp sprint. But Billy Elliott and Phar Lap composed themselves, and shot past the winning post to win by three lengths.

As the riders brought their horses back to the saddling enclosure, the course broadcaster announced, 'Ladies and gentlemen: Phar Lap, first; Reveille Boy, second; and Scimitar, third. The time of 2.2 and four-fifths is a new track record.'

Jockey Billy Elliott had only one thing on his mind: 'Where do I weigh in?'

'Big Red' had done his job, but one could see that he was becoming quite agitated by the big crowd around him. When actress Claire Windsor tried to put a garland of flowers around the great horse's neck, he jerked his head, stepped back, and stumbled against a step, knocking his foreleg and hoof, which started to bleed once again. All Tommy Woodcock could think about was getting Phar Lap back to the stables so that he could treat the wound.

After all the back-slapping and well wishes, Dave Davis and his wife returned to their hotel. One movie studio had been phoning every half-hour, begging Davis to return their call. There was also a stack of messages from well-wishers, with one that stood out from the rest: 'Verified, ex-London today – heartiest congratulations on great victory – King George V.'

All Woodcock could think of was returning to Australia to see his beloved wife of twelve months, his darling Emma. It was only a few more weeks before all the boys would be heading back home to Australia. A great relief came over the young trainer.

Later in the day, Davis had a meeting with Jim Crofton and was told that, after deductions, the prize money was only $48,000 – far less than the $100,000 that was originally offered. Davis was not happy, but accepted the cheque. The purse took Phar Lap's career earnings to £66,000, just £7000 pounds shy of the world record.

Now it was time for the big money to be made, with Metro-Goldwyn-Mayer (MGM) offering $100,000 for a series of short films. The rest of the contingent headed back to Menlo Park, California, where Phar Lap had been sent after his win.

On 5 April 1932, nearly five months to the day after Phar Lap carried 10 stone 10 lb (68 kg) in the 1931 Melbourne Cup, Dave Davis was in the film studios of Metro-Goldwyn-Mayer checking on the final clauses of the contract: 'Now, if you will just sign here, Mr Davis.' The phone rang, the movie mogul answered and passed the phone over to Dave Davis: 'Mr Davis, it's for you, sir.'

'WHAT? ... NO! ... It can't be – no, there must be some mistake!' Dave Davis was stunned.

Within hours the story had reached Australia. It was a day the nation will never forget.

'Phar Lap Dead!'

Old Harry Telford collapsed in his chair – 'Vi, the bastards have killed him. Those bloody yanks have murdered Phar Lap.'

More than 80 years later, the legend lives on!

Ready, aim, fire!

... not once, but twice!

On the morning of Saturday 1 November 1930, the young strapper Tommy Woodcock was walking two horses back to their stables. One was the stable pony; the other was the great Phar Lap, the odds-on favourite for the coming Tuesday's Melbourne Cup.

Woodcock sensed that something was wrong. He noticed two men sitting in a dark blue sedan, trying to ease their bodies back into the shadows of the car's interior.

With that, he quickly crossed the Glenhuntly Road and James Street intersection. He was immediately aware that the sedan's engine had started up and the car was closing in behind him. Something was seriously wrong.

His instincts clicked in. Mounted on the stable pony, he moved in front of Phar Lap, trying to shield him. The car sped up, and as it got close, Woodcock could see a sawn-off shotgun protruding from the passenger-side window. As the car sped past, the gun was fired and shot-gun pellets slammed into the wall, just missing Woodcock, Phar Lap and the pony. The strapper was thrown from the pony, and the poor horses went berserk. It was only due to Woodcock's experience that he was able to calm both animals down.

The Australian public was outraged. No-one could believe that somebody would actually harm the great horse. He was their idol, for God's sake! This was 1930s Australia, not the Wild West!

Police later concluded that in all probability Phar Lap was not a target but that the shotgun was fired to panic the horse so that he would injure himself. Even if that were so, they did a pretty damn good job of scaring the wits out of all concerned. That afternoon, Phar Lap was whisked away to St Albans Stud, and that was where he stayed until the late morning of the 1930 Melbourne Cup.

It is now in the history books that the great Phar Lap, carrying 9 stone 12 lb (62.5 kg), brilliantly won the 1930 Melbourne Cup, having started at 8/11 favourite. He was the shortest priced favourite in the 152-year history of the great race. It is estimated that the total loss for bookies all over Australia was £400,000, which is equal to a mammoth $29 million in today's terms.

No-one was ever arrested over the shooting incident.

Fast forward ten years and it was another Cup contender in the line of fire!

In the days before the 1940 Melbourne Cup, New Zealand champion Beau Vite became the hot favourite. If he won the LKS Mackinnon Stakes on the Saturday, he would be the shortest-priced favourite to contest the race since Phar Lap in 1930.

However, all hell broke loose on the Thursday before the Cup when two shots were fired in the vicinity of where Beau Vite was stabled. A horse was shot, but fortunately it was not Beau Vite. Unfortunately it was his stablemate, El Golea, the 1939 Newmarket Handicap winner.

Someone had drilled a hole in the back wall of the stable, large enough to poke through the barrel of a small calibre rifle. It was quite obvious that the felons had not done their homework in working out which horse was which: in fact, both Beau Vite and El Golea had almost identical colouring and markings, with both forelegs bandaged in a similar fashion. El Golea was shot in the hind thigh and hock area.

After the attempted shooting of Beau Vite, owner Ralph Stewart said:

As of tonight, there will be two night-watchmen with the horse. They will be armed and have been told to shoot first and ask questions later. El Golea's wounds are serious, but he is expected to make a full recovery.

Once the felons realised their mistake, they decided that they would now have a go at jockey Ted McMenamin by sending him threatening letters and making threatening phone calls. If they could not get the horse, they would certainly get to Ted.

Obviously Beau Vite wasn't affected by the shooting incident, because on the Saturday he came out and won the LKS Mackinnon Stakes. Come Melbourne Cup Day, McMenamin was a nervous wreck. One of the phone calls he received said that if he turned up on race day and mounted Beau Vite, he would be blown off the horse.

Maybe the nerves did get to poor Ted, because Beau Vite, the 7/4 favourite, could only run fourth in the Cup to the 100/1 outsider Old Rowley.

But what happened to El Golea? Well, he was successfully operated on, and the following year he ran second to Beau Vite in the 1941 LKS Mackinnon Stakes. Maybe the authorities felt sorry for the horse, because we now have the El Golea Handicap run each year at the Sandown Hillside racetrack in Springvale, Victoria.

As in the case of the Phar Lap shooting incident, no-one was ever arrested.

With a little help from our friends
... like the Beatles in 1967!

Barry and I have been surprised by the support given to us by not only friends and family, but also the many readers who have told us some of their stories. We have honoured them in the next series of yarns.

Some of these memories are recent and some go back more than half a century. The first five tales hail from Alice Springs. The last four stories were related to us by 81-year-old Tony Valli and 85-year-old Henry Lawrence. It was great to have triggered the memory banks of these two 'elderly statesmen' of our racing industry.

Periduki

... the Pride of Pioneer Park

Almost every country, state, city or town has one: a champion racehorse that captures the hearts and interests of all. We've had Phar Lap, Bernborough, Tulloch, Kingston Town, Makybe Diva and, from 2008 through to 2013, the mighty Black Caviar.

And we've also had the honest toilers, such as Mustard from Sydney, Taos Pleasure from Adelaide, Hawks Bay from Darwin and Geegees Blackflash from Tasmania. This yarn is about another honest toiler. Trained by Mick Whittle and ridden by Scott Westover, Periduki was the pride and joy of Alice Springs.

Foaled in 2004, Periduki is by Perugino, the unraced half-brother of the great Sadler's Wells. On his dam side he traces back to the great Nijinsky – yes, blue blood on both sides.

When Periduki first stepped onto the training track at Alice Springs' Pioneer Park, in 2007, racing patrons knew they were in for something special – and he did not let them down. He was a real flyer. In 2008, Periduki became the first three-year-old to win the Red Centre's premier sprint race, the time-honoured Pioneer Sprint, first run in 1990 and won by Rawedge.

A lot of water flowed under the bridge between Periduki's 2008 win and his attempt at winning the 2013 Sprint, this time carrying top weight of 61.5 kg. In the intervening years, he travelled to Darwin, Adelaide and even Melbourne, covering as many kilometres as the Leyland Brothers.

In 2013 he was back where his career began, Alice Springs. With his natural speed and a desire to lead in races, would Periduki be able to give up to 7 kg to most of the younger brigade, led by Outstandingly, Exceedingly and the challenger from the Top End, Alittlevolcanic? Only time would tell. The last 200 metres in the race could be the decider.

Alan and I had been invited to be guest speakers at the 2013 Alice Springs Turf Club Luncheon, and during the course of the Friday afternoon I asked race caller Shane Green if Periduki could 'carry the grandstand' and still win. With a wink and a wry smile, Shane said, 'Mate, why not! He is Periduki, you know.' God, why did I ask such a silly question?

Early in the afternoon on race day, one of Periduki's main rivals, Alittlevolcanic, became a late scratching due to a foot abscess. That made one less contender, and probably made sure that the Pride of Pioneer Park would lead 'on his ear'. Would Periduki save the greatest chapter of his illustrious career for today, 4 May 2013?

The horses made their way around to the starting gates, and the large crowd became silent. You could have heard a pin drop. Would the Alice's favourite horse get away to a good start, and by how many lengths would he lead the field? Yes, the crowd could hardly wait for Shane Green to announce 'They're off and racing!'

The crowd erupted as the starter said 'Go!' But there was something wrong, and you could hear it in Shane Green's voice over the loudspeakers: 'They've jumped as one, and they're going like the wind – but where's Periduki?' Yes, Periduki was nowhere near the leaders, and coming to the turn he was in second-last place. All you could hear was a large groan from the crowd. Periduki was not going to be part of history; he was going to be back with the 'cab catchers', closer to last than first. The crowd was absolutely shocked.

But the Pride of Pioneer Park was not going to give in without a fight. His young jockey, Scott Westover, must have had 'Georgie Moore's whistle', because on the turn into the straight, the field started to fan out and there, under his weight of 61.5 kg, Periduki was spotted by the race caller Shane Green weaving his way through the field – and didn't he let the crowd know: 'And here comes Periduki, and look at him go. He's coming with giant strides.'

With 100 metres to go, the Mount Isa raider Outstandingly still had a commanding lead, but Scotty Westover was throwing everything at Periduki. Would he get up under that big weight? Would he make history? Would he go down as one of the Red Centre's all-time great champions? Would this be the ultimate twenty-first birthday present for the young jockey?

'… And Periduki has burst through to win by a neck. Ladies and gentlemen, you have just witnessed one of the greatest wins you will ever wish to see. Periduki, you little beauty!'

That afternoon, Alan was privileged to be a guest in the broadcaster's box to watch and hear this fantastic race call by Shane Green. When he came downstairs, he told me, 'Baz, what a sight and what an unbelievable run. What a horse and what an amazing race call. Some things are just meant to happen.'

That win took Periduki's earnings to $668,335, a fantastic effort for a horse that went through the sales ring for $6000 as a yearling. We left Pioneer Park Racecourse with an indelible memory, never to be forgotten: black sand track, Periduki and a great race call. What else could we ask for?

Maybe Periduki was a nominee for that year's Alice Spring's 'Centralian of the Year' – who knows? On 16 December 2013, Periduki was retired from racing. From 84 starts, he had won 24 races and was placed fifteen times, with prize money of $674,095.

Alice Springs, you little beauty!

Eight from eight in the Alice

... now pay up, mate!

On 8 July 1970, Alice Springs punter Terry Webster claimed to have placed a $50 all-up bet with an off-course bookmaker on the Strathalbyn meeting in South Australia.

'You little beauty! They all won, with the last horse starting at 12/1.'

However, when the bookmaker was shown the paper profit of $65,000, he denied the bet was ever made.

After a complaint via the correct channels, the Northern Territory Betting Control Board believed Webster. It cancelled the bookie's licence and paid the Alice Springs punter the bulk of the bookmaker's $3000 fidelity bond.

It was a small win for the little blokes.

Clydesdales Quinella, race 3 at Pioneer Park

... the Wells Fargo stagecoach is in town!

No, this was not in America in the 1880s. These events happened in Alice Springs in the 1990s.

Our story starts at the Ross River Homestead, a tourist destination on 22,000 acres, just 80 km from Alice Springs in the East MacDonnell Ranges. It is the second-oldest homestead in the Northern Territory.

Back in 1994, Marilyn Wade and her partner, Greg Young, ran a tourist operation out of the homestead, called Wells Fargo. It comprised of a stagecoach drawn by two Clydesdales that went by the names of Commodore and Renown, named after the two battleships – yes, each was a big unit on four legs.

Wayne Kraft, owner of the Overland Steakhouse, approached Marilyn and Greg to see if they were interested in hiring out the Wells Fargo coach to take his party of twelve to the Pioneer Park Racecourse, in Alice Springs, on Melbourne Cup Day. A great idea! And they would not forget a seemingly endless supply of champagne for the slow, thirsty trip.

All tourist operators try to get an edge on their opponents, and so Marilyn and Greg put forward a proposal to John Fitzgerald, the general manager of Pioneer Park, to let the Wells Fargo coach give rides to the public on the racecourse between races.

John mulled it over for a while and thought, why not? The black racecourse surface was virtually bombproof, consisting of a mixture of oil and sand. What damage could two horses and a stagecoach do in four hours?

When Cup Day came, the Wells Fargo stagecoach delivered its passengers safely. So now it was time to make some more money, giving rides to the general public for a very modest fee.

The paying public was having a great time, until ...

Race time approached for the third race, and the track had to be cleared. Marilyn's slightly 'kamikaze' partner had decided to take a shortcut across a small ditch near the car park on their way back to the horses' resting place under the trees when – SNAP! The main pole attached to the carriage and attached by straps to the horses' collars splintered like a matchstick. If Greg had used the road like he normally did, nothing would have happened, but being a bit of a Crocodile Dundee, he probably thought, 'Nah, I'll save a bit of time and get back via the ditch', and he had taken off as though the stagecoach was being pursued by masked bandits.

What to do now with two giant Clydesdales and a stagecoach that can't be driven? They certainly couldn't leave the horses there.

Well, our hapless Ross River duo obtained permission to ride Commodore and Renown along the racecourse to the racing stables on the other side of the track – but they had better be bloody quick, because the next race was only five minutes away.

So, taking off the main harness – but leaving on the bridles, which had four metres of long reins – they clambered aboard the two 'giant racehorses'. To the cheering of the crowd, they rode bareback at a very fast trot to the other side of the track. As this was happening, it was announced over the loud speaker: 'Ladies and gentlemen, there will be no more rides on Wells Fargo today.' Thank goodness, 'Krafty' hadn't booked the coach for the return trip home.

However, all was not lost. Probably for their contribution to the day's entertainment, Marilyn and Greg enjoyed the hospitality of the Pioneer Park members for the rest of the afternoon.

And Commodore and Renown? They just did what horses do: R and R.

Unfortunately 'Kamikaze' Greg has since passed away. Marilyn now lives in Hampshire, England, in a typical 'olde English' farmhouse. She just happens to be one of the lucky racing enthusiasts, whose situation many of us would give our 'cunning kick' dollars for, because she lives about 30 minutes from the Goodwood Racecourse in West Sussex. In 2012, she was fortunate to see the mighty Frankel win at glorious Goodwood. Marilyn is a regular visitor to Alice Springs, and she is still a member of the Alice Springs Turf Club.

Ah, the good old days. It could only happen in the Alice!

Pink Champagne – only in the Alice
... man oh man!

'Hi! Let us introduce ourselves.

We are the Brown Brothers, Buddy and Ned. We are so fortunate to be able to enjoy life's little offerings. Our lodgings are at a respectable place run by Kath North: the beds are nice and comfy and the two meals a day very plentiful. Although sometimes we would like a change of the menu – probably a few more greens.

Believe it or not, we each have our own Facebook page.

Work's not too hard during the week, and occasionally we go to sporting events on a Saturday or Sunday, where they have organised races in front of cheering crowds. Well, actually, we are a couple of 'chaff bandits', and our real names are Passadane and Noir Rasoir.

Yep, we are racehorses.'

That's right, readers: two racehorses with their own Facebook pages. It could only happen in the Alice.

Lindsay and Annette Fuller are part of a syndicate with other friends, and their first entry into the wonderful and exciting world of horse ownership came in early 2013, when they acquired Passadane and Noir Rasoir. They now know how exhilarating it is to get up before sunrise, make their way to the training track and, especially in the winter months, try to keep warm in zero-degree temperatures. Yes, welcome to the real world of horse racing.

Now, becoming owners of racehorses for the very first time and proudly walking onto the track to see your horse perform that afternoon deserves a special kind of celebration. You could just imagine the look on the face of the then Alice Springs Turf Club CEO, Terry Hooton, when it was suggested that the Turf Club stock pink champagne for the syndicate of new owners, many of whom had never been to the races before. A wonderful host, Terry said, 'Not a problem.'

Yes, win, lose or draw, at the end of the day in the Members Pavilion, the syndicate could always be seen cheering and drinking – or more likely, drinking and cheering. One can only imagine the toasting of pink champagne whenever Buddy or Ned won.

At one Sunday morning visit to Kath North's stable, probably in a state of 'after the races' euphoria, the Fullers, on behalf of the connections, suggested that Buddy (Passadane) would run so much better with glitter on his rump.

We do not doubt for one moment that trainer Kath had seen all this owner enthusiasm before. She probably shook her head in wonderment: God, what next – bloody Twitter?

At the time of writing, Passadane (Buddy) and Noir Rasoir (Ned) had six wins and fourteen placings between them, with prize money totalling $105,635.

Meanwhile, back in the stables:

'Hey Ned, do you know that our owners have 'Buddy Days'? That's the Monday off work to recover from the pink champagne celebrations.'

'I know Buddy, I know. They have also put aside Fridays for 'Ned Day', just to prepare for the weekend.'

Yes, it's a syndicate of excited owners enjoying the camaraderie of the racing fraternity. Oh, what a wonderful world!

Racehorse does a runner in the Alice
… but where did he go?

'There was movement at the stables, for the word has passed around that the gelding from old Admirer had run away.'

Incredible, but true.

Not Abandoned, the 2007 Northern Territory Derby and two-time Buntine Handicap winner, certainly caused a stir in February 2008. Trainer Viv Oldfield had turned Not Abandoned out for a well-earned spell. The twelve-time winner – with earnings of $215,000 – was expected to eventually return to training, ready to start on another successful campaign. Being just a four-year-old gelding, there were plenty of racing years ahead of him.

However, when Oldfield went to pick up the horse from his paddock, he was gone.

As soon as Not Abandoned's disappearance was discovered, a helicopter was chartered to scour the bush, but nothing was found.

A reward was posted, and it wasn't long before Not Abandoned was headline news in the Alice Springs newspaper and the leading story on local television and radio. Photos were sent out to all the local farmers, but nothing resulted.

Some of the locals suggested that horse rustlers may have been involved, and some suggested that bike riders may have been riding through the paddocks and not shut a gate properly.

Who knows? Maybe Not Abandoned may have felt abandoned and joined the wild bush horses. Even today there may be a 'wild colonial' thoroughbred roaming the hills near Alice Springs. You just don't know.

Where's Clancy of the Overflow when you need him?

Miles and miles
... the Doc stumbles across the bleedin' obvious!

Here's a tale from the keeper of my health, Dr Allan Miles.

Those of us who have had the pleasure of owning or even naming a racehorse know the problems that can present themselves. Owning one is a sheer delight, but trying to have a name registered is another story.

Sometimes it can be simple, such as the colt foaled in 1957, Anything, which ran under the first name lodged. Actors Fred Astaire and Gregory Peck were in Australia filming *On The Beach*. To pass the time away, they purchased a colt that was ready to race but as yet unnamed. When they were asked by their racing manager what name to register the horse under, they replied, 'Just call it anything' – so he did. Anything went on to be quite a successful racehorse, winning the 1962 Ballarat Cup.

Other times it is much more difficult, such as in the case of Bart Cummings' brilliant horse Century. Foaled in 1969, he went on to win five Group 1 races, the highlight of which was the 1973 Newmarket Handicap. Suggested names were rejected time and time again; at the final hurdle, the 100th name lodged was accepted and, appropriately, he raced as Century.

This naming story is about a filly born in Australia in 2010, by

Stromberg Carlson from the American mare Pour Ma Mere. Now, what sort of name would be appropriate for a petite filly with that breeding?

Dr Allan Miles had bred this filly. One day he was in the process of taking his daughter to the airport, and the conversation turned to naming the filly. The doc's daughter, Claire, suggested that since she was going back to work in Shanghai, China, maybe 'Sally' could go with 'Shanghai', and she could be called Shanghai Sally.

Weeks later, that name was rejected, so they shortened the name to Shanghai Sal. No, that was also rejected. How about Super Shanghai Sal? No. So the good doctor tried Super Sal, but unfortunately that was already taken. Maybe having Sally or Sal in the name was going to be an ongoing problem. He wondered what to do next.

Because the horse was out spelling, there seemed to be no rush in naming her. But when she was brought back into the stables, the 'name game' was back on the agenda.

The doc took a trip to Barry Baldwin's stables in Brisbane, just to see how much the horse had grown. Did he expect to see a petite little filly? When he sighted her, he was amazed. She stood just under 16 hands high, but what else took the doc's eye was how long she had grown. Even the stable foreman mentioned how long she was. Obviously at such a young age she was still growing, so images of her height and length dominated Allan's thoughts. She was going to be quite a size.

Well, after seeing what the petite little filly had grown into, it was time to think of some more names to apply for. The doc wanted to keep Sally in the name, and then ... Eureka!

The filly's name had become obvious. She will do all her racing as Long Tall Sally. What else?

Sometimes the answer is staring you right in the face.

Bulla, the bully
... how 'the kid' got his revenge

Our first book, *Off the Track* (September 2012), produced a lot of interest in regions well away from the bookstores and the bright city lights. This is a tale from a well-known identity in the Top End, who wants to remain nameless; for clarity's sake, we will call her Aunty Linda. She was and remains today a real friend to a lot of people in the area, and even though she says that some of what she relayed to me may have been embellished a little, Aunty Linda will swear on a stack of bibles that a great percentage is true – so help me God.

Laura is a small town in the Cook Shire of Cape York Peninsula in northern Queensland. It is a good four-hour drive from Cairns, on the only road that heads north to the tip of Australia. You can't miss it: the town appears out of the middle of nowhere. Laura is on the southern end of the Lakefield National Park and in the 2006 census a population of 125 people was counted.

The town has two main claims to fame: it is home to the largest collection of prehistoric rock art in the entire world, and it holds the area's social event of the year, the Laura Race Day and Rodeo, held over three days in June.

Each year during the three-day carnival, the tiny township swells from its population of 125 to around 3500 people. In anyone's language, that's a real boost for the town and the surrounding area. Support for the rodeo and the races comes from many outlying areas and stations, some thousands of kilometres away. It is a must on any young buck's social calendar to come to Laura, race his horses and then do what comes naturally for a young person who wants to keep warm in winter. It is a real hoot.

Aunty Linda tells the story that a number of years ago, a group of racehorses were ridden from a station a few hundred kilometres away. They arrived at a small station near Laura to be held for safekeeping before competing on race day. The young bucks who rode them over took a community truck back to the station, planning to return a month later for the big race weekend.

A young bloke at the station near Laura was given the task of looking after the horses until their riders arrived back for the races. There was only one order given by the ringleader, a big fella called Bulla, and that was: 'Just let the horses pick on grass – definitely no grain. If you can't get that right, I will kick your arse for you when I get back.' They all laughed at the time, and the kid was embarrassed and just let his head drop.

The reason behind wanting no grain in their diets – opposed to the grain diet usually given to thoroughbreds – was that certain grains are stimulants, which can increase a horse's stamina but can make it very flighty. The guys travelling down from remote stations had the task of riding their own mounts back home after the three-day event. In some cases the ride would be over four days, with a few nights spent kipping under the stars. They certainly didn't want their mounts 'fired up' with grain after the races. All the boys wanted was a leisurely ride home.

Well, a few weeks passed by and 'the kid' mulled over the bully and his remarks. He thought to himself, 'I wonder what will happen if I feed his horse as much stimulating grain as I can find over the last week before the races.'

Race day came and while Bulla's mount seemed a little skittish, he took the kid's word that the horse had eaten nothing but grass, like the rest. The kid didn't tell him that the horse was 'hot', charged with energy like a kid on red cordial after a week on corn, barley and molasses.

Aunty Linda continued on to tell me that, no surprise to people in the know, Bulla's mount picked up the $1000 prize money for winning the main sprint on race day, posting a new race record. Bulla was suspicious, but could not find 'the kid'. Instead, he found that the joy of his new-found wealth and a few 'malt sandwiches' would put off the inevitable ride home on his horse, which was still as hot as a firetruck.

Word got through after the carnival that Bulla must have found a shortcut back to the station, because he and his 'hot' horse were off like a bucket of prawns in the hot sun on the return trip home. They reckon he broke all records and was home in a day and a half. His mount only stopped that first night through sheer exhaustion. Bulla then spent the next week soothing his blistered backside and vowing to kick the kid's arse when he saw him at the Laura Races the next year; he knew exactly what revenge the kid had served on him.

Aunty Linda looked at me with a twinkle in her eye and reached for her rum and coke. 'Serves the bastard right', she said. She laughed as she told me that 'the kid' was sent to a boarding school in Cairns soon after the races, and he looks like staying there for the rest of his life to keep away from Bulla the bully.

Legend!

Papua New Guinea
... they certainly love their racing in Paradise

Situated just north of the tip of Australia is the independent state of Papua New Guinea (PNG). It includes the eastern half of the island of New Guinea, with the west of the island being part of the Indonesian provinces. Port Moresby is its largest city and capital. The fledgling nation gained independence from Australia on 16 September 1975.

Papua New Guinea is one of the most diverse countries in the world when it comes to cultures, languages and traditions, and it is home to vast tracts of land containing great treasures of plants and wildlife as yet undiscovered. It is recorded that there are more than 800 languages spoken in PNG, with around ten of these languages so mysterious that there is no known written word on record.

Though there are hundreds of languages, there is one language that most people understand, and that is the dialect called 'Race Day in Australia'. Papua New Guineans just love racing and having a bet.

As in Australia, our book *Off the Track* (2012) found many homes and supporters in Papua New Guinea. One lady, Lorraine B, was good enough to give us this tale of the tropics.

To the envy of most Australians, SP bookmaking (that is, starting price bookmaking) is legal in Papua New Guinea, and there are heaps of betting shops in the cities and in some populated rural areas. When Lorraine spent some time living in Port Moresby, she had the 'pleasure' of working in one such SP shop, and she experienced firsthand the locals' love of Aussie racing and the punt.

Considering the population, the volume of bets that the Papua New Guineans make is incredible. In 2011, a census showed a little more than 7 million people in Papua New Guinea, with only around 1.25 million living in the urban centres.

Just to take the largest day in Australian racing as a yardstick, here are some of the statistics to come firsthand from one of the larger betting shops in Port Moresby. On Melbourne Cup Day, there would be no fewer than 150 – yes, that's right, 150 – pencillers working for that one betting shop and taking bets from the punters on the premises. As if that wasn't enough, the betting shop also employed at least ten expat Aussies onsite, taking all phone bets.

The above figures are for only one of many betting shops spread across the country. So, there you go: when you compare the average punter in Papua New Guinea and the local Aussie at his TAB betting shop, there is no doubt that our friends north of Australia can show us a thing or two about having a punt.

Many a punter today in Australia would love a return to the SP bookmakers, instead of giving more money to the government, that's for sure. But there are no SP bookies around today ... surely not?

Thanks, Lorraine, for these memories of this time of your life.

A day at the races

... *Fiji style*

Alan Fletcher shared this story from his adventures in Fiji.

This little yarn takes place in 1991. Friends of ours, Helen and Alan Fletcher, owned Fingerprint, one of Brisbane's leading fabric-printing companies. They also owned a small offshoot of the company in Nadi, Fiji. While Helen stayed in Brisbane, Alan spent two weeks at the Fiji workshop, making sure that things were running smoothly.

The Saturday after the Melbourne Cup is Emirates Stakes Day, and it happens to coincide with Fiji's running of the Suntours Local Bred Cup. This is where our story starts, on the way to the races.

Now Big Al (and I always refer to him as that, because he makes Mick Jagger look like he's on steroids), with his party of four, squeezed into one of his employee's small four-cylinder cars and headed off for a day at the races. Just a kilometre from the Skylodge Hotel, the little car 'died' and, yes, they thought the battery was cactus.

Just across the road was a motor mechanic shop, and their expertise and speed was something to behold. The 'head mechanic' said that he didn't have a replacement battery. He could get the car started with jumper leads, but he warned, 'When you stop, don't turn the motor off, because it won't start again.' Earlier attempts by a backyard mechanic to fix the clamping mechanism for the battery hadn't been successful, so the battery was tied to the main body of the car to stop it moving around under the bonnet while the car was in motion.

They instead headed off to a reliable battery supplier. Once the new battery was lashed down securely, it was a hurried return to the Skylodge Hotel for a quick cleanup.

Big Al came out of the bathroom. One of his staff had the radio blaring at full volume – obviously hearing aids had not been heard of in Fiji in the early 1990s. The announcer started talking about race 7, the Suntours Local Bred Cup.

'Ladies and gentlemen, the Cup is to be run over 1600 metres; first prize is $100 and a trophy, second prize $50, and third prize a bottle of Fiji Bounty Rum. The track is hard and dusty, and unfortunately cracks and potholes are starting to appear.'

The party of four made a quick dash to the car, squeezed in and hoped to make it to the races in time for the Cup. Big Al was dropped off at the entrance, and after paying $1.50 admission to the main pavilion, he purchased several tickets in an assortment of colours. Yes, this was the Fijian way: one colour ticket for food and one colour for something to quench your thirst.

Strolling through the Fijian section of the crowd, Big Al noticed something that the Fijians rave about: a large, oversized bowl of kava. The surrounding group was just staring into oblivion, eyes bulging and bodies swaying in the balmy breeze. Maybe they had been swimming in the oversize bowl. Who knows?

The starter announced that the Suntours Cup was about to begin, and with that, everyone clambered for the best view possible, even climbing the large trees around the track. As the horses came around the turn into the straight, the dust billowed like a snowstorm. Through the haze, Black Kava hit the front, and at the post he had won by a length.

After the excitement had settled, waitresses in colourful garments plied their trade, selling hamburgers and banana desserts and, yes, more of the dreaded kava: the stuff that makes your lips go numb and numbs your senses with pleasure.

The Cup had been run and won, but race 8 was the race that the locals were eagerly waiting for: the Carpenters Motors Nissan Heavyweight Cup, for jockeys 65 kg and over. Obviously a strict diet of hamburgers, cakes and Coca-Cola were what these jockeys thrived on.

The race was won by a horse with a very appropriate name: Rum Duty. Once the dust settled, it was more kava and Bounty rum for all the patrons – well, that is, the ones who were capable of standing. Fiji time and kava time, oh, what a deadly mix.

'Ladiesh and gentlemensh, we are getting ready … we are nearly ready for … raishe, ah, yesh, raishe 9. It ish our time honour … it ish our big raishe of the year. It ish the GCI Ghasti Raishe.'

Big Al had never seen or heard anything like this, especially listening to the course announcer trying to apply his craft. This bloke was definitely four sheets to the wind. How the bloody hell was he going to call the race? Or more to the point, how could he *see* the race?

Fast forward to 2014, and we were at the Fletchers' home, enjoying Sunday lunch and a few cleansing ales. Big Al was recounting that day more than 20 years ago. He said, 'You know what, Baz? You know why this race was their big event of the year? Believe it or not, the horses didn't have jockeys in saddles: they towed jockeys on pallets – yes, bloody pallets. Christ, I couldn't bloody believe it. And what's more, there were fifteen bloody starters in the race, and Baz, some of those jockeys looked like they had been on kava all afternoon. Bloody hell.

'Baz, the horses appeared chained to the pallets, and some of those pallets were all shapes and sizes. The flag goes up, a deathly hush fills the air, a large Fijian bloke farts, the horses take off in fright and the race is underway. Bloody hell.

'Dust flies over the crowd, the sound of hooves and pallets drown the cheers, and the bloody commentary box was swaying with one excited and drunk race caller. The dust settled a bit as they came into the straight and ready for the run home. But the first ten horses were riderless, and the number 11 bloke, who is leading the charge, dodges pallet after pallet, but eventually loses control, flies across the parched earth, skids under the running rail and comes to a screaming halt in a large pile of horse shite.

'And that's not all. The rest of the field dodges all the carnage, and crosses the line to the ecstatic pleasure of the wild crowd. The dust settles, and the caller announces that "the winner ish number 7". And a great cheer goes up.

'Now Baz, this is where the proverbial hits the fan. Number 4 is already in the winner's enclosure to claim the first prize, and on hearing the decision, he promptly grabs the cheque and trophy, and starts kicking at the presiding officials. As the officials try to retrieve the prizes, the course announcer bellows for police assistance in the winner's enclosure. Number 4 is then knocked to the ground and is ferociously kicked until the constabulary arrived. The police, in their fine cotton skirts, yank the dishonoured jockey to his feet and drag him from the track to the cheers of the energetic crowd.

'This is obviously what they had all come to see: utter mayhem. Another minor-placed jockey appears and starts to punch and kick before he can even make a grab at the first prize. The crowd cheers, more punches flying in the dust, and the course announcer asks for more assistance back in the enclosure.

'And would you believe it, two rather annoyed large policemen reluctantly drain their glasses of Bounty rum and waddle off to assist in the beating of the elfin jockey. Bloody hell, I couldn't believe it. And the real winner, number 7, he decides to forgo his prizes and stays motionless behind his horse.

'Now, the drunk race caller, after all that excitement, remembered to call for an ambulance to collect all the injured participants scattered in agony around the track. The ambulance arrives and majestically glides through the packed assembly to collect the writhing bodies.

'Then with lights flashing and sirens blaring in the warm afternoon sun, the ambulance makes its way to the local hospital in Nadi. But the crowd wants more, and it isn't long before punches and bottles of Fijian beer are flying into the crowd. Bloody hell – never, never again.'

Could we imagine that happening at Flemington or Randwick? No! Or maybe it did back in the 1800s – well, the fights anyway.

Meanwhile, back in Australia on that day in 1991, Pontomo flashed home to win what is now called the Emirates Stakes.

Yes, this was a day at the races that Big Al will never forget as long as he lives. Racing Fiji-style: there's nothing like it.

Tony and Henry's hijinks
... a trip down memory lane

Finally, here are some tales from our 'mature' contributors, Tony Valli and Henry Lawrence.

Nerves ... as told by Tony Valli

'Hi boys.

'Here is a story from my own experience. In the late 1950s to early 1960s (before TAB), I was clerking for an SP bookie to supplement my wages from the brickyards. We were at Arncliffe in southern Sydney, using a shed in a lane between the pub and the Catholic Church. We had this punter, a skinny, sickly looking bloke, who always had two bob on the longest-priced horse in a race. Anything at 100/1, he loved it. He would chew his nails and make groaning-moaning sounds every time the broadcaster mentioned his horse's name, even if the horse was running last. We nicknamed this bloke "Nerves".

'One day his horse hit the front in the straight and poor old Nerves was tearing his hair out and making all of these very weird sounds. The favourite comes at his horse, and "photo" is the call. Nerves goes down in a heap. I raced around from the counter and couldn't feel his pulse. I called in Ron Hanson, a Leichhardt Stadium wrestler and our "keep-the-peace" man, who was the guard man on the gate at the time.

'"I know what to do", says Ron, coming up with one of his very good ideas. "Let's drag him out in the lane behind the church and blame it on the Catholics." Horse got beat and Nerves did recover.

'True story, fellas.'

Water … as told by Henry Lawrence

'Gentlemen,

'I once knew a bookmaker in Rockhampton, Bob Baxter. He was known as a punting bookmaker and was also the punter for trainer Dom O'Malley.

'In 1945, a horse by the name of Cruzore, trained by O'Malley, was firm favourite for the Rockhampton Cup, a big race in those days.

'At the time, the great Australian jockey Neville Sellwood was in the army and was stationed at Townsville, but was granted leave to come to Rockhampton and ride Cruzore in the Cup.

'Just before the race, O'Malley, the trainer of Cruzore, came up to Baxter and said: "Don't back my horse because Sellwood's mates have jumped in and taken our price so it is too short to back now. I've given him a bucket of water." (This was a popular way to stop a horse in those days.) Bob went white and said, "Hell, I wish you had told me ten minutes ago; I've just had £250 on him." Today, that would equate to several thousand dollars. Cruzore ran unplaced and ended back with the tailenders.'

A big drink of water on race day kept some sneaky punters at bay.

The Man in the Red Coat … as told by Henry Lawrence

'In 1942, as a fourteen-year-old, I used to help the barrier attendants at the Rockhampton Races, just to get a few pennies.

'At the time there was a jockey riding there by the name of Des Evans [a pseudonym to protect the innocent], quite a pleasant bloke, but crikey, what a bit of a larrikin. Jockeys then did not make much of a living and often had another job. So, it wasn't surprising that they often employed tactics not within the rules of racing, just "to make a quid".

'Des had a reputation for using electrical assistance to convince his mounts to do their best. Often, just before starting time, the stewards would signal the starter to hold the start, come around to the barrier in their car and take Dessie back to the stewards room to search him for a battery – in colloquial terms, "a jigger".

'Des would get out of the car, cheeky as you like, slapping his whip against his boot, not a care in the world. Needless to say, the stewards never found anything.

'Des and his "way with horses" were always on my mind, and on Sundays I used to go to the stables of an old trainer by the name of Arthur Watson and take his horses for a bit of a pick at the grass.

'One Sunday I said to "Watty", "The stewards searched Dessie again yesterday, and did they find anything? Does he carry a jigger?"

'Now Arthur was trying to give up the smokes, and would often have an empty cigarette holder in his mouth. He took the empty cigarette holder out of his mouth and said, "Oh, yes."

'I said, "But they never found one." He took his cigarette holder out of his mouth again, and said, "Watch the man in the red coat."

'The following Saturday, Des Evans had a ride on a horse called Himalaya, which was quite a barrier rogue. The owners and trainer had been warned that if Himalaya didn't jump with the field this time, he would be banned.

'At the start, Himalaya kept reefing away from the barrier, so the man in the red coat – as you know, the clerk of the course – came up to lead him in. As he did, he slipped the jigger into Des's hand. I saw it with my own eyes.

'Himalaya jumped with the field, and although he didn't win the race, he wasn't banned from future racing. Would you believe, the trainer of Himalaya was none other than Arthur Watson?'

The man in red giving out gifts again.

How did I miss that? … as told by Henry Lawrence

'In your book *At the Track*, on page 61, you mentioned the Lincolnshire Handicap. As a young bloke in 1951, I was fortunate to see the Cambridgeshire Handicap, run on the third day of the Lincolnshire Race Carnival [in Lincolnshire, in the East Midlands of England].

'The race is over 9 furlongs (1800 metres), and is run down the straight Newmarket "Rowley Mile" course.

'There had been relentless rain over the past month, and with the jumping season finished, day three had become a quagmire.

'This day there were 30 starters in the Cambridgeshire, and being a true blue Aussie, I backed "Scobie" Breasley's mount,

Fleeting Moment. Now, back then, race callers in England were very inexperienced, and with such heavy rain, large fields, and runners spread all over the track, one must forgive mistakes.

'At no stage during the running of the race did the race caller mention my horse, Fleeting Moment. Who knows? He may have been a late scratching at the barrier. There was a photo finish, and after a lengthy delay: "Here is the result of the photo fin– ... um ... ah ... ah ... Ladies and gentlemen, I regret to say that due to the blinding rain, I did not mention the winner of the race. The winner is Fleeting Moment, ridden by Arthur 'Scobie' Breasley. My apologies."

'A nice win at 28/1 for a 22-year-old lad 12,000 miles from home.'

Thank goodness for TV broadcasts today.

The Joe and Archie Show
... *a remarkable beginning, then a drug slur!*

It is well documented that when times are tough, the average Aussie looks for something or someone they can look up to, aspire to, live the dream with – because if we don't have dreams, life can be terribly boring. This tale is just a reminder that racing belongs to the average man on the street and not just to those hanging out in the boardrooms.

The story begins in 1999 at Meringo Stud, near Moruya on the southern coast of New South Wales. A colt by the stallion Celtic Swing, out of a well-bred mare, Shady Stream, hit the ground running. It was an easy decision to syndicate this thoroughbred to three successful businessmen. The boardroom businessmen were all involved in the takeover of Melbourne's Crown Casino for Kerry Packer, so naming the colt Takeover Target was a logical choice.

The well-respected trainer John Morish, at Randwick, was selected to get their investment ready for the track. As can sometimes be the case, the following two years were full of disappointment. Takeover Target had a problem with his suspensory nerve, which was very painful for the horse and which contributed significantly to him being one very cranky customer.

Because of the injury, there was no chance of a race, so the businessmen decided to cut their losses. Next stop for Takeover Target was a dispersal sale, in 2003.

At the next Inglis Dispersal Sale, there were four bidders. The bidding started at $500 and then escalated to $800; it finally concluded with a cabbie named Joe Janiak, who paid the princely sum of $1250 for the horse. Joe thought at the time that the price he paid for this cranky son of Celtic Swing was a little steep but, nevertheless, what was done was done. Joe and his trusty steed wound their way back to Queanbeyan and to Joe's home, a caravan.

Takeover Target's cranky disposition was highlighted the very first day in the stables when he reared, sending Joe packing to the local hospital to get 30 stitches for a head wound. Not a great start.

No-one could possibly imagine that this trip to the hospital was the start of a union that would result in 21 wins and ten placings for 41 starts, with winnings in excess of $6 million across Australia, Great Britain, Singapore and Japan. Here are just some of his Group race wins in Australia and overseas:

- 1st, 2004 – Group 1, Flemington Salinger Stakes
- 1st, 2005 – Group 3, Doomben Summer Stakes
- 1st, 2006 – Group 1, Flemington Lightning Stakes
- 1st, 2006 – Group 1, Flemington Newmarket Handicap
- 1st, 2006 – Group 2, Royal Ascot King's Stand Stakes, UK
- 1st, 2006 – Group 1, NAKA Sprinters Stakes, Japan
- 1st, 2007 – Group 1, Doomben 10,000
- 1st, 2008 – Group 1, KrisFlyer International Sprint, Singapore
- 1st, 2008 – Group 2, Perth Winterbottom Stakes
- 1st, 2008 – Group 3, Perth AJ Scahill Stakes
- 1st, 2009 – Group 1, Randwick TJ Smith Stakes
- 1st, 2009 – Group 1, Morphetville Goodwood Handicap

Some horses have a preference for particular tracks and conditions, but Takeover Target raced at his peak everywhere and in all conditions. He won on twelve different tracks all over the world. He always gave his best – and all any punter wants is for his horse to put in. 'Archie', as he was fondly known, was always in the leading bunch and never let you down. That running style was reminiscent of the great Vo Rogue and Might and Power. To top off this exciting story, there is also something deeply satisfying about cheering on a horse that is owned and trained by a real-life Aussie battler.

Takeover Target has written his name in the annals of Australian history through his ageless ability to win at the highest possible level when many thought that his best was behind him.

To support this ageless theory, it should be known that Takeover Target was the oldest horse on the card on Doncaster Day at Randwick in April 2009. He astounded all and sundry by taking out the TJ Smith Group 1, beating a champion in his own right, the well-credentialed performer Apache Cat.

The crowd erupted that day when 'Archie' led them around the turn and just kept on increasing his lead. Joe had a tear in his eye as he admired his champion – nay, the people's champion. He had always known that the horse could do it, but very few others had believed.

Our great sporting commentator Ken Callander said of Takeover Target on that day, after that win: 'Well, I've never seen anything like him. What a champion.'

Now the drug slur ...

Joe Janiak's third Royal Ascot campaign in England with Takeover Target was soured by accusations in the British press that described Takeover Target as 'the drug runner from Down Under'.

The accusations were made by Mark Johnston, a qualified veterinary surgeon and one of Britain's leading trainers. He questioned the authorities as to how they could allow this horse to have another stint at the riches of Royal Ascot and why Joe Janiak's training licence was not suspended.

Johnston was quoted in *The Times* as saying:

As I understand the rules of racing in this country on drug use, it is an offence to administer a prohibited substance to a horse with intent to affect the racing performance. ... It strikes me that Mr Janiak is guilty under those rules and that if I was to admit administering anabolic steroids to one of my horses I would be liable to have my licence to train withdrawn. I cannot, therefore, understand how a horse which has previously tested positive for a prohibited substance and whose trainer has freely admitted administering the drug, can be invited to participate in a race in this country.

This sorry saga began when Takeover Target arrived in Hong Kong in October 2006 to prepare for the HK$14 million Hong Kong Sprint. He had travelled from Japan, where he had recently won the prestigious Sprinters Stakes.

Joe advised the Hong Kong officials that a drug (HPC) had been administered to Takeover Target to assist with his air travel and flight out of Japan. He had been assured by a vet in Japan that the substance would clear out of his system within two weeks.

Minute traces were found in his system on the morning of the Hong Kong Sprint, so stewards had no option but to insist that Joe withdraw his horse, and they also slapped a HK$200,000 fine on him. Despite all the assurances given by veterinarians, these were the strict rules of racing and they had to be adhered to.

In Australia at that time, the drug known as HPC was not a banned substance. It was widely reported to have a calming effect on horses, as well as being a mood stabiliser and appetite stimulant. Reflecting on Mark Johnston's unprecedented outburst before Royal Ascot, we don't suppose it had anything to do with Takeover Target being victorious over his runner in Japan's prestigious Sprinters Stakes the weekend prior.

Mark Johnston's outburst was viewed with great suspicion by Australians. Australians are still vehemently against anything that smells of a class structure. We do not accept our culture being contaminated by pomp and ceremony, nor do we accept any comment that hints of class distinction, especially when it is seen as a thinly veiled attempt to deride one of our great champions.

Joe Janiak and Takeover Target: the people's champions.

The Sydney Racetrack was a bog
... so they changed to a different track mid-program

Saturday 20 June 2009 started like any other race day for the officials who were to oversee the race program at Royal Randwick. Well, it started like any other day with the exception of the weather, because it had been a shocker in Sydney, and many people were eagerly waiting for the report from the course authorities on whether the races would go ahead.

Very early morning, in winter's darkest shadow, Chief Steward Ray Murrihy and racecourse manager Dave Hodgson braved the conditions to see if the track was safe for racing. Apart from the two of them nearly being skittled by a horse and work rider in the morning darkness, Ray and his cohorts decided that the races could commence that day on time and in safe conditions. In everyone's interest, if the rain persisted, they would continue to check during the day and take advice from the jockeys.

Well, the program started under rainy skies, and after three races. Murrihy and Hodgson were forced, on advice from the jockeys, to again cast their experienced eyes over the course proper. The course was now rendered unsafe, in their opinion, and the rest of the program would have to be abandoned, unless ...

Whether you are a worker in the members stand, manning the many security areas, a bookie or a punter, there is nothing worse than getting to the races – in rain, hail or shine – and then having them cancelled. It's a waste of all that effort to get there and set up. To abandon a race meeting mid-stream is a great inconvenience to many, and it can also cause financial hardship for some, such as the food and beverage suppliers.

To understand what Ray Murrihy announced next, you need to understand what is available at Royal Randwick. Inside the course proper, there is the all-weather Kensington track, which is used for training and barrier trials. That course in itself is kept in reasonably good order, and the only difference, naturally, is the circuit distance and consequently some barrier-start positions.

The announcement that the last five races on the program were to be switched to the Kensington track was greeted with silence, bewilderment and, for many of those who didn't understand the changes that would have to be made to continue racing, sheer delight. It was a very brave step by Ray Murrihy.

The circumference for Royal Randwick is 2224 metres with a 410-metre straight. This is not much different from Kensington, the inner racetrack, which has a circumference of 2100 metres. Adjustments could be made to accommodate a finishing straight of 410 metres.

But there was one problem: the next race was the Coach and Horses Handicap over 1200 metres, but there was no 1200-metre chute. There was only a much narrower chute to accommodate barriers at the 1100-metre mark. There were just too many horses for the race. The decision was made, and Ray Murrihy, much to the disappointment and criticism of some trainers, announced that he would have to ballot out some horses to allow the field to start in a safe manner.

Murrihy took off his trusty hat and placed in it the names of all the two-year-olds having their first start in a race. Much like picking the winners in a raffle, names were pulled out of the hat – but these horses were scratched from the race. Some old-timer said that it was the first time he had seen it done since World War II, more than 60 years before.

The smaller field lined up and the races continued for the rest of the program on the Kensington track. Maybe it was an omen: the winner of the Coach and Horses Handicap was Cleanup. We dare say the jockeys had to after each race.

Brave man, that Mr Murrihy.

CHAPTER 2
Ring-ins and Rogues

Very simple explanation, Your Honour
...from the King of Ring-ins and Ringers

In the United States and, at times, in the United Kingdom, horses substituted with other better-performing horses were known as 'ringers'. In Australia, they are known as 'ring-ins'.

Peter Christian Barrie (1888–1973) was known as 'King of the Ringers'. Much of his life involved the dubious art of ringers, and most of the time Peter Barrie seemed to be one step ahead of the authorities. He was said to have at least 20 aliases, and he was the master of dyeing horses so that the colour would never wash out with water.

The following are just a few things that were said about or by the King of Ringers.

In 1928, writing for the *New York Press*, E Phocion Howard reported:

> Barrie is an engaging cuss. You could not help but admire his brazen frankness. He's the best con-man I have ever met.

In 1931, the *New York Worldwide Telegram* reported the New York Jockey Club had banned Mrs Jean Browning for her involvement in irregular betting patterns and the possible substitution of a horse named Saintlite. It stated:

We know Peter Barrie is possibly involved in this and will probably suffer the same fate, as this is not a novelty to him. He has already been banned from tracks in England, Canada, Maryland and Miami.

In 1932, Peter Barrie told the *New York Daily News*:

> You can't hold on to crooked money, because it is as slippery as a fish, and like a fish it won't keep.

This extract from the British newspaper *The Observer* (October 1935) is from a statement made by Peter Barrie:

> People in England haven't got the foggiest notion of what really crooked racing means. Over in the United States, the Sport of Kings is just another racket, with gangsters and gunmen pulling most of the strings. Ringers are everywhere. I know.

Something else Peter Barrie was renowned for was his ability to manufacture a kind of 'miracle concoction' that was legal at the time. It consisted of glycerine, strychnine, cola nut and heroin, mixed with digitalis, which was a medication used by heart patients. In 1951, *People* magazine republished an article from years earlier advertising 'Barrie Tonic'. The tonic was for sale at 25 shillings, and the instructions on the bottle read:

> Barrie Tonic – Shake the bottle well three-and-a-half hours before a race and give your horse a few shots. Watch him go and you will have a winner.

Barrie had told the magazine, 'I am looking forward to this tonic to give me the fortune I intend to have before I retire to a life of ease in Australia.' He never made it to Australia, and died in 1973 at the age of 85. He spent his last days in the Greenwich District Hospital, England, suffering from senile dementia.

Once, when questioned by a magistrate to please explain the terminology of a 'good thing', he said, 'Easy, Your Honour: a useful three-year-old in a moderate two-year-old race.'

QUICK ... THEY'RE ONTO US ... RIP OFF THOSE STICKERS!

ACME STICKERS

Reporter Paul Gallico summed up Peter Christian Barrie, 'The King of the Ringers', in two words in the *New York Press* in 1930: 'Utterly brazen!'

The look-alikes had a day to remember
... and the bookies took a bath in Bath

The race in question was the Spa Spelling Stakes at Bath, tucked away in the county of Somerset in south-west England. It is a town that is well known for its universities and the natural hot water springs commonly referred to as the Bath spa.

It was a summer's day in July 1953. The sting had been set a little earlier, with the purchase of two French thoroughbreds: Santa Amaro, which was potentially a very good horse, and Francasal,

63

which was a very mediocre performer and very rarely finished in the first five of the race he contested. But the horses had one thing in common: they were very much 'look-alikes'.

The sting revolved around that obscure race meeting in Bath. As usual, the on-course bookmakers determined the starting price of a horse based on what money was wagered on the day. There was a small group of five people involved in the sting; some of them were on the perimeter and didn't know the ins and outs of the scheme, but they knew that whatever was going on, they best keep their traps shut and just do what they were told. There was plenty of money available. As long as the on-course bookmakers could not communicate with the off-course bookies, then no-one would wise up to what was about to go down. (One has to remember that, in 1953, the only 'mobile phone' was the one you carried across a room with a long extension cord so your nearest and dearest could have a conversation with the person on the other end.)

The well-deserved favourite, Empire Magic, was priced at 6/4 in the Spa Spelling Stakes; the unwanted and poorly performing Francasal was at 10/1. No-one knew, except for a couple of those involved, that the real Francasal was tucked away in a stable box a few miles away, feeding on his chaff. Santa Amaro took his place in the field under the name Francasal, and no-one suspected anything – not at that time, anyway.

Nearby, two luckless participants in the scam had been given a job by the main man. They stopped their van not far from the Bath Racecourse, and out from the back came an extension ladder. The ladder was placed against the telephone pole, one holding it steady while the other scaled its heights. With about 30 minutes until the start of the race, *snip, snip,* all communications to the course were gone.

Well, the five main conspirators had their prearranged bets placed all over England. As long as the off-course bookies, who were being 'belted' by the punters, could not communicate with the on-course bookies, then their scam could not fail. All that had to happen now was that the horse called Francasal in the race book had to win – and win he did, at those juicy odds of 10/1.

Santa Amaro, after the right weight was declared, was quickly whisked away to another set of stables, not far from where the real Francasal was enjoying a feed and a kip.

However, there were two little problems for our conspirators, the first being that our two friends who had scaled great heights to cut the telephone lines had been noticed by a nearby maintenance worker. Thinking to himself that they did not look like people from the telephone company, he jotted down the registration of the van. The second thing was that, although the bookies off course could not contact those on course, just prior to the race they had grave suspicions about the trend in the betting. There were some bookies who took bets of £2000 and £3000 on 10/1 Francasal. The suspicious activity was reported to the appropriate body.

Of course, the ring-in, Santa Amaro, had proved too good for his opposition in the race, and those involved thought everything looked settled. But it wasn't long before the 'Bill' came knocking on their collective doors. To the cheers of the bookies throughout England, in March 1954 at the Old Bailey courthouse, London, four of the conspirators were found guilty of conspiring to defraud the Bath Racecourse. Their sentences ranged from nine months to three years, to be served as 'guests' of Her Majesty's Prisons.

A few years later, one of the gang, Cardiff bookmaker Gomer Charles, who had been sentenced to two years' jail, answered a knock on his front door and was shot dead.

Even though it had been a small racecourse and it was just the one telephone line cut, bookies around the country said that the sting had netted the gang the equivalent of £4 million today. Had they not been so greedy, they probably would have gotten away with it.

Both Francasal and Santa Amaro were held under guard in a stable by the police during the trial, and they were sent to auction once the verdict was handed down. Some people just wanted something to remind them of that day in Bath; nonetheless the horses were knocked down by the auctioneer for a sum far less than their original purchase price in France.

Mobile phones put a stop to that lot.

Belmont Park and the Belmont Stakes
... *home of champions and a ring-in*

Belmont Park in Nassau county, New York, is one of just a few racetracks that would be considered hallowed ground when it comes to describing the part it plays in American racing history. The Belmont Stakes is the third leg of the famous US Triple Crown, run five weeks after the first leg, the Kentucky Derby, and two weeks after the next leg, the Preakness Stakes. It is run over 1.5 miles (2.4 km) in early June every year, and it is open to all three-year-olds – colts, geldings and fillies. It is nicknamed the 'Test of Champions'.

The very first winner of all three races was Sir Barton in 1919, but it wasn't until Gallant Fox won all three races in 1930 that this was referred to as the US Triple Crown of Champions.

There have been only a handful of champion thoroughbreds that have managed to win all three races in the one year; it is no doubt a feat that sets them apart and allows them to truly be called great champions. Other winners are the son of Gallant Fox, Omaha (1935), War Admiral (1937), Whirlaway (1941), Count Fleet (1943), Assault (1946), Citation (1948), Secretariat (1973) and Seattle Slew (1977). At the time of writing, the last one to achieve this rare distinction was Affirmed in 1978.

The year of controversy at Belmont Park was 1977. A little over three months after Seattle Slew won the Triple Crown, there was another race at Belmont Park that caused more headlines and more dinner table conversation than even the winner of the unique thoroughbred treble that year.

The key player was a well-respected vet at the leading New York raceways, Mark Gerard. Born in Brooklyn in 1934, he went on to study veterinary medicine at Cornell College. To supplement his income during summer, Mark worked at the tracks as an exercise rider and walker. He soon came to the attention of the legendary trainer 'Sunny Jim' Fitzsimmons, who trained for the leading owners at that time.

Dr Mark Gerard qualified as a vet, and with his connections on the course, he soon headed a flourishing practice where he attended such greats as Kentucky Derby winners Secretariat, Riva Ridge and

Canonero II, and one of the greatest horses of the modern era, Kelso. Gerard had a great reputation, and everything was going along just dandy.

In the mid-1970s, the doctor bought two thoroughbreds in Uruguay. One was Cinzano, a three-year-old that had won seven out of his last eight races; the other was Lebon, a four-year-old that one could rightly say 'could not run out of sight on a dark night'.

Why would these two opposites be bought? Maybe it was because they looked remarkably alike. They were then brought to the New York area where, you could say, there was some shuffling of the registration papers, and unbeknown to the racing public, Lebon became Cinzano and Cinzano became Lebon.

On 23 September 1977, a few months after Seattle Slew took out the Triple Crown, Lebon was nominated for and contested a modest race at Belmont Park. With the abysmal form of this ex-Uruguayan racehorse, it was no surprise that he was quoted at nearly 60/1. In one of those rare events that happen on a course, for a reason known only to the horse and connections, Lebon proved too good for his opposition. There were a few head scratches, but everything was in order. Paperwork was okay, weight was right, so it was pay-up time.

Dr Gerard must have had some confidence in his horse, because he managed to have $1200 to win and $600 to place. If you use your calculator, as I am sure the cashier at the payout window had to, his winnings came to a very healthy $80,400 and some change. In today's money, this would be around $500,000.

Everything was hunky-dory. The good doc had his small fortune and nobody was the wiser. It simply looked as though Lebon had an amazing change in his form line and had brought the bikkies home for his stable and connections. Except ...

A racing editor at a racing newspaper in Uruguay read about the unexpected victory of an old favourite of his, Lebon, so from his office in Uruguay he requested a photo of the winner from the Associated Press. He also knew and admired another bright star of the Uruguayan thoroughbred industry – you guessed it, he had a soft spot for the best three-year-old at the time that he could recall, Cinzano.

The editor was sent the official shot taken in the winner's circle after the race. Bingo! He noticed the difference straight away. He could see that the winner was in fact the excellent three-year-old performer Cinzano. He didn't know how widespread this fraud went. Was it an honest mistake or was it a controlled ring-in operation perpetrated on the good folk of New York using ex-Uruguayan racehorses? He immediately contacted the New York Jockey Club with his allegations.

When the appropriate authorities had tracked down both horses in question, despite the registration papers it was clear that the five-year-old was the real Lebon and the four-year-old was the real Cinzano.

The complicated web slowly unravelled. While Lebon was bought by Dr Gerard for a paltry $1600, he had paid $81,000 for Cinzano. I'm sure you're thinking: 'Wait, he only won about that much on the ring-in Lebon.' But there was an earlier money-making part to Dr Gerard's scam.

What had happened when the two horses were first brought back to New York? Dr Gerard, it was believed, had initially sold the real Cinzano to a racing enthusiast. As many racehorse owners would know, sometimes you don't see your horse from one month to the next when they are spelling and training. Dr Gerard made a sad call during that time and told the new owner of Cinzano that, unfortunately, the horse had contracted a virus and had to be put down. (Untrue!) The good doc even arranged the insurance claim for the owner. Before the sale, the owner had been told of the horse's ability, so he had him insured for $150,000.

Everyone was satisfied. The owner in New York, who had paid Dr Gerard a little over $80,000 for Cinzano, received a payout of $150,000 from his insurance company, and the good doctor still had Cinzano and Lebon tucked away. The registration papers were shuffled and altered.

So the sting was working. Apart from the sharp eye of a racing editor in Uruguay, Dr Mark Gerard would have been home free.

The well-respected veterinary doctor was charged relating to the conspiracy. He was found guilty of only 'fraudulent entries and practices in contests of speed' and was fined $1000 and sentenced to one year in jail. His lawyer appealed, and Gerard ended up serving a much lesser sentence in Nassau County jail. Dr Mark Gerard died on 21 June 2011, aged 76 years old.

Cinzano and Lebon: not a good mix.

The mystery of the 1844 Epsom Derby
... where the winner was killed months before the race

As the years roll on, the facts of many a true story in the racing game have been distorted, reinvented or blatantly changed, as per the old adage 'you never let the truth get in the way of a good story'. When I was researching Lord George Bentinck (1802–1848), once a happy punter and owner of thoroughbreds in England, his story yielded some information that I felt I must further research. While there are many reports written about the 1844 Epsom Derby, there is no doubt that in all of these tales, there is the same thread of historic fact. I have tried to represent these 'facts' here and limit any liberties in telling 'a good story'.

As stated previously, Lord George Bentinck was a great supporter of horse racing and, by all accounts, a very profitable owner, trainer and punter, before he turned his efforts to horseracing administration. Lord Bentinck poured his efforts into cleansing horseracing of fraudulent activity, and supported this push by proposing a Set of Rules to cover all contingencies. Through the British Courts, he was able to change outdated legislation regarding the corruption involved at that time with settling debts. He was so committed to this role that he sold all of his racing interests and stables, so that there would be no other distraction nor any nefarious implications of conflicting interests made by others.

The Epsom Derby is Britain's richest Group 1 horserace, the most prestigious race on its racing calendar and the second leg of its Triple Crown. It is run in June each year at Epsom Downs, Surrey, over 1 mile, 4 furlongs and 10 yards (2423 metres). Only three-year-old colts and fillies are eligible to participate.

In 1844, the Epsom Derby was won by a three-year-old horse

called Running Rein, owned by Abraham Levi Goodman. Second in the race was Orlando, owned by Colonel Jonathan Peel and ridden by Nat Flatman. Everything seemed to be in order, until the doyen of the racing industry, Lord George Bentinck, stepped up to the plate and convinced Colonel Jonathan Peel to lodge a protest against the winner on behalf of his jockey and horse.

This was a very unusual step on Lord Bentinck's part but, as his main objective as a racing administrator was to rid the industry of fraudsters and charlatans, it was thought that he obviously knew more about the winner than everyone else.

Those readers who can recall the 1984 Fine Cotton ring-in affair at the Doomben Racecourse, Brisbane, may have a feeling of deja vu when reading about the 1844 Epsom Derby. Apparently, as word got around of a protest and possible ring-in, it was not the ground-breaking news that one would expect it to be. A lot of people that day had heard of the possibility – and when one person tells another person a secret, we know it is never a secret again.

In one account of the great race in 1844, it was described as an extraordinary racing event where the favourite was not allowed by the jockey to run on its merits. There was a firm belief that the second favourite had been 'got at', and one three-year-old was found to be in fact a six-year-old when it had to be put down after breaking its leg during the course of the race. The 1844 Epsom Derby had it all!

When Lord Bentinck announced the protest and inquiry, he went through the appropriate bodies and had all prize money suspended. It was up to the bookmakers if they wanted to settle and get on with life. Lord George Bentinck's claim was that the three-year-old first past the post, Running Rein, was in fact a four-year-old from the same stable, called Maccabeus.

As Lord George Bentinck began asking questions, it was found that the scam to produce a win in the 1844 Derby had started about two years earlier, when Running Rein and Maccabeus were switched in name at the stable. They were very similar in appearance, although poles apart in performance, with Maccabeus being a year older than his stablemate.

A local horse dealer by the name of George Odell was called to give evidence. He said that he recognised the distinctive markings on the leg of the winner, which pointed to the Derby winner being the four-year-old Maccabeus, not Running Rein.

When the request was made of the owner, Mr Abraham Levi Goodman, to produce Running Rein for an examination, the investigators were advised that the winner had been abducted.

Eventually the facts were revealed. The real Running Rein had been killed months before the race – just in case there were any questions, only one Running Rein (the real Maccabeus) would be found. One of the most telling factors when deciding the age of a horse is the examination of the horse's teeth. Later that same year, the Running Rein imposter was eventually found and a dental examination was made, finding that he was indeed a four year old, and therefore ineligible to run in the Derby.

Lord George Bentinck became the hero of the racing public, with his relentless push to clean up the scams that were being perpetrated on the public through the greed of a few. After all deliberations, Orlando was promoted to first place in the 1844 Epsom Derby and the history books state this now, but they don't mention the drama behind the horse Running Rein, who won the Derby but died months before.

Running Rein couldn't outrun the truth.

The good Doctor Poison
... a result of being in the grip of horses and gambling

There are many sayings and colloquialisms in the English language; some of their origins are mysterious, some obvious, and with some we are left guessing as to how they came into use. There is one such saying that many of us have used over the years when inviting someone to have drink and before we order their 'tipple'.

After reading this next story about a deadly attraction to racehorses and gambling that resulted in murder and mayhem, you may come to think that this gentleman is indeed the originator of that saying: 'What's your poison?'

William Palmer was born in Rugeley, Staffordshire, England, on 6 August 1824, and died at the ripe old age of 31 years old on 14 June 1856, in Stafford Prison. His death was a result of a public execution by hanging, after having been found guilty of murdering John Parsons Cook. Palmer's evil trail is said to have been littered with at least ten more victims. All were murdered for money – or the lack of it, to be more precise – as Palmer chased his next big win on the horses.

Palmer was twelve when his father died, and his early life was not very easy. He found himself in and out of trouble with the authorities, but he finally managed to secure a place to study medicine in London, where he qualified as a surgeon in 1846. His life certainly seemed to be turning around for the better.

When he returned to Staffordshire fresh from his academic triumph, he had a thirst-quencher at the local watering hole, where he challenged a local businessman, George Abley, to a drinking contest. Brandy was his favoured indulgence. This may sound like rather innocent fun, but it turned out to be a deadly game for George.

Palmer insisted that they 'gulp' down the drinks, as this was the best way to enjoy the taste. George did as the good doctor said, was carried home by friends an hour later and died in his own bed later that night. It was said that the good doctor had his eye on George's very attractive wife, the now Widow Abley.

Palmer married Ann Thornton in 1847. He became quite the successful physician and surgeon in his town and region, and his attention to horses and gambling started to become a major interest in his life. From all reports he was a terrible gambler, but he always found the money to keep on returning to the track. His reputation on the track was one of a 'quiet and friendly nature' and a man who liked a drink on a hot day.

Being a good son-in-law, he invited his widowed mother-in-law to come and stay with him and his wife at their home in early January 1849. Alas, only two weeks after she had arrived, she became very ill and died. The good doctor called in Dr Bamford, an elderly man of medicine, to pronounce the death of the mother-in-law. Dr Bamford issued a death certificate that stated death was caused by apoplexy (due to bleeding from internal organs). The mother-in-law left her money and estate to Ann, Palmer's wife. It was a timely windfall.

Dr Palmer also made acquaintance with Leonard Bladen at the races, and after a number of losing bets, the doctor borrowed £600 from Bladen. Leonard Bladen found himself at the Palmer residence after that day at the races, and he was soon invited to a 'gulping' contest with Palmer. He too succumbed to terrible pain, which led to his death within just a few hours of having first arrived at the doctor's home.

When Bladen's wife arrived at the Palmer residence after hearing the news of her husband's death, she was very surprised to see that his wallet was empty and his betting book had disappeared. Leonard Bladen had won quite a substantial amount of money at the races the previous week and would have had some on his person – but, no, there was nothing. In his betting book, he had listed all of his bets as well as any monies that he lent out. Palmer's £600 debt would have been listed here, but the betting book had disappeared too.

It probably will not surprise the reader to know that soon after this, Palmer took out a life insurance policy on his wife, Ann. She died in 1854, at the tender age of 27 years, from cholera – at least, that is what is stated on the death certificate.

Dr Palmer, grief-stricken, reluctantly accepted the insurance payout of £13,000. His gambling continued, and so did his bad luck, so the good doctor took out an insurance policy on his brother, Walter Palmer. Now, Walter was already in the 'grip of the grape', and when he died after a 'gulping' session with his dear brother William, he died a quick and painful death.

Again full of grief, Dr William Palmer fronted up to the insurance company to collect the insurance money. This happened to be the same company that had insured his wife, and the insurers had questions for Palmer. There was no payout, but plenty of suspicion.

With his gambling debts at the races spiralling out of control, Palmer made acquaintance with the unfortunate John Cook. John Cook and Palmer were frequent punters at the same track, and over a three-day racing carnival, including the Shrewsbury Handicap Stakes Day, John Cook won plenty. Keeping his record intact,

Dr William Palmer, the surgeon from Rugeley, lost heaps. The more the doctor lost, the more he saw that it was a sign that his next bet would be a winning bet. His stakes got higher and higher, but his winner never came. Within a week of John Cook's very successful day at Shrewsbury, Dr Palmer went and visited Cook, who was feeling poorly, and administered to him some medicine.

That night after Palmer's visit, John Cook died an agonising death. When Cook's brother was called by his wife, he found that Cook's money and betting book had disappeared. He should have had plenty of money, and his betting book most certainly would have contained a notation of the thousands of pounds that the good doctor owed him.

At least Palmer was consistent. Again he rolled out the elderly Dr Bamford to issue the death certificate, stating John Cook died from apoplexy.

Two and two finally equalled four. It was thought that John Cook had been poisoned. It was said that Dr Palmer's poison of preference was more than likely strychnine.

After what some would call interference in the postmortem process by the good doctor, the eminent Dr Swaine Taylor issued a statement. In his findings, he stated he could not find conclusive evidence of poisoning, but other matters had been brought to his attention surrounding Dr William Palmer's involvement in the affair. He went on to say that Palmer was more than likely responsible for the death of John Cook.

Palmer was arrested and charged with John Cook's murder. He was subsequently found guilty and sentenced to be hung by the neck until dead. It was said at his trial that the 'gulping' contest – Palmer's innocent and boyish game – was nothing more than a way to disguise the taste of strychnine as it went down the throat.

More questions were asked and an investigation followed. It was stated that there was no doubt that in his short life, the good Dr William Palmer of Rugeley had been responsible for many other murders in his desire to fund his gambling on the horses.

Known victims of 'Dr Poison'

It is reasonable to assume that in his pursuit to settle his massive gambling debts, Palmer murdered his wife, his mother-in-law, his brother, two people that he owed money to and, of course, the unfortunate John Cook. Were there more victims?

Four of Palmer's five children died in a matter of weeks after their birth. Infant mortality was quite common in those days, but there are suggestions that Dr Palmer would rather have gone to the races than feed yet another mouth. Suspicious! He was also responsible for many illegitimate children, and nothing is known of them or their mothers' fates. Imagine the mothers of the illegitimate babies seeking out Dr Palmer for money to help them support his children. That would have been a dangerous task.

It is said that when they were leading Dr William Palmer up the rickety stairs to place the noose around his neck, he stopped at the very top step and said to his executioner, 'Is this structure safe?' I don't think that really mattered, do you?

So whenever you are at the local watering hole and someone offers to buy you a beer, or whatever it is you are drinking, and they ask 'What's your poison, then?', don't slam the door behind you: run for your life!

The ring-in at Plumpton

… you wonder how many times these mistakes are made

The events of our next story all happened at the Plumpton Racecourse, which is a National Hunt racecourse in Plumpton, East Sussex, a friendly neighbour to Lewes and Brighton, and an hour's train ride from London.

The year was 2003. One of the hot favourites to contest the Cantor Mobile Handicap Hurdle was Investment Force, trained by Charlie Mann. Unfortunately for the horse and its connections, he fell during the race; with two broken legs, Investment Force had to be destroyed. It is never a good sight on a racecourse to see a horse put down, and the scene always serves as fodder for those people who protest and demand that these types of races be banned.

A few days later, when Charlie Mann was going about his work at his stable, he had one of those moments – one of those times when you just stop in your tracks and say to yourself, 'This can't be happening.' Charlie must have thought it was a dream, but there it was, standing in one of the boxes right in front of him: Investment Force, as bold as you like.

A devastated Charlie Mann had his own theories as to what was in front of him in the stable, and he had no option but to contact The Jockey Club and tell them of a possible error at the previous meeting. The club then put the wheels in motion and ordered a DNA test of the euthanised Investment Force.

To everyone's shock and amazement – except Charlie Mann's – the destroyed horse was found to be Investment Force's stablemate, Trump Card. He had been mistakenly sent to Plumpton, cleared through all of the identity safety nets and raced as Investment Force.

There is no doubt that the Plumpton Racecourse has now tightened all checking procedures on horses entering races. After The Jockey Club hearing, Charlie Mann was fined £5000 and was warned that any further mishaps – like in the Trump Card and Investment Force saga – would result in the suspension of his training license.

The irony of it all was that the real Investment Force was a five-year-old winner of above average ability, while poor old Trump Card was a six-year-old plodder that was struggling with form. There was no suggestion that any of this was done intentionally. However, Charlie had already been found guilty of racing the wrong horse on three occasions in the last three years. Apparently a few punters were considering suing Charlie for their losses on the day.

Something tells me Charlie's stable system is flawed.

It was Vital he won
... then he disappeared without a trace!

These events happened many years ago in the goldfields of Kalgoorlie, Western Australia. The story centres around a horse and a very select band of four punters, who no-one had ever seen before. To this day, no-one knows whether the winning horse was a ring-in. The horse in question was Vital, and the year was 1936.

Vital turned up in Kalgoorlie to contest the feature double, the Hannan Handicap and the Kalgoorlie Cup. The four cloak-and-dagger punters backed him as if there was no tomorrow; so much so, they were taking some very short odds right up until the running of the first leg of the double.

After Vital won the first leg quite easily, word got around that the bookies were going to be in deep strife if Vital won the Cup the following week. The four punters refused to be interviewed by journalists from the local newspaper, the *Kalgoorlie Miner*.

By the time the Cup came around, there still had not been even a whisper from the Vital camp. They just waited inside their rooms for the whole week, only coming out for meals and to check on the welfare of the horse.

Race day came around and still no-one could get anything out of the cloak-and-dagger four. 'Mum' was the word.

In a close finish to the Cup, Vital won, defeating First Consul in race record time. The previous year, First Consul had won the WA Sires Produce Stakes. It was reported that connections of Vital had cleaned the bookies out to the tune of £30,000, an incredible amount at the time.

In the early 1970s, *Daily Telegraph* writer Keith Nolan wrote an article about that coup way back in 1936. He stated that Vital was definitely no champion and that his previous best was just a restricted middle-distance race in Ballarat, Victoria. Nolan also wrote that he believed that the connections of Vital were:

hard-bitten people from the Eastern States, who would not hear of Vital being beaten and kept backing him and backing him for the double, at any price they could get.

Back to the day after the 1936 Kalgoorlie Cup win. It was revealed that Vital and the cloak-and-dagger four had disappeared. They were never seen again.

It was rumoured that Vital was a ring-in and that he was, in fact, a major Cup winner from the eastern states, who had identical colouring and markings to Vital. Some 78 years later, no-one is the wiser and we will never know for sure.

Say nothing to no-one!

How do you know that?
... the holiday that saved the bookies heaps

On 19 March 1983, Victorian bookmaker John Hallam was on holidays and decided to attend the St Patrick's Day meeting at Broken Hill, New South Wales. The last race on the program was the 1100-metre Orlando Improvers Handicap.

It was a quiet day, until there was a massive betting plunge on a horse by the name of Foden. On course, it had been backed in from 50/1 to 2/1 equal favourite. In the race, it was never going to lose and it was eased down to win by two lengths.

Hallam knew that something was wrong, and immediately informed the stewards of his concern. He said, 'I know Foden, and this horse is not Foden. The real Foden is a very moderate performer and I have seen him race down south. He is only a picnic horse and has been placed in picnic steeplechase races. This horse won too easily over a short distance, and believe me, it is not Foden.'

This set off the alarms bells, and the siren sounded before correct weight could be notified. The stewards inspected the horse, and on checking the horse's papers and his markings could not be sure if the chestnut was indeed Foden.

As a result, the stewards suspended any betting payouts and immediately disqualified the horse. Obviously, house rules applied here. Correct weight was then signalled and the amended placings were given: first, Eastern Crisis; second, Clear The Deck; third, Duncan Lass.

Once again the bookies were blessed and there was a large sigh of relief. John Hallam had just saved his colleagues a mammoth $250,000 payout. One bookmaker said, 'One of my first bets on Foden was $30,000 to $600. I knew the horse's form, and could not see it even finishing in the first half of the field. However, they just wanted to back it for anything. I shut up shop and would not take any more bets on the horse.'

Foden's trainer was questioned. He told the stewards that he had been given the horse to train only three weeks prior and was told specifically to set the horse for this race. The only times he had seen the owner was the day the horse entered his stables and the morning of the race. He was told not to back the horse, but that there would be a good 'sling' for him if the horse won. And no, he never had one dollar on the horse.

The horse was impounded by the stewards for further investigations of his branding and markings.

Detectives from the Victorian Racing Bureau were called in by the Australian Jockey Club (AJC) Stewards to investigate the ownership of Foden, who it seemed had done his early racing in Victoria. This had all the indications of a possible ring-in. Time was of the essence.

Detectives questioned Wonthaggi owner-trainer Maurie Hill and his wife, Betty, who were the previous owners of the chestnut gelding Foden. They declared that even though the horse had won a 2000-metre picnic race at Woolami in Victoria on 14 February, they had decided to sell him. The horse was sold on 22 February.

When interviewed by *The Age* newspaper, Victorian Detective Senior Sergeant Bill Kneebone said that his squad was making inquiries in conjunction with the Broken Hill CIB, and they would leave no stone unturned.

A reporter from *The Age* then interviewed Maurie Hill, and was told that Hill and his wife had sold Foden for $1000 to a man named Arthur West, who wanted to buy the horse for his daughter to learn to ride. That seemed fair enough, because Foden was a seven-year-old gelding, with a very placid nature. As a racehorse, he didn't have much of a future.

Further inquiries led the police to a property in Victoria's Western District to check on the ownership of another chestnut gelding, once trained at Mortlake. No horse at that property resembled Foden.

Detectives then received a tip-off that finally got the ball rolling. Further information had come to light that a seven-year-old chestnut gelding with very similar markings to Foden was sold at the Dalgety

Bloodstock Mixed Sale in New South Wales in January for $6000. That horse was a multiple Moonee Valley winner, who had won against very good company, and was registered as Nordica. It was now obvious that the horse that had been impounded by the stewards that day in March was Nordica, the ring-in for Foden. Further investigations failed to unearth any more evidence.

Thanks to a holidaying bookie's keen eye, the sting came unstuck. The real Foden and Arthur West were never seen again.

It was another day that the bookies were winners.

The winner was a dead-set certainty
... but someone had their eyes wide open

January 1941 saw the running of the Trial Handicap at Brisbane's Eagle Farm Racecourse. Once betting opened on the race, punters came from everywhere to back only one horse, Russell Maddock's mount, Daylate.

Daylate won brilliantly and it seemed the plunge had come off, but before 'correct weight' came through, it was announced: 'Could you please hold all tickets.'

That day, country racing steward Steve Brown decided to have a day at the Brisbane races and was a guest of the Queensland Turf Club (QTC) Stewards. When Daylate came back to the enclosure, Brown said to the chief steward, 'Sir, that horse that has just won is not Daylate, but the Toowoomba horse Brulad. However, there is another problem. Brulad is dead.'

To the joy of the bookies, the stewards took immediate action and disqualified Daylate. At the subsequent inquiry, all roads led back to Brulad's owner, the farmer Fred Bach. Yes, Brulad was alive and well. The QTC disqualified Bach for life.

One wonders how many other ring-ins Fred Bach and the 'dead' Brulad had been involved in. A couple of months prior, Fred Bach's son, Jack, attended a dispersal sale and purchased the eighteen-year-old broodmare Bern Maid, with a foal at foot by Emborough. That foal was later registered as Bernborough. Due to the Bach family's history, Bernborough was exiled to race only in Toowoomba. In 1945, he was sold to Sydney restaurateur Azzalin Romano and went on to become one of Australia's greatest post-war gallopers.

You've got to know your horses.

Cough, cough ... splutter ... what?
... it rained on the connections parade

Whenever there was a race meeting at the Hawthorne Racetrack in Cicero, Illinois, United States, Lou Grainger never missed going to his favourite track. To Lou, who was nicknamed 'Milwaukie Lou' by his mates, it was a ritual.

On this cold wet day of 18 November 1978, Lou's two punting mates, Bill Reynolds and Jack Sloane, knocked on his door, fully expecting Lou to be ready for the 90-mile (145-km) trip to the races.

However, Milwaukie Lou had one look at the weather and made an exception. Today, he would stay at home in front of a very warm fire. He told Bill and Jack that he would see them at their favourite haunt that evening. He wasn't even going to listen to the races.

That evening his mates arrived at the restaurant, and after dinner and drinks were ordered, the subject got round to the races at Hawthorne.

'Who won the double today?'

'Nervous Tortilla won the first leg, and Charollius won the second.'

On hearing this, Milwaukie Lou nearly choked on his Jack Daniels and said, 'Impossible! Charollius, no! A buddy of mine used to own that bag of bones, and it just about cried every time it saw a sloppy track. No! Impossible!'

Lou explained to his two mates that Charollius's form was very ordinary to say the least, that it had won only once and run only two placings in its previous 21 starts. At his last start at Thistletown in Ohio, Charollius had run a shocker on a wet track, coming in last by four lengths, in a $2500 claiming race. And here he was today in a $3500 claimer. No, Lou was sure something was not right.

Bill and Jack then went on to tell Lou that Charollius opened up at 30/1 – and that was the appropriate price, according to Lou – then was backed in to 8/5, and finally eased to 4/1. They said that the horse romped in by two lengths and paid $10.80 for the $2 betting unit. Its win formed part of the daily double that day with the 2/1 favourite and first leg winner, Nervous Tortilla; the double paid a very healthy $113.60 for the $2 bet. The reason for such an inflated winning amount was that all bets on the double closed before the first leg, so the double was paid out on the 2/1 and 30/1 odds, not the 2/1 and 4/1 odds. There must have been some very well-informed punters.

Lou just shook his head and said, 'There is no way in the world that the second leg winner was Charollius – NO WAY! Impossible!' He realised that this had all the indications of a very well-organised sting, and he reckoned someone had won big time. You just don't back a horse that is completely hopeless in the wet, taking it from 30/1 to 8/5.

The next day, the TV evening news led with the story: 'Hawthorne Racetrack's grandstand burns to ground. Other facilities slightly affected, including wiring used for the Totaliser board.'

This certainly caught Lou's attention, and he was now convinced more than ever that there was something amiss. The one building that had escaped the fire housed the offices and records of the racing stewards.

The win by Charollius had not escaped the eyes of the stewards, and one month later, all investigations led to trainer Charles Lee (Charlie) Wonder. At the racing inquiry, Wonder was charged with producing a ringer at the Hawthorne Racecourse on 18 November 1978.

Milwaukie Lou's judgement had been spot-on. That day in November, Charollius was actually a wet-track specialist by the name of Roman Decade, who had raced in a $20,000 claiming race in the winter of 1977 at Meadowlands Park, New Jersey. In early 1978, he won an $18,000 claiming race at New York's Aqueduct Racetrack in sloppy conditions.

Unknown to Charlie Wonder and his cohort, William Combee, they had been under investigation by the Thoroughbred Racing Protective Bureau for other incidents relating to betting results. Also at the inquiry held into the ring-in of Charollius by Roman Decade, an Illinois Racing Board official produced proof that Charles Lee Wonder and William Combee had engaged in a staggering 27 of 32 attempted ringers in the last couple of years.

According to one source, it was alleged that on one occasion Wonder and Combee bought a broken-down hack for $500, sent him down to an Ohio racecourse and entered him in a $2500 claiming race. They then substituted the horse with one that was eligible for a $15,000 claiming race. Wonder and Combee made all their money betting only on claiming races.

Two very busy boys!

No bones about this one
... a ring-in on the merry-go-round

At Flemington Racecourse, Victoria, on 8 June 1931, the punting public was enjoying a normal race day, without incident. The Rothsay Trial Stakes, over 7 furlongs (1400 metres) with seventeen starters, was going to be just another race, until the stewards were alerted that there was a mammoth betting plunge on a horse by the name of Gagoola. He had been backed in from 33/1 to become 6/4 favourite. The horse had been backed to win £30,000, which was some very serious money at that time.

The race got under way, but things started to go horribly wrong for the plunge horse Gagoola, and he was beaten by three lengths by the 80/1 outsider, Stephanite, having his first race start.

After 'correct weight' was announced, the stewards wanted to check the credentials of Gagoola, but the horse and its connections were nowhere to be found on the course. Soon after, they located the horse and owner-trainer Mr Henry Graham in another stable complex, and he produced papers to show that he had bought the horse from a breeder called Mr HJ Forrester in July 1929. Gagoola's papers were in order.

The following day the stewards went back to the stable, but the horse was gone and the owner-trainer could not be found either. Stablehands told the stewards that very early that morning, the horse had been taken to the local train station.

Because of this suspicious activity, the stewards acted quickly and found that Gagoola was booked on a train to Sydney. When the racing authorities interviewed a railway official, however, they were told, 'No horse by that name was loaded, but a horse by the name of Wellfire was.'

The Victorian Racing Club (VRC) Stewards immediately notified the Albury stationmaster and asked him to verify if there was indeed a horse by the name of Wellfire in transit to Sydney. The answer was yes and that he was the only horse on the train. Australian Jockey Club (AJC) officials and the Registrar of Racehorses, Mr Loddon Yuille, were alerted and asked to inspect the horse as soon as the train arrived in Sydney. It was believed this was the horse 'Gagoola'.

Around the same time, Mr Loddon Yuille received an anonymous phone call saying that Gagoola was really Simba and that the horse was on a train headed for Sydney.

Wellfire was gone, but now Simba was in the frame. Could this be the answer? Was it a ring-In?

The train arrived in Sydney, but there weren't any horses on board. The stewards learnt that a horse had been unloaded at Cabramatta, outside of Sydney, and was now at a property at Mulgoa. When the horse was unloaded, it was so well rugged up there was not an identifiable mark to be seen.

The VRC chairman, LKS Mackinnon, then requested that police, AJC officials and Mr Yuille conduct a raid on the Mulgoa property. No horse was found, only the remains of a smouldering horse carcass. Any identifiable markings had been destroyed by the fire. The property caretaker, Fredrick Lawrence, stated that on arrival, Gagoola had snapped his off foreleg and had to be put down. His body had been burnt. How convenient.

Poor Gagoola was gone, but what about Simba?

On 20 June, the AJC was alerted that a former New Zealand horse, the well-performing gelding Simba, had gone missing. In New Zealand he had been trained by Jack Jamieson and had won four of his five starts. Hello Simba. This sounded encouraging. The hunt was on again.

The owner, JS McLeod, had sold the horse for £1000 to a client of Sydney trainer Joe Smith. It was later confirmed by the AJC that a month earlier, on 5 May, Sydney wharf officials had contacted Joe Smith, as specified on the ship's manifest, to collect the horse that had arrived on board the *Ulimaroa* from New Zealand.

Smith informed the officials that he had no knowledge of the consignment, and he refused to pick up the horse. He also claimed he knew nothing about the sale of a New Zealand horse by the name of Simba.

At around 4pm that same day, a float operator by the name of Bill Calnan arrived at the wharf to pick up a horse 'for a man named Smith'. When questioned by officials, he claimed the only direction he received about the 'pick-up' was to collect a consignment – a horse – for a 'Mr Smith'. Being late in the day, the wharf officials were keen to off-load the horse, so with that it was released to Bill Calnan.

It was later reported that Bill Calnan delivered the horse to a property of 'Mr Smith'. The AJC searched this property of Joe Smith, but no Simba.

Simba had gone again.

On 30 June, the AJC received information that the horse thought to be the missing Simba had tripped and broken his leg at a stable near Randwick Racecourse, and the horse had needed to be put down. Racing officials urgently visited the stables, and were then directed to other premises and found a horse's carcass in the process of being boiled down. Some of the markings seemed to correspond to those of Simba, but it was not possible to make a positive identification.

When contacted in New Zealand, trainer Jack Jamieson revealed that the owner, Mr McLeod, had sold the horse to a Sydney buyer, George Guest. Apparently Guest raced many horses at unregistered race meetings in Sydney.

Based on all that evidence, the AJC opened an official inquiry on 2 July. When questioned, George Guest revealed that at no stage did he want the horse trained by Joe Smith, his regular trainer. When he was asked why, the silence was deafening. He admitted he sent Calnan to pick up the horse from the Sydney wharf and take it to a certain property. He also admitted the horse was in his care, had been gelded and was being given time to recover. He then went on to say that he purchased Simba for the sole purpose of racing it at registered race meetings in Sydney.

What was it Mr Guest – registered or unregistered?

He then said he knew nothing about a horse breaking its leg at stables near Randwick. He told the AJC Stewards that Simba was spelling at a property at Warren, western New South Wales, but he refused to say where, as advised by his solicitor.

The inquiry was then taken over by the VRC Stewards. Finally on 21 July 1932, some twelve months after the betting plunge on Gagoola, it was concluded that the horse that had raced as Gagoola was, in fact, Simba. Photographs showed that the markings of the two horses were extremely similar.

Which horse had died first at the Mulgoa property, and which horse had died at the stables near Randwick? Galgoola or Simba?

George Guest pleaded guilty to being involved in the whole substitution saga and subsequently lying to stewards about the horse's whereabouts. He was disqualified for five years, but not jailed. It was said that he expected a far heavier sentence and, when interviewed, he stated that he could have kissed the VRC Chairman, LKS Mackinnon, on top of the head, for such a lenient sentence. At the time, Guest had expected disqualification for ten years or life.

Back on 8 June, when the alleged Gagoola was competing in the Rothsay Trial Stakes, the owner-trainer Henry Graham testified that the horse that had raced was indeed Gagoola. The VRC were not satisfied with that answer, but they could not find any proof that Graham knew about the switch. He was not charged with any offence.

Very complicated, but where there's smoke, there's fire.

Miller, Miller and Miller
... and nothing to do with flour!

Jockey John Miller is best known as the rider of Galilee, who won the 1966 Caulfield and Melbourne Cup double. He also rode Galilee to win the 1967 Sydney Cup. Miller retired with over 2200 wins to his credit.

However, Miller could have had quite a few more winners but for a few indiscretions, such as weight problems, which led the volatile jockey to make many 'visits' to the stewards rooms and which resulted in suspensions and disqualifications. A total of 30 penalties meant Miller spent around seven years on the sidelines.

John Miller is also remembered as the rider of Rocket Racer, owned by Laurie Connell, the sensationally backed nine-length winner of the 1987 Perth Cup. On returning to scale that day, the horse was in such a distressed state that it took six handlers to get him back to his stalls.

Two weeks later the horse was dead. It is generally regarded in racing circles that the unfortunate animal was under the influence of the banned substance 'elephant juice'. A postmortem was never carried out on the horse.

John Miller was inducted into the Western Australia Hall of Champions in 1995.

Miller and his wife, Kay, had three sons: Ray, Shane and Mark, the latter two blossoming into very competent jockeys. On 10 March 1986, John's youngest son, sixteen-year-old apprentice Mark Miller, got himself into quite a bit of strife over an incident at the Pinjarra Race Cub, some 87 kilometres south of Perth, in Western Australia.

Young Miller had been riding for only twelve months, with three winners from 63 rides. The race was won by Echoing, ridden by apprentice Jim Taylor, defeating Miller's mount, Lemarc, by a long neck. On returning to the scale and after weight was declared, Taylor put in a complaint to the stewards. The Western Australia Turf Club (WATC) Stewards immediately opened an inquiry and called the two young riders into the rooms. Jim Taylor accused Mark Miller of pulling his horse's reins during the race, and in doing so, pulling Taylor's horse's head towards Miller's mount. Not only that, Taylor said that Miller had also grabbed his whip, preventing him from riding his horse out to the finishing line.

Young Miller's mount, Lemarc, was trained by his grandfather, 77-year-old John Miller Senior. He too was asked to attend the inquiry. Miller Senior refused. In his absence, the stewards suspended him until 19 June.

Miller denied the accusations and said, 'I was riding my mount out, and had my whip in my left hand, so how could I reach out and grab his whip with that hand? No, I did not; and he claimed that I also grabbed his reins with that hand. If that was right, I would have had to have dropped my own whip. No, he is wrong.'

Apparently, the stewards were not having a word of that, and to the shock of all the racing fraternity, apprentice jockey Mark Miller was disqualified for fifteen years – one of the longest sentences in the history of the Australian turf. On appeal, his disqualification was reduced to two years.

Once he resumed riding, Mark Miller soon began riding winners. In 1995 he travelled east to ride Starstruck to a brilliant victory in the Australian Cup at Flemington. The horse was trained by his mother, Kay.

It seems the racing gods must be against the Miller jockeys. While riding in Malaysia on 9 November 2002, Mark Miller rode Hurricane Warning into second place. The stewards were not happy with the ride and Miller was banned from riding for twelve months. He appealed his suspension, but to no avail.

In 2006, one of John Miller's other sons, Raymond Miller, received a life ban from all racetracks worldwide, imposed by Racing and Wagering Western Australia.

Plenty to talk about around the kitchen table, no doubt.

CHAPTER 3
The British Isles

Tipperary Tim and Foinavon
... never give up, no matter what

Both of these thoroughbreds share a rare distinction: they each ran in and then won the Grand National at Aintree, Liverpool, England. Tipperary Tim's momentous win came in 1928, and Foinavon was the 1967 Grand National winner.

Tipperary Tim was friendless in the betting at 100/1. He was being mounted by his rider, William Dutton, in the enclosure when one of the jockey's friends in the crowd, knowing that the horse and rider had no chance, yelled out, 'Billy, the only chance you have is if all of the others fall over!'

... And they did.

Forty-two horses started in the race, and by the time they had jumped the Canal Turn on the first lap, there were only seven horses left. The race continued with its usual share of carnage. As the dwindling field prepared to jump the last fence, it was down to three, with Tipperary Tim bringing up the rear. On the very last jump, the leader, Great Span, dislodged his rider when the saddle slipped, and then the second placegetter, Billy Barton, lost his rider. Tipperary Tim was left to run down the straight all on his lonesome.

Billy Barton's jockey remounted and took chase, but Tipperary Tim had a significant lead. He greeted the judge at 100/1 – just proving how important the saying is, 'never, ever give up'.

Then 39 years later, along came Foinavon – a 100/1 starter, like Tipperary Tim.

The 1967 Grand National began with 44 starters. With one and a half laps completed, they had already seen sixteen horses bow out of the race. The remaining 28 horses were approaching the twenty-third fence, which was the smallest of all the fences, at 4 foot 6 inches (1.35 metres) high.

A horse that had lost its jockey at the very first jump was running with the pack, and it suddenly veered erratically as it approached the fence. Many leading horses were knocked out there and then. Not being content with that, the rogue horses then ran up and down in front of the twenty-third fence, ensuring many a competitor pulled up or dislodged its rider and refused to go any further.

Foinavon was travelling well in the rear, as one would imagine of a 100/1 chance. His jockey, John Buckingham, seeing what was happening in front, went right to the outside of the course and successfully jumped the fence and continued on. At the next jump, the Canal Turn, Foinavon's rider had a peek over his shoulder and realised he had a 30-length lead with only six fences left to negotiate.

Seventeen riders managed to remount and give chase. By the time Foinavon had approached the finishing line, his lead had been cut to just 20 lengths. John Buckingham waved his whip in the air in triumph as he guided his mount across the line at 100/1.

And the name of the horse to cause the carnage at the twenty-third fence? Popham Down. It says it all really.

The events in the 1967 race entered Grand National folklore. Even though it took a few years, in 1984 the Aintree Executives bowed to pressure and renamed the twenty-third fence the Foinavon Fence.

Never, ever give up, no matter what the circumstances are. Just ask William Dutton, the rider of Tipperary Tim in 1928, and John Buckingham, the rider of Foinavon in 1967.

100/1 – our favourite number.

Sir Winston Churchill
... a quiet drink, a verbal stoush, then a hefty punt

Over the years there have been countless stories told of Britain's wartime prime minister, Sir Winston Churchill (1874–1965), who was a very keen gambler on the horses as well as at the casino tables.

A quiet drink

Of champagne, Sir Winston Churchill said, 'In victory, deserve it; in defeat, need it!'

In 1908, Churchill drank his first glass of Pol Roger champagne, and it became his favourite drink throughout his lifetime. During World War II, the underground war bunker in London was renowned for its champagne-fuelled lunches, and Churchill for his afternoon naps.

A verbal stoush

During his years in British Parliament, Sir Winston Churchill had many a verbal stoush with Lady Astor. The most famous of all anecdotes is when Lady Astor confronted Churchill and said, 'Sir, if you were my husband, I would poison your tea!'

Churchill responded, 'Madam, if I were your husband, I would drink it!'

That hefty punt

Many stories have been written about Sir Winston Churchill's battle with clinical depression – or as he called it, 'the black dog'.

After World War II, people were going about their lives, while trying to rebuild what was left of Mother England. Relaxation and a holiday was one way of trying to get some normality into one's life, and this was also true for Sir Winston Churchill.

In 1946, Churchill thought that gambling might just be the way to beat a bout of depression. And where was the place to be at the time? The Casino in Monte Carlo, of course.

One evening, it is reported, Churchill lost £170,000 playing cards, and he had to settle his debts by writing out a cheque. Well, how fortunate for Sir Winston Churchill that the Casino's owner decided not to bank the cheque, but instead had it framed and then gave it pride of place in his office.

One thinks that if that cheque had been banked, Sir Winston Churchill may have suffered another severe bout of depression.

Long live the Casino owner.

England solves great American mystery
... the invading Romans and their horses held the key

One great oddity in American transportation is their railway lines or, to be more precise, their standard railroad gauge. The railroad gauge is the measurement between the two rails of line. It is set at exactly 4 feet 8½ inches (1.42 metres) – now isn't that strange?

Urban legend tells us that the first part of the mystery is explained by the fact that the US rail system was designed by English expatriates living in America. These expats built them the same way as the railway lines were built in England. And the railway lines in England had been built by the same people who had built the tramways, before rail. But why had the tramways used that gauge?

Well, the people building the tramways had used the very same tools and machinery that were used to build the wagons that travelled England's roads. But why did the wagons use this spacing? Some of the long distance roads in England had deep wheel ruts impregnated into the ground. The wheels of new wagons had to fit into the ruts – if they were wider, the wheels and axles tended to break.

Hold on, why did all these wheel ruts on English roads have that spacing? Well, if we take another step back in time, we find that it was Roman chariots that first made the ruts in the roads, as the Romans guided their legions through early England. Therefore we now have half the answer to our question. The railway gauge of the great American railways is based on the wheel ruts made on tracks used by Roman chariots in England.

But the ultimate question is still to be answered: why was the measurement of 4 feet 8½ inches used as the base gauge for a chariot's wheels? It is simple really. The Roman Army's chariots were standard, and this was just over the width of two backsides of their warhorses.

So when we pause to think why the American railroad gauge is set at 4 foot 8½ inches, we can thank those pairs of horses, side by side, pulling the chariots and wagons of thousands of years ago as they traversed through Ye Olde England. The English expats followed with the same for the American railway, because that was simply the way it had always been done.

Long live bureaucracy.

The 1993 Grand National
...false starts, red flags and the race that never was

Here we have undoubtedly one of the most watched races in the history of horse racing – the great Grand National steeplechase, raced at Aintree in Liverpool, England. This race is adored by the racing public. Over the decades, the working man has forged champions, legends and folklore, in the time it takes to run the 4 miles and 3½ furlongs (7141 metres). First run in 1839, this National Hunt horse race has given us the legends of Arkle, Red Rum and many others.

The 147th running of the race, on 3 April 1993, is a farcical story. The unthinkable happened in what has gone down in history as 'the race that never was'.

The Grand National is one of the richest races in Europe; in 2013, the prize money was just shy of £1 million ($1,664,350, in June 2013). The race attracts both punters and non-punters, and the nation stops to see if their selection can, first of all, finish the gruelling race and then greet the judge. It is regarded as the ultimate test for horse and rider. They must run two complete courses of the track, and they are challenged by 30 fences in total.

Some of these fences strike fear into even the most experienced horseriders, and if you think the horses don't have feelings, take a look at the whites of their eyes in recent colour photographs as they find themselves at the top of a 6-foot (1.8-metre) fence, looking down at a 5-foot-wide (1.5-metre-wide) ditch. There is Becher's Brook to terrorise them, and there is the Canal Turn that makes sure they not only have to jump tall buildings at a single bound but also turn their 500-kilogram frames on a penny to continue the run home.

The famous Becher's Brook, named after Captain Martin Becher, who had the distinction of being the first jockey to fall in the first official running of the race, is a 4-foot 10-inch (1.5-metre) fence immediately followed by a 5-foot 6-inch (1.65-metre) wide brook. Becher's, as it is affectionately known, has been made 'easier' over the years; it did have a much higher fence and a much wider water challenge.

So, the remarkable race of 1993 was being watched by around 600 million people, in around 140 countries. And the unthinkable happened – a bloody flag fails to unfurl and we have 'the race that never was'.

There was the customary large number of combatants in the race, totalling 39 brave horses and jockeys. Party Politics started favourite at 7/1, and at the other end of the hopefuls was Tarqogan's Best at 500/1, with plenty of other odds in between.

The first attempt to start the race was called a false start when a few horses and their riders got entangled in the starting tape. The system of notifying those jockeys who were unaware of the false start was to have an official starter wave a red flag to a second official about 100 yards down the track, so that he in turn could produce a large red flag and wave it at any horse and rider that ventured his way. The horse and rider would stop and proceed back to the start – which they did, this first time.

Then there was a second attempt to start the race. This time some horses and their riders were again too close to the starting tape. On activating the 'go', the starter noticed that the tape had worked itself around of the neck of Richard Dunwoody, riding Won't Be Gone Long at 16/1. The starter waved his red flag furiously to his 'wingman' further down the track, signifying yet another false start, and the wingman in turn ran out onto the track and signalled.

Guess what? Only a handful had stopped for the second false start. Most of the field was away, despite the furious attempts at waving them down. Officials tried furiously to get the attention of the remaining field, but by the sixth fence, Becher's Brook, there were 29 horses remaining in the race that had no idea that a second false start had occurred.

On they raced, until after much carnage, there were only seven runners remaining as they raced the final 2 furlongs to the line. The 50/1 outsider, Esha Ness, stormed home and greeted the judge first, with second place going to Cahervillahow at 25/1, and third place to Romany King at 15/2.

Imagine the shock and dismay when officials told each of the finishing brigade that the race was 'null and void'. Well, here were the interesting findings after a top-level inquiry held by High Court Judge Sir Michael Connell. It appears they took the events very seriously indeed.

Keith Brown, the official starter, had been officiating in his last race before retirement – he retired soon after.

Ken Evans was the man responsible for alerting the field of the false start 100 yards down the track. He bore the brunt of criticism; but why?

One of Ken Evans' responsibilities on race day was to make sure that his red flag unfurled. For the second false start, it did not. He waved furiously at the 30 horses charging towards him, but he probably looked like nothing more than a man waving a stick in the air, and the field charged on. Indeed, the club had problems with protestors at that spot earlier in the day.

After the judge's findings, it was decided that the official and the red flag should be replaced by two officials, who would be in radio contact with the starter. In case of a false start, both of these gentlemen would wave fluorescent yellow flags at the approaching horses and jockeys. If for some reason the fluorescent yellow flags did not alert the field to the false start, another official further on had the power to stop the field and pursue them in a vehicle if need be!

Here is the wash up of the 'race that never was':
- Finished the course: 7
- Pulled up: 13
- Did not start: 9
- Fell, unseated rider or refused to jump: 10

Bookies had to repay punters a total of £75 million (AUD$125 million, in July 2013), because the race was declared a 'no race'.

Just to add insult to injury, Esha Ness – the unofficial winner at 50/1 – had run the second-fastest time in the history of the Grand National that day. How would you have felt backing this 50/1 winner? Somewhat cheated, I would imagine.

Just another way to blow your dough.

King's horse kills woman in the 1913 Epsom Derby

... the lady never stood a chance

This is the grand stage of horse racing in England: the Epsom Derby, a Group 1 race run at Epsom Downs, Surrey, south-eastern England. It is for three-year-old colts and fillies, and it is run over 1 mile 4 furlongs and 10 yards (2423 metres) in early June each year. It is Britain's richest race.

The Epsom Derby is traditionally a huge event on the racing calendar in England. Kings and Queens attend, accompanied by all the pomp and ceremony that they can muster. The British royals even have some of their best thoroughbreds contest the race.

In the early twentieth century, in the other corner, we had the suffragettes – women who fought hard to have their voices heard, demanding equality, freedom, a say in their own destinies and the right to vote. At the time, women were treated as second-class citizens. They had no say in many decision-making processes that affected them. The men made all the decisions for them.

'Suffragette' was a term penned by journalist Charles E Howard, writing for the *London Daily Mail* in the 1880s. The term referred to all the women around the world who were campaigning for the right to vote. However, women in the United States over the age of 21 were allowed to vote in the territory of Wyoming from 1869, and Utah from 1870. The English were a little behind the times.

During the early years of the suffragette movement, the suffragettes were seen to be part of a radical movement that used extreme measures to illustrate their right to be heard. There were reported cases of women throwing themselves to the ground in front of moving animals or 'horseless' carriages, disrupting events and functions, and doing anything else to get their movement recognised. These demonstrations eventually became commonplace, with women chaining themselves to the gates of important male-dominated institutions and trying to put forward their message in very large public forums, such as the running of the Epsom Derby.

In 1913, King George V's horse Anmer was going to contest the great race. A suffragette by the name of Emily Davison believed that she could bring the suffragettes' fight for equality to the attention of the large Epsom Derby crowd. Davison was one of the most famous suffragettes. In the latter part of her 41 years, she had been jailed on nine occasions and force-fed 49 times.

On that fateful day, Davison had in her possession a flag in the colours of the suffragette movement: purple, white and green. Plan A was to attach the flag to Anmer's riding gear in the parade ring – but she could not get close enough.

The race got underway. As the horses rounded Tattenham Corner in the run home to the finishing post, Emily positioned herself on the inside rail, waiting, waiting. After the bulk of the field had passed her, the King's horse, Anmer, running third-last at this point, approached the turn.

It is still debated to this day whether it was Emily Davison's intention to sacrifice her life or whether she did not realise what she was doing was that dangerous. Davison stepped out in front of Anmer, onto the course proper, and took the brunt of a half-tonne thoroughbred running at around 40 miles (60 km) per hour front on. She was tossed aside like a rag doll. She made the ultimate sacrifice for her cause, dying in hospital from her injuries four days later.

To add to the theatre, Queen Mary, the wife of King George, was unsympathetic and exclaimed at the time, 'She is nothing more than a lunatic woman.'

A journalist at the time remarked, 'What a stupid woman, placing the horse at great risk.'

There is no doubt that society has changed considerably since the running of the 1913 Epsom Derby, but many commentators would say that society still has a long way to go before women achieve real equality. In September 2006, the London newspaper *The Guardian* was instrumental in a campaign to persuade the Epsom Racecourse to 'honour' the memory of Emily Davison. Upon construction of the newly developed Queen's Stand at the course, journalist Tristan Hunt wrote, 'There is no recognition of Emily Wilding Davison, her role within the suffragette cause, or the significance of her sacrifice. Campaigners want a plaque placed on the racecourse with the inscription from her gravestone – "Deeds not Words".' Thus, on 18 April 2013, to celebrate the centenary of Emily Davison's death, one hundred guests were invited to the unveiling of a plaque at Epsom Downs.

Now back to 1913. Sixteen days after what was known as 'the Suffragette Derby', the field turned for home in the Ascot Gold Cup at Epsom. The 1912 St Leger winner, Tracery, was some six lengths clear of the field, when all hell broke loose.

The London Evening Post the following day reported that:

This demented fanatic rushed from trees carrying a revolver in one hand and a flag in the other. The rider of Tracery, Albert Whalley, also known as Snowy Whalley, tried desperately to avoid the lunatic, but failing to do so, both he and his horse were brought down. The lunatic was Trinity College student, Harold James Hewitt, who suffered extensive injuries. He was also a member of the suffragette movement.

When interviewed by *The Guardian*'s Kenneth Elsy, fellow jockey Steve Donoghue stated:

Whalley was booked to ride a good horse in the race, Mr August Belmont's Tracery, and at dinner Whalley told us that he had a horrible presentiment that suffragettes would make an attempt at interference with horses during the meeting, and said: 'They're sure to try it on during the race for the Gold Cup,' he said. 'If they come at me, well, there's only one thing to do. I shall drive straight at 'em.'

The previous year's winner, Prince Palatine, had to jump over Tracery and went on to win his second Ascot Gold Cup in race record time.

Now to the Antipodes. Australia had a similar case of racecourse disruption back on 19 September 1854, when more than 5000 people flocked to see Adelaide's Thebarton Grand Annual Steeplechase.

There was plenty of cheering from the large crowd when the favourite, Duke Of Wellington, raced to the front. But the punters' hopes for a collect from the bookies soon turned to dismay when, in a bizarre incident, a woman broke from the crowd, rushed onto the racecourse and thrust her parasol at both horse and rider.

Duke Of Wellington shied, jumped sideways and came down on his rider, who died the following day of internal injuries. The woman was arrested and taken away.

Today we only have streakers.

Arise Sir Gordon Richards
... he received a knighthood while still riding winners

When you are the first of anything, you should shout it from the rooftops. Here is one of the greatest accolades that could be bestowed upon a great jockey: to be made a Knight of the Realm while still competing and riding winners.

Born the son of a coalminer in Shropshire, England, on 5 May 1904, Sir Gordon Richards met his maker on 10 November 1986, after an exceptional career. As a child, Gordon developed a love for the pit ponies that his father kept. His great love of the horse paved the way for his future.

Sir Gordon Richards won the British Flat Racing Championship on no fewer than 26 occasions, and his career wins totalled 4870. He was knighted for his services to horse racing while he was still competing. Today he remains the only jockey to be given that honour.

The year 1953 was a great year for the Commonwealth. On the world stage we had the coronation of Queen Elizabeth II, and feats such as the climbing of Mount Everest by New Zealander Edmund Hillary. For racehorse lovers, this was the year that Sir Gordon Richards was knighted, and then capped that memorable time by winning the English Derby on the three-year-old champion colt Pinza. In a twist, he beat the Queen's horse, Aureole.

Sir Gordon Richards retired the following year, in 1954, after suffering a pelvic injury. His 4870 wins remains today a British record. He still also holds the record for the most consecutive winners, which was twelve in a row over a couple of meetings.

The Racing Post listed Sir Gordon Richards as number one in their 'Top 50 Jockeys of the 20th Century', an award that can now never be beaten.

Arise Sir Gordon Richards, arise.

King Henry II in 1174
... tally ho and off to the races

It is acknowledged that Roman soldiers were the first to organise horse races in England – in the area now known as Yorkshire, around 200 AD – but the first recorded race meeting in England was arranged during the reign of King Henry II (1133–1189). King Henry II is probably better known in the line of British monarchs as being the father of Richard, the Lion Heart. The race meeting was at Smithfield in 1174, in the Greater London area, and it was advertised as a Horse Fair.

The relationship between horse racing and the British royals continues to this day, with the current monarch, Queen Elizabeth II, often enjoying watching her horses compete at Royal Ascot. In fact, the Queen was in the winner's box in June 2013, after her horse Estimate won the prestigious Gold Cup by a neck. History dictates that the monarch awards the Gold Cup to the winner, but because the Queen was in fact the winning owner, the authorities had to do some quick thinking. Her second son, Prince Andrew, the Duke of York, stepped forward to present the Gold Cup to the delighted Queen. She became the first reigning monarch to win the Gold Cup in the race's history.

It all started at Smithfield in 1174.

Here comes Abscess on the Jaw
... and Lady Churchill had everything to do with it

Just pause and ask the following question, like CJ Dennis did in his book, *Songs of a Sentimental Bloke* – and like William Shakespeare did before him, of course. We have translated it to twenty-first century 'speak' for you.

> What's in a name she says,
> and then she sighs,
> and clasps her little hands
> and rolls her eyes.
> A rose, she says, by any other name
> would smell as sweet.

What is in a name? A damn lot, apparently! We often reflect on whether the name makes the horse, or whether it is the other way around and the horse makes the name that it has been called.

What would you think if you were at the races, you read the form and then you heard the race caller make a call in his commentary something like this: '... and here comes Abscess on the Jaw around the outside making her way to the front?' You would have every right to think that the horse was obviously owned by a dentist or a doctor or a total 'whack job'.

Well, it was a long time ago, but the owners gave the punting public no other information to interpret the name that the horse was given. But all those people who followed racing, who were without the benefit of a much higher education and upbringing, just took this name in their stride.

The horse in question was foaled in 1886 in the United Kingdom, from a union between the sire Trappist and the dam Festive. Her record shows that she had 24 races for nine wins, three seconds and one third. Here are some of the races she won:

- Epsom Oaks: 1889
- Manchester Cup: 1890
- Portland Stakes: 1890
- Hardwicke Stakes: 1891

She was owned by Lord Randolph Churchill and Lady Frances Churchill, the mother and father of Sir Winston Churchill. Lord Randolph bought the little black filly as a yearling for £300 from the Doncaster Horse Sales and then gave his wife the task of finding a suitable name for her.

Lady Frances was well educated and well versed in the finer things in life. She turned to the French historian Ernest Renan for a name for her little black beauty. Ernest Renan wrote a play about the French Revolution, which was a personal favourite of Lady Randolph's. The play's title was none other than *L'Abbesse de Jouarre*.

So was it any wonder that the working class could not get their mouths around it and for its very successful racing career, the horse was affectionately called Abscess on the Jaw?

Believe it or not.

Those horse names
... that make the officials cringe

Whatever happened to the stiff upper lip on the racecourses of the British Isles? It looks as though the working and middle classes have forged a way into racing folklore that cannot be denied. English resilience and restraint in the face of great danger and adversity seems to have evaporated, and the stiff upper lip has given way to the quivering bottom lip of the officials: 'Can we have that name? Is there a hidden meaning there? Does that horse name mean something else in another language?'

Whatever the reason, it is now a game of chance when you submit a name for your champion horse. Hopefully it gets through the screening of the Jockey Club, now named the British Racing Authority.

A few basic rules protect the legends of the great horses that have graced our racecourses over history. All names are protected for a period of twenty years, but the names of great champions, such as Shergar, Arkle and many others, can never be used again.

At any one time in Britain, there are about 250,000 thoroughbred horses running around. This has put great strain on the British Racing Authority, which must make sure that everyone toes the line.

No horse name that is R-rated or even remotely blasphemous will be approved; however, you cannot stop individuals playing with letters and camouflaging their real message. There is always a way.

When some owners in England requested that their horse be named Big Tits, quite rightly it was refused. It didn't stop the owners having that name registered in France though, because in the French language those words do not mean anything at all. So the owners got their way.

Here is a short list of horse names that were proposed to racing authorities – some were banned, and some found their way to be approved.

- Chit Hot
- Norfolk Enchants
- Oilbeefhooked
- The Fooker
- Arfur Foulkesaycke
- Passing Wind
- Fuchu
- Cockney Wanker
- Hucking Fell

It would appear that at some stage, their thoughts on naming their gee-gee never wandered too far above the navel or out of the gutter.

Odds of 11 million to 1

... and it was the 1 pence bets that paid off his mortgage

This very lucky punter never wanted to be identified, and all we can ascertain is that, once more, William Hill Bookmakers had to pay out. In mid-2013, this gentleman placed a number of accumulator-style bets for his own entertainment and spent the princely sum of just over £15 on these online bets. The gentleman made different types of bets, and some of his selections are detailed here. (The simplest way to explain an accumulator bet is that you select a number of horses to win and place a wager on the very first horse only. Your winnings go all up on the next one, and if it wins, then the next. If at any time any of the horses don't win, then the bet is useless.)

One of his 'accumulators' was a selection of eleven horses in eleven different races. His bet was that at least eight of his selections would have to win their respective race for him to collect. He was successful with his 2-pence bet and won £112,000.

Three other bets for 1 pence each were for four of his selections to win, five of his selections to win and six of his selections to win. They did, of course, and that added approximately another £100,000 to his coffers. Here were the selections in his eleven-horse accumulator and the results.

- Stencive, Newmarket: 5/2, lost
- Gabriel's Lad, Newmarket: 5/1, lost
- Sky Lantern, Newmarket: 10/1, WON
- Sun Central, Salisbury: 9/2, WON
- Swing Easy, Salisbury: 7/2, WON
- Fleeting Smile, Salisbury: 15/8, WON
- Nasharra, Hamilton: 6/1, WON
- Flipping, Hamilton: 8/1, lost
- O Ma Lad, Hamilton: 11/2, WON
- Coral Sands, Hamilton: 25/1, WON
- Two Turtle Doves, Hamilton: 11/1, WON

A spokesperson for William Hill, Kate Miller, said:

No doubt this is one of the luckiest bets we have ever seen. This type of betting is very popular and a couple of times a year we have a large winner. This one is unique as his stakes was mere pennies.

Pennies from heaven.

Odds of 1 million to 1
... and the punter pulled it off

When you try to find 'Thirsk' on the internet, the search engine will state that it is a small market town in the Hambleton district of North Yorkshire. The 2001 census recorded a thriving population of 4700 people. It is a popular tourist town, and the home of author James

Herriot and the birthplace of Thomas Lord, after whom the Lord's Cricket Ground in London is named.

A quick internet search will fail to tell you that probably the most famous Thirskonian is none other than Fred Craggs. And why is he famous? Fred managed to pull off a bet on the ponies that paid 1,000,000/1. We think that is something worth mentioning.

On a fateful Saturday in 2008, Fred had a bet that was a '75-pence-throwaway punt' on an eight-horse accumulator. In simple terms, he put his 75 pence on each of the chosen horses all up to win. If any of them failed to greet the judge, the bet would be useless. You may agree that it is hard enough putting your 'hard-earned' on one gee-gee to win and come up trumps.

The races that were bet on in the accumulator that day were being held in Sandown, Dubai and finally at Wolverhampton. International form was not a worry for our man Fred – it was just lady luck, and a whole lot of that into the bargain. Below are the six of the eight horses that ran and won that afternoon. Whether it was written in the stars or not, just take particular notice of his first winner, at Sandown, and his last winner, at Wolverhampton. We were unable to find the names of the other two winning horses; there is just one man who could tell us and that would be Fred himself.

- Isn't That Lucky
- Racer Forever
- Frosty Secret
- Sun Classique
- King's Fable
- A Dream Come True

The William Hill betting shop was 'thrilled' to hand over Craggs' £1 million (the equivalent of around $1.5 million). Just to top things off, the stars must have really been aligned because it all happened on Fred's sixtieth birthday.

Happy birthday, Fred!

The Queen Anne Stakes of 1974

... the winner wasn't in the first three to cross the line.

Here is a very famous race that has stood the test of time and was elevated to Group 1 status over the years. It began its life in 1840 as the Trial Stakes for horses three-years-old and older, over a mile (1600 metres). The race was renamed in 1930 in honour of Queen Anne (1665–1714), who founded the Ascot Racecourse in 1711.

In 1971, the race was classified as a Group 3. It was promoted to Group 2 in 1984, and it was given the prestige of being classified as a Group 1 race in 2003, with participating horses now being four-years-old and older. The Queen Anne Stakes is now the opening event on the first day of the great Royal Ascot meeting held at Ascot, Berkshire, every year in June.

It is hard enough to win a race anywhere in the world, let alone such a prestigious race in the Ascot Carnival. In 1974, a full field of hopefuls set off over the mile to claim victory. There were no holds barred in what was tactically a very hard fought race, and when the horses crossed the line, it was Confusion first, Gloss second and the 6/4 favourite Royal Prerogative third. When the horses arrived back at the mounting yard, the siren sounded to warn everyone on course that a protest had been lodged. A very enterprising bookie, hearing the news of an inquiry, quickly placed odds on his board as to which horse out of the first, second and third place-getters would be judged the eventual winner; at those odds of a winner being one in three, many jumped on board.

In an unprecedented move, the racing stewards disqualified all three horses, and awarded the race to the fourth place-getter, Brook. The stewards deemed that the rough-riding tactics of the leading jockeys warranted such action.

That enterprising bookie must have thought all of his Christmases had come at once; all of the wagers that were laid on which horse would be awarded the race would stay in his bookie bag.

Now, as a punter, that is just the worst luck.

Boys will be boys!

... when doing the weekly shopping, no less

In June 2004, the English newspaper the *Swindon Advertiser* reported that local horse trainer Sylvester Kirk had fractured both arms in a somewhat unusual accident. No, it was not a stable accident, but a joyride in a supermarket trolley.

When quizzed by the *Racing Post*, his wife, Fanny, replied, 'I'm not going to tell you how he did it, because it will probably end up in a divorce court and I am not ready for divorce yet.'

And Mr Kirk's response to what happened? 'I tripped in the supermarket, so let's just leave it at that.'

However, a Tesco supermarket spokesperson stated, 'Mr Kirk was apparently riding one of our shallow trolleys down the aisle, and we do not wish to elaborate any more on the subject.'

But the best was still to come from fellow shopper Mrs Sandy Holmes: 'He was just like a bloody kid thinking he was on a bloody roller-coaster, the bloody idiot. What was he thinking of?'

It was also reported that there were quite a few 'injured' bottles of champagne, wine and beer.

The next day, while the family attended the Royal Ascot meeting, Sylvester Kirk was in hospital, probably wondering where he went wrong on that infamous ride.

Better off riding horses no doubt!

Don't patronise me, mate!

... history lesson about the sinking of the Bismark

One of Britain's best-known on-course bookmakers, Barry Dennis, was also known for his role on Channel 4's Morning Line show, where he would tip what was known as 'Barry's *Bismark*', a favourite who he thought could not win. Barry was also known as a bit of a 'motormouth'.

At England's Windsor Racecourse in July 2006, one lucky punter – as Barry put it, 'some sharp-looking old geezer' – had £1000 on a horse at 9/4. It duly won, and when the punter came to collect his £3250, he asked Barry, the bookie, what he should back in the next.

Just fancy asking any bookie that type of question. He would probably say a 100/1 shot. Maybe the punter was trying to get under Barry's skin.

Before Barry could say anything, the 'sharp-suited old geezer' leaned over and grabbed a £1 coin from the bookie's tray, saying: 'Tails, I'll back number 2; Heads, I'll back number 5.'

The coin came up tails, and our lucky punter put £3250 on number 2, which happened to be the 2/1 favourite. Now, our bookie was hoping that he could put 'Barry's *Bismark*' on the horse, hoping it would lose and take that silly smirk off the punter, in his smart attire and all.

This time the *Bismark* curse did not work, and the punter came back to collect his £9750. When he received his money, he pocketed £9000 and handed back £750 to Barry to 'spend on a drink'.

But all our friendly bookie could say was, 'You bloody tosser!'

And I'll only say this once!

Barry Dennis was also well known for having no time for drunks nor the fairer sex while giving the odds. He recalled this little incident from a Royal Ascot meeting in 2004: 'One day a woman came up and asked for £1 each way on the 5/1 ON favourite. Could you bloody well believe it?! So I said, "Listen luv, here's your two quid back, and here's another pound to go with it.

'"Now, pretend the bloody thing won, and just p**s off!"'

Yes, a good case of customer relations.

As luck would have it!
... or lack of luck

Back in the early nineteenth century, Scotsman Captain George 'Bay' Middleton was recognised as one of the most popular sporting personalities of his day. He was also an outstanding rider.

It is believed Captain George Middleton's nickname, 'Bay', was derived from the 1836 Epsom Derby winner, Bay Middleton. One of Captain Middleton's horses, Lord of the Harem, won seventeen consecutive races between November 1882 and April 1884, and on retirement it had won a total of 26 races.

However, on Saturday 19 April 1892, Captain Middleton's luck ran out when he partnered his own gelding, Night Line, in the Sportsman's Cup Steeplechase at Lord Willoughby de Broke's estate at Kineton Valley, Scotland.

The race got under way, with all horses and riders negotiating each of the fences with great dexterity. In a compact field of five runners, things changed for the worse when the horses approached the last jump. Only 50 yards from the finishing line, tragedy struck.

As Middleton was about to take off at the last fence, his horse, Night Line, shied, threw his head back and caught Middleton on the chin, immediately snapping his neck. 'Bay' Middleton was dead before he hit the ground.

Talk about having a bad day or what?

Where did he go?
... yet another way of losing

As the starters lined up for the 1991 European Gold Patrons Handicap at Lingfield in Surrey, England, friends and family were patting excited owner Leonard Searle on the back, wishing him well with his horse, Super Sally.

In a torrid finish to the race, Super Sally and Rapporteurs went head to head. At the finish, the judge called for a photo.

However, while waiting for the outcome of the photo finish, no-one could wish Leonard Searle the best of luck. Why? Unfortunately he had a massive heart attack and dropped dead at their feet during the running of the race.

The result of the photo finish was: Super Sally first, the 11/4 favourite.

It was just plain bad luck.

Death at Royal Ascot
... and 'God protects the toffs!'

Timing is everything and one has to say, if your time is up, then there is not a damn thing you can do about it. The year was 1955 and the

King's Vase (changed to the Queen's Vase in 1960) was being held at the Royal Ascot meeting in June. The perpetual trophies for the Royal Hunt Club and the Gold Cup were up for grabs.

A major rail strike was about to be held, which would bring the country to a standstill, so the racing authorities took it upon themselves to protect the integrity of the running of important races, and rescheduled the day to be run in July to escape any transportation issues. However simple that may have sounded, there was one small thing that they never counted on happening on that day in July – a severe storm.

The Queen had previous engagements arranged for the new July date on the racing calendar. She was an avid racegoer, so she was very disappointed that she would be unable to attend. Nevertheless, the racing public turned out in all of their summer finery to watch the Classic races and to enjoy the pomp and ceremony that only a Classic race can offer.

It was just after the running of the Gold Cup, late in the afternoon, that the dark clouds that had threatened all day opened and a deluge descended upon Royal Ascot. As the winner was being led back to the enclosure, the thunder growled and lightning flashes lit up the sky. People were dashing everywhere for cover, and it felt as if the lightning had hit the course directly. There were two metal fences: one was surrounding the Royal Enclosure and the other was surrounding the course enclosure for the ordinary folk. Yes, there was a direct hit on the latter.

More than 50 people were knocked off their feet, and many of the racing public were walking around in a daze from the strike. The end result was that 42 people were recorded injured, with 18 people taken to the local hospital and admitted. Unfortunately, there were two racegoers who never made it back to racing ever again. Barbara Vera Batt, from Reading, and Leonard Tingle, from Sheffield; both died as a result of that direct lightning strike on the course fence. Of course, the negative feeling between the Royals and some 'workers' was not lost, as someone in the crowd yelled out, 'God protects the toffs!'

Because of her previous engagement, the Queen was not in

attendance. She was hosting a garden party back at Buckingham Palace.

Wrong place, wrong time.

Royal Ascot 2012
... simply the best!

What a promoter's dream. The dates of 19 June and 23 June 2012 will go down in history as two of the all-time great race days the racing world has ever seen. Two undefeated champions – Frankel, from the United Kingdom, and Black Caviar, from Australia – showed us what racing is all about.

Having Frankel racing on the opening day at Royal Ascot only whetted our appetites for the coming days. He did not disappoint the racing world: he showed just how great he was. In an amazing end to the one-mile (1600-metre) Group 1 Queen Anne Stakes, Frankel absolutely demoralised his opposition by eleven lengths. Excelebration, by the Australian sire Exceed And Excel, once again had to play second fiddle to this mighty equine athlete.

The BBC television host Claire Balding made a formal announcement to the lords and ladies: 'The best racehorse we have ever seen.' And the *Guardian*'s Greg Wood wrote, 'It is not that no horse in the world could have lived with Frankel yesterday. It is unlikely that any horse ever foaled would have beaten him either.'

Even Black Caviar's trainer, Peter Moody, was completely blown away by what he had just witnessed: 'Seeing is believing – he's the best horse I have ever seen.' Wow! What a statement!

Within a couple of days, Frankel's Timeform rating rose to a record of 147. In other words, he was recognised as the greatest horse the world had ever seen.

Day two of the Royal Ascot Carnival saw Aussie expat So You Think brilliantly win the 150th running of the Group 1 Prince of Wales Stakes. In doing so, he defeated Queen Elizabeth's horse, Carlton House, which ran in second place.

Now what would the Aussie invader Black Caviar offer when she took centre stage in two days' time in the Group 1 Queen's

Diamond Jubilee Stakes over 6 furlongs (1200 metres)? Would 'Nellie' demoralise her opposition as easily as Frankel had done on day one?

Back in May, Black Caviar had won the Group 1 Goodwood Handicap in Adelaide, South Australia. All the talking was over and the action was about to begin. Black Caviar would go to Ascot and show the world that Australia has the best sprinters, and she would remain undefeated. In the coming weeks it was all systems go. When 'Nellie' was finally loaded onto Flight SQ7297, she was all suited up in her custom-made 'bat suit'. This was it, no turning back.

When Black Caviar landed in the United Kingdom, observers were in awe of her size – there was over 600 kg of her. She looked more like a stallion than a mare. The British media were fascinated. There would be no excuses if Black Caviar lost, but deep down all the Aussies were thinking, 'Roll on, race day. Let's show 'em what "Nellie" can do.'

In the days leading up to the Diamond Jubilee, Black Caviar showed the British media what she was capable of in a track gallop. It prompted the *Racing Post*'s track watcher David Milnes to write: '… that Black Caviar showed a Frankelesque acceleration between the two and six-furlong pole in a solo gallop. That will long live in my memory.'

However, things were not as they seemed, and 'Nellie' started to lose weight. Trainer Peter Moody had always said that if things weren't right at any stage, he would 'pull the pin' and scratch her. But it wasn't long before things started to look better, and Black Caviar started to perk up. She seemed to be back on track for her biggest assignment yet.

Race day. This was it. No excuses, just luck in running … and it was a very wet track.

Things were definitely not right with 'Nellie'. In the saddling enclosure, former jockey and now television presenter Simon Marshall remarked that this was the worst he had ever seen Black Caviar in a mounting yard. He also said that you would like to see a horse happy on race day, and she did not seem that at all. 'Mate, something is not right.'

The horses proceeded up to the starting gates for the Diamond Jubilee. As they were being loaded, jockey Luke Nolan was biding his time, looking at the other starters and probably asking himself, would 'Nellie' begin brilliantly? Would she lead the field 'on her ear'? Surely there would not be another horse to go with her. Surely the top UK entrant, Morning Cloud, could not get within lengths of her – or could she?

The field jumped as one, and after going a short distance, something was definitely wrong. Black Caviar could not get a clear break on the field. She seemed as flat as a biscuit. In the running, Nolan pulled the whip on her, just to shake off Soul, a horse that could not get within cooee of her back in Australia.

Still in front of the field, albeit by a very slender margin, 'Nellie' was labouring. All the Aussie contingent and everyone back home in Australia knew that this was not the real Black Caviar. About 200 metres out, we could all see that the tank was empty – something was clearly wrong. Where was the acceleration? The field was closing in on her. Surely to God this would not be the same result that the great undefeated American mare Zenyatta had experienced in going for her twentieth straight win, only to lose by a nose to a horse called Blame.

Luke Nolan just urged and urged her. She was hurting but still giving her best. Then, just before the post, instead of cruising to the finishing line, she started putting in the short strides, thinking her work was done. Nolan pushed her hard – no whip! – just nursing her, as they came at her, one by one.

And the result? Black Caviar won the Group 1 Queen's Diamond Jubilee Stakes by a nose from Morning Cloud. It was the closest any horse had ever been able to get to her at race's end.

Black Caviar had made it 22 from 22. She was simply the best, but the media were now having a field day. Back in the enclosure there were cheers, tears, back slapping and absolute relief, and of course the question: 'Mr Moody, will Luke Nolan be her jockey in the future?' Peter Moody probably wanted to deck that reporter for asking that question, but he was there to defend his jockey, not to criticise him. 'When Trumby brought 'Nellie' back in to the enclosure, I looked into her eyes, and mate, she was exhausted, absolutely cactus. I knew she was running on empty, I bloody well knew that.'

Black Caviar was spent. However, she did lift her head to receive a pat from the British monarch, Queen Elizabeth II. How appropriate – from one Queen to another. With that, 80,000 spectators erupted with delight.

As soon as he could, Peter Moody got Black Caviar back to her stable in Newmarket, fed her and waited to see how she pulled up after such a torrid run. Was there something wrong with her? Would tomorrow morning answer many questions?

Now the armchair knockers lined up. The British media played their part the following day and did not hold back with their news headlines: 'Flukey Lukey' – 'The Blunder from Downunder' – 'The Moment of Strewth' – 'She Won, But Too Close For Comfort' – 'What Was He Doing?'

Yes, there were also many back in Australia who could not believe what they had seen. The questions were asked by more armchair critics: Why didn't Nolan use the whip on her? Why didn't he ride her out to the finishing post? Was he going to sleep thinking that this was just another day in the sun?

Now, what was it that these armchair trainers or armchair jockeys were not aware of? Black Caviar had always been prone to soft tissue damage, probably due to her will to win at all costs; no doubt, her massive size played a major part in her injuries, too. The morning after the Diamond Jubilee Stakes answered all the questions, and the truth was revealed.

Black Caviar had re-torn two quadriceps muscles and had sustained severe bruising to both her hind legs. With each stride in the race, as her hip flexed and her leg extended, 'Nellie' probably wanted to scream out with pain. However, like all champion athletes, she fought through the pain barrier. Finely tuned champion athletes always seem to find that extra will to win, and all pain seems to be put aside. But even most footballers would have limped off the ground with that type of injury, and some might even have needed to be assisted off the ground.

Where did the injury occur? Was it as they jumped? Was it after going 100 metres? Was it at the halfway mark? Was it only at the

100-metre mark? We don't know, because horses can't talk, but the damage to her was huge.

After spending time in quarantine, Black Caviar returned home to Australia. Peter Moody was asked the inevitable questions: Would 'Nellie' be retired to the breeding barn? Would she be spelled and race in the spring or would she be given a much long period of 'R and R' and return in the autumn of 2013? It was the latter.

In April 2013, after winning her only three starts after her long spell, all at Group 1 level, Black Caviar was retired. In August 2013, it was announced that she would be mated with the 2012–13 Australasian Champion Sire Exceed And Excel.

Australia would never again see those familiar racing colours of salmon pink and black spots. Those of us who had witnessed one of the world's great racehorses will cherish those remarkable years of 2008 to 2013 forever. The legend retired undefeated: 25 wins from 25 starts.

But what about Morning Cloud, the horse who got so close to her in the Diamond Jubilee Stakes? Well, after her narrow defeat by Black Caviar, she crossed the channel to France and won the Group 1 Prix Jacques le Marois at Deauville. In 2013, Morning Cloud returned to France and won that same Group 1 race for the third year running. She has been recognised as Europe's Champion Sprinter for the last five years.

Both Frankel and Black Caviar can certainly hold their heads high. They raced and defeated the best.

Here is a summary of two of the world's greatest racehorses:

- Frankel (Galileo × Kind by Danehill) – 14 wins from 14 starts, 10 Group 1 races and £2,998,302 in prize money. Timeform rating: 147, the highest of all time.
- Black Caviar (Bel Esprit × Helsinge by Desert Sun) – 25 wins from 25 starts, 15 Group 1 wins and $7,953,936 in prize money. Timeform rating: 136, the equal-highest ever for a mare.

The likes we will probably never see again!

What, just me?
... *well, goodness gracious*

We all dream of backing 100/1 winners – or even better, 200/1 winners. One of this book's authors was fortunate enough to back Moville Peter when it won the 1991 Tramway Handicap and paid around $260 on the Queensland TAB.

Now, spare a thought for Mrs Catherine Unsworth way back in June 1929. She wandered into the local betting shop, Joe Coral Bookmakers, and after perusing all the race fields, decided to have her 10-pence bet on a horse at Haydock, England.

Well, this horse, Coole, had just one bet placed on him – and he won. Mrs Unsworth found that she had the only winning ticket, and she received the princely amount of £314.

Yes, that represented odds of a cool 3410/1. It would be nice to have that as a winning leg of the quadrella.

Great, he's racing today
... *so who else will I back?*

There are some horses that bookies just fall in love with. You know, the 'gunnas', the ones that keep putting in a great run, get backed for quite a few dollars, but always come up short. Yes, a good enough run for the punters to back him next time.

This story is about a horse that, if he could talk, would probably say, 'Don't worry, back me next time and I will get all your money back.'

Well, the horse in question was Ribofilio, who in 1968 was crowned English two-year-old of the year. The bookies' favourite horse just could not deliver for the punters in his three-year-old year. He started favourite in the four Classics in 1969 – the English 2000 Guineas, the English Derby, the Irish Derby and finally the St Leger – and he lost the lot.

Ribofilio was retired in October that year after starting favourite in the St Simon Stakes. Yes, he lost that one too. At least he was consistent.

No rocking chairs for these golden oldies
... Harry and Frank rode to the end

Harry Beasley, often called the Doyen of Gentlemen Riders, passed away peacefully on 18 October 1939 at home in Curragh, County Kildare, Ireland, in his eighty-eighth year. Well, may we say to one and all, what a great innings. If one reaches that milestone of becoming an octogenarian, then we say what a great effort.

Harry was not the sort to sit around and look out of the window at life. To recap, in 1876 he had ridden his first winner in a steeplechase at Ballydoyle, just north of Dublin, in Ireland. He became a legend in his own lifetime at courses in Punchestown – the home of Irish jumps racing – and the legendary Aintree, the home of the Grand National in Liverpool, Merseyside.

Now, Harry rode through the years and, let it be known, his greatest pleasure was when he rode his own horse, Pride of Arras, to victory in a maiden plate at Punchestown. Why did it give Harry so much pleasure? Well, he was a spritely 71 years of age at the time.

Harry rode in thirteen Grand Nationals; he managed to win just the once on Come Away in 1891, when he was a babe in arms, at the age of 39 years. Harry was also well known in France where he had won their Classic chase and hurdle races in Paris before the turn of the twentieth century.

But the best part is saved for last, and this should give everyone heart: just because the years are passing us by at the rate of knots, it doesn't mean we should not be as active as we can. After all, Harry was. In 1935, he finished unplaced on a horse called Mollie when he competed in Ballydoyle's Corinthian Plate – and he was a spritely 83 years of age.

Now for another golden oldie

Frank Buckle enjoyed a similar life to Harry, but he was born a little earlier, in 1766. He passed away in 1832, at 65 years of age. He was to flat racing in England what Harry Beasley was to jumps racing in England and Ireland.

Frank's father was a saddler at Newmarket, and young Frank was determined at a very young age not to follow his father's footsteps. At the age of nine, he packed his bag and found work and lodgings with Lord Grosvenor's Racing Establishment. His love of riding started to flourish. He was labelled a gentleman rider of his time, and many said that he brought an air of respectability to jockeys and their craft.

Frank had a long and successful career and held a record for the most number of British Classic races won (27), and this record stood for more than 100 years. He won the 2000 Guineas on five occasions, the Oaks on nine winners and the 1000 Guineas no less than six times. To top that remarkable career, he rode five English Derby winners, in 1792, 1794, 1802, 1811 and 1823.

As is often the case, the moment you stop doing something you have done all of your life and put your feet up, the man upstairs comes calling. Just three months after he rode his last race, Frank Buckle passed away from a diagnosis of 'inflammation'. Still riding at the age of 65 years, he was held in such high esteem that the following inscription is found at his grave site:

> No better rider ever crossed a horse;
> Honour his guide, he died without remorse.
> Jockeys attend – from his example learn
> the meed that honest worth is sure to earn.

Harry and Frank: two great golden oldies.

CHAPTER 4
The United States

Dayjur and the 1990 Breeders' Cup Sprint

... he lost by jumping at shadows

Once dubbed the fastest horse in the world, Dayjur had an outstanding career. But it was his last race that ended up being talked about for years to come.

Dayjur was American-bred, foaled in Kentucky in 1987, and British-trained. His sire was the champion Danzig and his dam was the well-known sprinter Gold Beauty. Bought in 1988 by Hamdan Al-Maktoum, he was sent to be trained in England by Dick Hern in Berkshire. Dayjur had eleven starts for seven wins and three seconds. He was ridden in all of his races by Scottish jockey Willie Carson.

This son of Danzig was a specialist sprinter, and he ran during the racing seasons of 1989 and 1990. In 1990 he dominated European sprint racing by winning the King's Stand Stakes, Nunthorpe Stakes, the Ladbroke Sprint and the Classic sprint race in Europe, the Prix de l'Abbaye de Longchamp.

Dayjur took his fearsome reputation to America in 1990, to contest the Breeders' Cup. His main adversary was going to be America's sprint queen, Safely Kept, who was by the sire Horatius.

During her illustrious career, Safely Kept won 24 of her 31 starts and remarkably finished 'in the money' in no less than 30 of those races. Safely Kept contested the 1989 Breeders' Cup Sprint but could only finish second, behind Dancing Spree; at season's end, she had won eight Stakes races. She was now lining up in the 1990 Breeders' Cup Sprint, and she was heavily favoured to defeat the sprint champion from across the ocean, Dayjur.

As a four-year-old, Safely Kept had won her first six races. In her seventh and last race of her season, on 27 October 1990, she was going to take on the best the world had to offer, as part of the field of fourteen under starter's orders in the Breeders' Cup Sprint at Belmont Park. The distance was the Classic sprint of 6 furlongs (1200 metres).

Just to make it interesting for Dayjur, this was going to be his first ever run on a dirt track and his first ever run around a bend. He was drawn the outside of the field – in any sprint race this can be a curse, because all the other contestants, if riding strategically, can leave you out in no-man's land and tire you out before the run to the wire.

At the start of the race, Safely Kept showed her credentials and went straight to the lead, and Dayjur was left out on the outside, facing the breeze like a shag on a rock. There was too much at stake for the other jockeys to give him an easy ride: *our country, our race, our rules*. With her blistering speed, Safely Kept had no trouble putting a few lengths on the field.

With dogged determination, jockey Willie Carson urged Dayjur from the outside to finally take up a close third and then a close second behind Safely Kept. There was no doubt that these two champions were going to have the race between them in the straight. It was daylight third, as Safely Kept held on to her slim lead. Dayjur just kept on coming, inch by inch.

About 100 yards to go, Dayjur slowly but surely put his big nose in front; it was still just the smallest of margins. Each jockey tried to get the very best out of their mounts. At about 40 yards to go, Dayjur's lead would have been about 6 inches (15 centimetres) and he was looking like he was just holding on, when the strangest thing happened.

It was late afternoon and the sun was behind the main grandstand, which was positioned down the straight, at the winning post. Part of the grandstand roof had a peak. The shadow the roof cast on the track, down the length of the straight, was a straight line down the centre, giving the effect of a two-tone track, with the shadow of the peak jutting out from this line.

Poor Dayjur – running his heart out and heading towards victory by the smallest of margins – came to the shadow of the peak on the course and jumped it. He lost his momentum momentarily and Safely Kept, running on the rails and in the sunshine, kept up her speed, poked her head in front and went on to win by no more than a short head. It's a definite YouTube watch.

Safely Kept: first; Dayjur: second; and Black Tie Affair: third. Jumping at shadows: who would have thought?

Kingston, the world champion of winners
... owed his success to a pair of butcher boys

It is not very often that you can look back on a career and say, 'Well, no doubt about it: he was the best of all time and we probably won't see another one like him.'

Kingston was born in 1884 and died in 1912, and there was nary a dull moment in between. There was a peculiarity in his breeding: his sire was Spendthrift and his dam was Kapanga, but his grandsire was Australian. No, he was not from Australia, but by the British champion sire called Australian, who had nothing to do with the convict colony on the other side of the world. He was bred and owned by James Keene but, as in some tales of great success, Keene suffered financial hardship and sold Kingston before he had a chance to prove his greatness.

The amazing statistic that highlights Kingston's status and his undisputed claim in thoroughbred terms of being the world champion of winners is his form. He raced on 138 occasions for:

- 89 wins
- 33 seconds
- 12 thirds.

He was out of the prize money just four times in his 138 starts – unbelievable. Anyone who has owned a racehorse knows just how great this record is; we will detail more of it later.

James Keene sold Kingston to Evert Snedecker and his partner, J Cushman. They bought him as a yearling and only raced him as a two-year-old. During his first year of racing, he showed some promise and won two from six starts. Two of the horses that beat him that year were the champions Hanover and Tremont.

Both of these remarkable thoroughbreds were owned by brothers Phil and Mike Dwyer, commonly nicknamed the Butcher Boys. The brothers were well known in the Brooklyn borough of New York City, where they started their business in meat. They made their money when business expanded into general meat-packaging, and they supplied meat directly to restaurants and hotels in New York and the surrounding areas.

The Butcher Boys had to do something with their money. Mike, being a gambler of note, thought the best thing would be to win some money from the other side of the rails – how true it turned out to be for them both.

They had witnessed their well-credentialed horses Hanover and Tremont successfully defeat the young Kingston in his two-year-old year, but they also saw much more in the immature Kingston, and they just had to have him. Their theory at the time was that Kingston looked as though he had the makings of an exceptionally talented thoroughbred, and they simply never wanted him to run against Hanover or Tremont again. So they bought him.

Hanover was also foaled in 1884, and he had won his first seventeen starts for the Dwyer brothers. Mike and Phil must have had a damn good eye for horseflesh, because their yearling purchase of Hanover ended in a career worth noting. From 50 starts, Hanover returned:

- 32 wins
- 14 seconds
- 2 thirds.

Hanover was out of the place and prize money just twice in 50 starts.

The other champ in their stable was their other yearling purchase, Tremont, also foaled in 1884. What a great year 1884 proved to be for the brothers! Tremont had thirteen starts as a two-year-old and won all thirteen races by an average of six lengths. This is a record that he still holds today. The Dwyer brothers were known for over-racing their horses and the thirteen wins that Tremont strung together were over a ten-week period. He broke down afterwards and then went to stud.

Now back to Kingston, the world champion of winners. You would have to wonder how Mike and Phil would explain having three such exceptionally talented horses in their stable, all the same age. Consider how difficult it is trying to find one good horse, let alone three that would set the tracks on fire. No wonder they never wanted any of them to race each other.

Here, below, is the full record of Kingston over 138 starts. The wins never stopped, right up until his ten-year-old season.

- 2-year-old: 2 wins from 6 starts
- 3-year-old: 13 wins from 18 starts
- 4-year-old: 10 wins from 14 starts
- 5-year-old: 14 wins from 15 starts
- 6-year-old: 9 wins from 10 starts
- 7-year-old: 15 wins from 21 starts
- 8-year-old: 13 wins from 20 starts
- 9-year-old: 9 wins from 25 starts
- 10-year-old: 4 wins from 9 starts

It is interesting to note that as a nine-year-old that 'only' won nine from 25 starts, Kingston was in the prize money pool for all of those 25 starts, and as a ten-year-old, he won those four races, beating much younger horses.

At the ripe old age of ten, it was off to the breeding barn. When you ask the experts about a horse's chances as a stallion, they will tell you that a horse should never commence his duties too old and you should never consider a horse for stud duties if it has had a lot of racing, as it is generally considered that stallions sour if raced for too long. Well, Kingston was a ten-year-old that had seen 138 starts. We would say that he had not a snowball's chance in hell of stud success.

But, again, we are talking about an exceptional horse. His progeny carried on just like their 'old man' and won races such as the Belmont Stakes, the Futurity Stakes and the Doncaster Cup. Kingston led the

American sire list up until 1910. He died peacefully at the age of 28 years old in 1912.

When the American National Museum of Racing and Hall of Fame was created in 1955, 43 years after his death, he was one of the first horses inducted. Kingston, the World Champion of Winners.

Just to add a little more about Kingston, his half-brother, Bankrupt, was also by Spendthrift. There must have been longevity running through their veins: Bankrupt managed to chalk up 348 starts for 86 wins – amazing.

We don't think the Dwyer boys saw a sausage on their table for many a year.

Not him again!
...Jacinto had the wood on the greatest

One of America's greatest racehorses of all time was undoubtedly Secretariat. Foaled in 1970, the son of Bold Ruler and Somethingroyal was named in a very unusual way. Meadow Stable Farm's Elizabeth Ham was responsible for applying to register names for all their horses. After the colt's first ten names were rejected, she was having trouble with the next ten names for application. So she decided to put forward a name that was a broad description of her own previous employment, and it was accepted. Secretariat was named, and the rest is history.

A brilliant two-year-old, the flashy chestnut stepped up to the plate in his three-year-old career, and gained equine immortality by becoming the ninth winner of America's Triple Crown, winning the Kentucky Derby, Preakness Stakes and Belmont Stakes in 1973. In front of a crowd of 68,000 people, Secretariat was responsible for everyone's hearts in their mouths as he crossed the finishing line in the Belmont Stakes. He won by an astonishing 31 lengths, in the world record time of 2:24.00 for the 12-furlong (2400-metres) journey.

When his racing career was over, Secretariat had the enviable record of 21 starts, for sixteen wins, three seconds and one third. He had won prize money of US$1,316,808, a staggering amount back then.

Over the years, Secretariat has been remembered as a wonderful broodmare sire. His link with Australia is that he was the sire of Kingston Rule, the 1990 Melbourne Cup winner.

There was something quite interesting about Secretariat's three second placings in his career. He was defeated by three separate horses: Onion, Angel Light and Quebec. Well, there's nothing remarkable about that – only that they were all ridden by Jacinto Vasquez.

Watch out, Secretariat, here I come.

Exterminator – the galloping hat rack
... he was lucky just to be alive

Exterminator was sometimes called 'Old Bones' and 'Slim', but sticks and stones may break his bones but names would never hurt him. You can take from these descriptions that he wasn't the best looking athlete in the field, but there were one or two things he had on his side – a little bit of luck that stems all the way back to his grandsire and, most importantly, a little bit of talent.

First of all, let us look at his grandsire. White Knight was pretty slow in the breeding barn so after producing one foal, he was gelded. That one foal ended up being McGee, the sire of Exterminator. Just to add a tag of 'ordinary' into the mix, Exterminator's dam, Fair Empress, failed miserably in her only two race starts, so she was turned out into the paddock for breeding purposes. So here we have an unlikely young foal born at Almahurst Farm in Lexington, Kentucky, on 30 May 1915. Nothing much to look at – just a gangly young colt – but nevertheless, one that was lucky to have his four feet on the ground.

Cal Milam, a local horse trader, bought the bony colt as a yearling, for just over $1000. For reasons known only to Cal, he had him gelded as a two-year-old and then set about trying to find a buyer for him. Cal Milam's wife one evening jokingly said, 'He will probably kill off all of his competition, so why don't we call him Exterminator?'

Before we look closely at the remarkable career of this 'galloping hat rack', you can see that his record, from 99 starts, was:

- 50 wins
- 17 seconds
- 17 thirds.

During his career, Exterminator won 34 Stakes races; this is a record that has never been beaten in North America. He was inducted into the American National Museum of Racing Hall of Fame in 1957. To top off all of his awards, he was rated number 29 in *The Blood-Horse* magazine's top 100 US thoroughbred champions of the twentieth century.

In one of those unforgettable tales of the turf, Exterminator became such a traveller that the racing fraternity likened him to a favourite dog or cat at home. When it came time for bedding down for that well-earned sleep, these pets would walk in circles on their bedding and then lay themselves down to rest. Exterminator travelled throughout his career in a railroad box car. Through the United States, Canada, Mexico – wherever there was a racecourse and prize money on offer, he would be there. They said that all you had to do for him was to put plenty of straw on the floor. He would walk into the box car, walk around in circles, seemingly making his 'bed' more comfortable, and then just lie down on the floor and rest or sleep. He always arrived at his destination fully fit, awake, rested and raring to go. He travelled thousands of kilometres like this.

But back to the horse trader Cal Milam and his gelded two-year-old Exterminator. The horse's purchase as a pace-setter for a young champ was about to change his future.

There was a wealthy racehorse owner by the name of Wills Kilmer. He owned the champion two-year-old Sun Briar, who carried all before him in his two-year-old season; in 1917 he was made the early favourite for the Kentucky Derby. As can happen to youngsters, after a spell to bring him back for his tilt at the Derby, Sun Briar wasn't training strongly at all, so his owner gave his trainer an order: 'Go and find another horse for me that will work with Sun Briar and see if we can get him into galloping fitness to have his crack at the Kentucky Derby.'

Well, lucky for Cal Milam, he was only too pleased to part with Exterminator at a handsome profit; after all, that is what he was in the business of doing: buying and selling. 'Old Bones' had found another home, and now his job was to race beside Sun Briar on the training track to get the champ's mind back on the business of winning.

Well, Wills Kilmer's idea amounted to nothing and Sun Briar just could not find any form at all. Wills was left without a runner to carry his colours in the 1918 Kentucky Derby – but hold on, maybe we can saddle up Sun Briar's training partner? He hadn't had a run since his ten-month spell from his injury as a two-year-old, but he had been doing some solid workouts with Sun Briar. He shouldn't embarrass the stable, and Wills thought at least he would have a runner in the Classic race – even though Exterminator was unwanted in the betting, at 33/1.

The truth was that Kilmer did not want to run a 'billy goat' in his colours to contest the Derby, when it was first suggested to him after Sun Briar was scratched. It took the persuasive manner of the Churchill Downs Race Club President to change his mind – or so the story goes.

In the forty-fourth running of the Classic first leg of the US Triple Crown, the 1918 Kentucky Derby, that bag of bones they called the Exterminator ran away from the field and won by a length. Needless to say, Wills Kilmer took all the credit for masterminding the result with his 'smokey', the Galloping Hat Rack. The legend was born.

Exterminator's success, they say, was due to the ease at which he travelled. As we have said, he was always relaxed, especially in a box car, and he was able to get that restful sleep before competing. He ran throughout the years. Probably his best year was in 1922 as a seven-year-old, when he won ten of his seventeen starts, carrying weight between 133 pounds (60 kg) to a high of 140 pounds (64 kg). He raced on as an eight-year-old and nine-year-old with limited success, before being retired from racing in 1924.

Exterminator raced in the shadow of a horse that was and is still today regarded as one of the best thoroughbreds of all time, Man o' War. Legend states that many a follower wanted a match race between Man o' War and Exterminator, but it is said that Sam D Riddle, the owner of Man o' War, did not want to test his brilliant three-year-old at that time against 'Old Bones', the seasoned veteran.

Exterminator, 'Old Bones', 'Slim' or the 'Galloping Hat Rack' – whatever name you wish to remember him by – died peacefully on 26 September 1945. He was buried beside the horse 'who would be king', Sun Briar, in Birmingham, New York.

The Galloping Hat Rack was a sight to be seen.

The legendary Shoe
... born and placed in a shoe box

Willie 'The Shoe' Shoemaker was, and probably remains today, one of the most loved jockeys who has ever been hoisted into a saddle in the history of American thoroughbred horseracing. The term 'legend' is often bandied around, but in this case it certainly fits this 'giant' of horse racing – who stood all of 4 feet 11 inches (150 centimetres).

Shoemaker was born on 19 August 1931 at Fabens, El Paso County, in Texas. His birthweight was 2½ lb (1.1 kilogram) and he was a measly 10½ inches long (26.7 centimetres). He was so small he was not expected to live through the night. His wily old grandmother, however, was not about to lose one of her grandchildren, so she placed him in a shoe box, all wrapped up, and put him beside her oven in a bid to keep him warm.

You must wonder whether his grandmother had inadvertently tagged him with his eventual nickname of 'The Shoe'. That shoe box on the night of his birth was his saviour. He survived the night, and there was a whole new world out there waiting for him.

It wasn't a really happy time for Willie, family wise, as his mother and his dad divorced. After dropping out of school, Willie found himself in southern California with his father, scrubbing out stables on a thoroughbred ranch – and the connection was made. There are some unions that are inevitable, and so it was for this diminutive young man and horses. A month later, the connections of the ranch thought so much of young Shoemaker's ability with horses they gave him his first professional ride, on 19 March 1948. He was only seventeen years old, and just a few months short of his eighteenth birthday.

His first race was a claiming race at Golden Gate Fields in California. He was legged atop a filly called Shafter V, and his record began – she won. At the tender age of 18 years old, Willie found himself earning money that he had never dreamed of and that he could never spend in one day even if he tried. The Los Angeles Superior Court stepped in, after some well-intentioned whispers in the right ears, and appointed an attorney as his guardian to control his estate, with the consent of both his parents.

Shoemaker's greatest achievement in the saddle was that he rode a total of 8833 winners, with the last victory being when he guided Beau Genius in first to greet the judges on 20 January 1990 in the Hallandale Handicap at Gulfstream Park, Florida. His very last ride was on a seven-year-old just a month later on 3 February at Santa Anita Park, California. The horse was called Patchy Groundfog, and even though the punters made him the sentimental favourite, he could only finish fourth. The very next day Willie Shoemaker announced his retirement from racing.

His 8833 winners remained a world record until it was beaten by Laffit Pincay Jnr in 1999. On his retirement in 2003, Laffit set the bar at 9530 wins. Will that ever be beaten?

Some of Shoemaker's greatest achievements were in the three races that make up the US Triple Crown rank. Even though he was never able to secure the Triple Crown (winning all three races in the one year), he won eleven of these premier races.

- Kentucky Derby: Swaps (1955), Tomy Lee (1959), Lucky Debonair (1965), Ferdinand (1986)
- Preakness Stakes: Candy Spots (1963), Damascus (1967)
- Belmont Stakes: Gallant Man (1957), Sword Dancer (1959), Jaipur (1962), Damascus (1967), Avatar (1975)

There is one Kentucky Derby Willie would have been happy to forget. The year was 1957. At this time, Willie Shoemaker and the champion three-year-old Gallant Man were on top of their game. The team was expected to be the best chance in the Kentucky Derby of that year, and the 'Run for the Roses' was on everyone's minds and lips. Early in 1957, the racing authorities at Churchill Downs made some changes to the course proper. They lengthened the straight by

110 yards (100 metres), thus changing the position of the winning post.

Willie had not ridden at Churchill Downs that year, with the new straight in place. On race day in 1957, racegoers witnessed something quite remarkable. When the horses rounded the turn into the straight, Willie, on Gallant Man, had a brain snap where the old winning post used to be. He stood up in the irons, as one does after finishing the race, but there was a slight problem – there were still 110 yards to the new finishing line.

Just as Willie stood up in the irons to acknowledge the cheering crowd, thinking that he had won the prestigious race, up scoots Iron Liege, ridden by Bill Hardtack, taking advantage of Willie's mistake. Willie took after him like a man possessed, realising immediately what he had done, but he failed to catch Iron Liege on the line.

One would have thought that Gallant Man's owner Ralph Lowe would have been sick to the stomach with rage after what Shoemaker had done in America's most important race, the Kentucky Derby. But, no, he knew it was going to happen. The day before the great race, he had told friends and family that he dreamt his horse had lost the race because the jockey misjudged the finishing line and stood up prematurely in his stirrups, waving his whip to the crowd. Lowe took it in his stride and forgave Shoemaker. Being a Texas oil millionaire probably helped ease the pain of not winning the $107,000 first-prize money.

After that Derby day in 1957, it was definitely head down and bum up for Willie Shoemaker. Some four weeks later, Shoemaker and Gallant Man combined to win the third leg of the Triple Crown, the Belmont Stakes, in race record time.

There was some good news for Willie and connections of Gallant Man, with the recording of the 1957 Derby. The footage that you can see on YouTube of the race is very old and unclear, but if you look hard enough, watch it a few times and recognise Gallant Man in the maze of black and white, you will see for a fleeting moment that action that robbed Willie and Gallant Man of their Kentucky Derby win. If you don't see it – and it is difficult – then Willie's good name and memory remain intact.

Willie wanted to forget that 1957 race and erase it from his memory, but in 1986 he went from zero to hero in the Kentucky Derby. He turned things around and etched his name into the history books when he guided Ferdinand to victory at 18/1, becoming the oldest jockey to ride a Kentucky Derby winner.

The irony of Shoemaker's years in retirement will not be lost on those who 'roll the dice'. After nearly 40 years in the saddle, gambling with his safety in every race he competed in and never sustaining any real serious injuries, the unthinkable happened to this great champion of American horse racing. On 8 April 1991, he was involved in a single-car accident, losing control of his Ford, which left the road and crashed down a steep embankment.

Willie Shoemaker was paralysed from the neck down, and he was confined to a wheelchair for the rest of his life. And the Ford model he was driving? A Bronco.

Shoemaker eventually got his life back into order. He continued his training career, before retiring from that on 3 November 1997. He died peacefully at San Marino, California, on 12 October 2003, aged 72 years old.

'The Shoe' from the shoe box.

Donerail's Kentucky Derby
... the longest-priced winner in the history of the race

To have any sort of record still standing after 138 years is amazing, and it should be highlighted for that reason alone. The famous Kentucky Derby has been run every year since 1875. It is an institution in America. It is held each year on the first Saturday in May, at Churchill Downs, Louisville, Kentucky. It is run over 1¼ miles (2000 metres), and it is the first leg of the prestigious US Triple Crown.

The race is steeped in tradition. It is often described as 'the most exciting two minutes in sport', for the time it roughly takes to run it, and as 'the Run for the Roses', for the blanket of roses that is traditionally draped over the winner.

It was just over 100 years ago, in 1913, that seven of the best three-year-olds in the country were ready to line up and contest the great race – actually there were eight starters, but that eighth starter was not figured to have any chance at all. His name was Donerail, and his starting price was well suited to his form, at 91/1.

To add insult to injury to all of Donerail's connections, and to add to the mirth of the punting public at large, the local paper *The Courier-Journal* published a cartoon on its front page on the morning of the race, depicting just the seven starters. Yes, poor old Donerail never got a look in.

History was made that day. Donerail, ridden by Roscoe Goose, went on to win at 91/1 and, even today, he remains the longest-priced winner of the Kentucky Derby. The closest to him was Mine That Bird, who started at 50/1 before winning the 2009 Kentucky Derby. From that day on, Donerail's jockey was known as 'the Golden Goose' – is it any wonder?

Laugh with me, fella, don't laugh at me.

Murder was on their minds
... but Uncle Frank Harper escaped to the races

'Uncle Frank' pretty much kept to himself, along with his sister and brother, Betsy and Jacob Harper. None of the siblings were married, and they lived in a small cottage on their 1000-acre farm in Midway, Kentucky. The property was a small horse farm called Nantura Stock Farm, and Frank dabbled in thoroughbred stock and breeding.

At a nearby stud, a British-bred sire was standing, and Frank put his mare Nantura to their import, Leamington. The sire was well bred but he had not shown much on the racecourse back in England. The result was a young colt in 1867, all legs and every bit looking like he may travel well over ground.

Now to the events that changed Frank Harper's life. His young colt was named Longfellow, because of his length and height of 17 hands. Longfellow was to have a match race against another well-credentialed horse, called Pilgrim. It was to take place at the Kentucky Association Track. The night before, Frank Harper thought so much about the security of his horse that he left his comfy bed on the farm and bedded down with Longfellow in a barn at the track.

That very night, someone broke into the family cottage and brutally murdered his sister, Betsy, and his brother, Jacob. They were hacked to death. If Frank had been home at the time, he would probably have suffered the same fate, and if that had happened, then the family estate would have been divided up between a couple of nephews, because Frank, Betsy and Jacob had no children of their own. One of these nephews, Adam Harper, was openly accused of the murders. Strong evidence pointed to him, but for whatever reasons, he was never charged.

Well, 'Uncle Frank' Harper made the most of the 'luck' that was afforded him and he continued to race Longfellow with great success. He won many Stakes races and when he looked as though he was training off, Frank turned Longfellow out into the breeding barn at home on Nantura Farm. At 17 hands tall, Longfellow's stride was measured at 26 feet. Both Man o' War and Secretariat had strides of 25 feet, so he could certainly glide over the ground.

Longfellow went on to sire great champions of his own: both Leonatus and Riley, who went on to win the Kentucky Derby. As a three-year-old, Leonatus was so talented that in one seven-week period of racing, he won ten Stakes races. Longfellow became the number one sire of the decade. He died at the age of 26 years, in November 1893, and the inscription on his gravestone read, 'Here lays Longfellow, the King of Racers and the King of Sires'.

Just so 'Uncle Frank' Harper could rest easier after the murder of his brother and sister, he had a private investigator look into the nephew that everyone was pointing the finger at, Adam Harper. It is interesting to note that Frank never revealed the outcome of that investigation, but it may suffice to say, after his own death, his will was read and he had left his estate to another nephew, young Frank Harper.

Justice served.

Richards, Longden, Shoemaker, Pincay and Baze
... records were made to be beaten

There have been many jockeys over the years who have enthralled us, thrilling us with their daring and amazing us with how good they are at their craft. All of the gentlemen named above had at some stage something in common. They all but one held the record of being the 'winningest jockey' on American racetracks, and each paved the way for the next.

Every time a record number of wins was set, collectively the racing public must have thought, 'Well, that's not going to be beaten,' but as sure as night follows day, records are made to be beaten.

If we need to have a yardstick, let us start with a person who broke all the records on the other side of the world. Sir Gordon Richards was English and he remains today the only jockey ever to be knighted while still riding and competing. He started riding in 1921 and he retired from the saddle in 1954 with a world record of 4870 wins. He rode for 33 years – so that would make it around 147 winning rides per year, or nearly three wins per week.

The man to break his record was American jockey John Longden. Longden was not only remembered for breaking this record, but also for something else quite interesting. He was actually a 'Pom', born in Yorkshire. When he was a baby, his mum had taken him by British rail to catch a boat to America to join this father. Luckily for baby John and his mum, the train they were travelling on broke down and they missed their passage. We say 'lucky', because the vessel they were due to leave on was the *Titanic*. Yes, we would consider them lucky – very lucky.

Longden started riding at Santa Anita, California, in 1927, and he retired from the saddle in 1959. His world record of wins was an astounding 6032, soundly beating Sir Gordon Richards' record of 4870. Longden rode for 32 years, so he averaged 189 wins per year in the saddle or just over 3.5 wins per week.

Along came Willie 'The Shoe' Shoemaker, who started his riding career in 1948 and retired in 1990. His riding career spans 42 years, and his 8833 wins can be calculated to around 210 wins per year or just over four wins per week. Now, how could you better that?

Next on the merry-go-round was Laffit Pincay Jnr. Born in Panama City, Panama, in 1946, he began his riding career in 1966, competing mainly in the United States. He retired from competitive riding in 2003, with 9530 race wins. He competed for 37 years, which works out to be nearly 260 wins per year or around five wins per week. It was a staggering amount and he was the new world record holder.

Then Russell Baze came on the scene. He was born in 1958, and we can report that on 7 July 2013, in Pleasanton, California, Russell rode a horse called Handful of Pearls to record his fourth win of the day and his 12,000th win for his career thus far. Up to this time, Russell had been in the saddle 39 years, which equates to 307 wins per year or around six wins per week – and Russell Baze has not announced his retirement as yet.

Baze quite clearly holds the record for the most number of horseracing wins in North America. Well, he holds it at the moment – until the next great rider makes his or her way to the podium. What a task he or she has to catch up to Mr Baze.

Who's next? Records are just made to be beaten.

Okay, who's next?

... 'And you better be good!' said young Julie

Born on 24 July 1963, US jockey Julie Krone went on to ride a total of 3158 winners. In 2002 she was inducted into the Michigan Sports Hall of Fame.

As a youngster, she always wanted to be a jockey. After completing her sophomore year at school, Julie set off with her mum to Churchill Downs, with a forged birth certificate organised by a family member.

After quite a bit of door-knocking, Julie was introduced to trainer Jerry Pace, who took one look at the 4 foot 10 inches tall (147-centimetre), 100 lb (45-kilogram) little girl and said, 'So, you want to be a jockey?'

With that, Julie replied, 'No, I'm gonna be a jockey!'

Krone's autobiography, *Riding for My Life,* and the feature film of her life, *The Boys Club,* show her determination to achieve what she set out to achieve. During her career as a very successful jockey there were many times when she lived on the edge, experimenting with drugs and fast cars. However, there was something else that was brought to the attention of the racing authorities: a feisty attitude that saw her become involved in the art of what we may call 'pugilism'.

Here are just a few cases reported in racing newspapers.

Krone vs Rujano

In 1986 at Monmouth Park, after a clash at the racetrack, jockey Miguel Rujano tried to drown Julie Krone by holding her under water, after throwing her into the racecourse swimming pool. Krone stated that during the race, 'He hit me with his whip and split my ear open. After the race, I retaliated and threw a punch at him and got him right in the mouth, splitting his lip. We fell in the pool, dumping water everywhere.'

After escaping Rujano's drowning attempt, Krone climbed out of the pool and threw a poolside chair at her attacker. Miguel Rujano was subsequently suspended. Julie Krone received a warning – probably to pick on someone her own size.

Krone vs Bravo

During a race in September 1989 at the Meadowlands Racetrack, New Jersey, Julie Krone and Joey Bravo got into quite a bit of roughhouse riding. The jostling started when Bravo manoeuvred Krone's filly Mosquera dangerously close to the running rail. Desperate to avoid a fall, Krone said, 'I reached over and hit him. He then hit my horse in the face.' After the horses passed the winning post, both riders were seen to be pushing and shoving each other all the way back to the weigh-in.

Krone said, 'When we reached the scales, Bravo took a swing at me and hit me in the mouth. I hit back before trainer Jerry Percival intervened and shoved Bravo out of the way. I then shoved Bravo into a metal railing. It was impossible to know who knocked his teeth out, the trainer or me.'

Both riders received a fine, and Krone was suspended for fifteen days.

Krone vs Turcotte

In 1987, at Gulfstream Park, Julie Krone and Yves Turcotte found themselves in the stewards room after a very roughhouse race. Krone said, 'During the race Turcotte hit my horse across the face, and when we returned to the weigh-in, I threw my saddle on the floor and started throwing punches at him.'

When interviewed by racing journalists, Krone said that both riders had been suspended: 'Yves for hitting my horse across the face, and me for hitting a jockey.'

Krone vs Marquez

At Garden State Park in 1988, jockey Armando Marquez was so desperate to win, he reached over and grabbed the reins of Julie Krone, causing her horse, Carousel, to stumble and interfere with other horses. Krone refrained from lashing out at Marquez and decided that she would 'take a deep breath, count to ten and leave it to the stewards'. When interviewed by journalists, Krone said, 'His actions could have seriously hurt my horse, me and other riders.' Armando Marquez was later disqualified and suspended.

Krone vs Alligood

Last but not least, there was someone to match her. During a race at Maryland in 1989, fellow jockey Mary Ann Alligood's mount was seriously interfered with by Krone's mount. Just as fiery as Julie, Mary Ann screamed, 'You bitch, I'm going to get you.' Yes, this was one lady Julie did not want to get into a fight with. After both riders weighed out, Mary Ann went on the attack, throwing punches left, right and centre.

'Boy, she was really mad at me and I was frightened of her,' Krone recalled. 'So I took off and locked myself in the first-aid room and hid there. I was more afraid of that woman than any other jockey alive. She was downright dangerous.'

Just settle down, okay? Just settle down!

A champion killed while game hunting
... it was just a shot in the dark

The American filly Ruthless was one of the great champions of her era, and possibly one of the greatest champions of all time. However, her time with us was to be short-lived.

Foaled in 1864, Ruthless was the daughter of the champion English stallion Eclipse. She won the inaugural Belmont Stakes, now the third leg of the US Triple Crown. She is one of only three fillies to win the race, the others being Tanya (1905) and Rags to Riches (2007). Ruthless was retired, having won seven from eleven races and $11,000, which equates to $1,181,000 today, quite a tidy sum.

It was now time for the breeding barn. One of her first offspring was the 1873 Kentucky Stakes winner, Battle Axe.

It was common practice for owner Francis Morris to let his mares and foals roam the fields of his property at Westchester, New York. A gentleman of the day, Mr Morris also invited his friends to be guests on his property and enjoy some game-shooting.

One weekend, after a late Sunday afternoon shoot, one of the guests hurried back to the main house, knocked on the door, and when Mr. Morris appeared said, 'Francis, I have some bad news for you. One of the hunters spotted an animal moving through the brush at quite a distant, took aim and fired. I am sorry to say it was one of your horses, and more deeply sorry to say that unfortunately it was Ruthless.'

One hopes that there was some insurance involved.

When your colour decided your ability
... you're in and you're out!

During the mid to late nineteenth century, many of the best jockeys in the United States were African Americans, and none were better than these two men.

Willie Simms won five legs of what we now call the Triple Crown. He won two Kentucky Derbies, on Ben Brush (1896) and Plaudit (1898). His compatriot, Alonzo 'Lonnie' Clayton, won the 1892 Kentucky Derby on Azra, and two Kentucky Oaks (1894 and 1895).

Now, let us go back to the 1860s. At this time, African Americans were not welcome to attend horse races, and a report from the archives of the *New York Daily Tribune* of 11 August 1865, shows just how bad things were. This is an extract from the newspaper describing the races at Saratoga that day:

> I should mention as a symptom of this era, when the capacity of the human races are to be demurred, that half of the jockeys are the blackest Africans, and I have yet to learn that their color interferes with their fitness for this most responsible business.
>
> One of them, who passes by the sobriquet [nickname] of 'Old Abe', is highly spoken of as a judicious jockey. The same democracy of feeling does not extend to the spectator's galleries ...

An added addendum to the program says, 'Colored persons not admitted to the stand, whites only!'

Yes, they wanted the best African-American jockeys, but not the African-American public. Thank goodness many years later for the likes of Dr Martin Luther King Jnr.

Shame, shame, shame!

The People's Champion shows his versatility
... it was country against country

He was the people's champion. He was the consummate underdog. He was the horse that people would travel miles and miles just to watch race. He was the horse that became an American legend.

He was Seabiscuit.

Yes, the horse that defeated the Triple Crown champion War Admiral in that 'Match of the Century' race, in November 1938, was the epitome of what horse racing is all about. By the time he retired, Seabiscuit had won 33 races from 89 starts and had earned prize money of US$473,730.

Seabiscuit, however, had been involved in another match race. It happened a few months earlier, in August 1938.

Legendary American entertainer Bing Crosby was one of the founders of the Del Mar Racetrack, built in 1937, in southern California. In partnership with Lindsay Howard, the son of Seabiscuit's owner, Charles Howard, Bing owned the South American champion Ligaroti, who raced in the colours of the Binglin Stable.

Now, Bing Crosby was always on the lookout for ways to promote the Del Mar racecourse and its seaside facilities. He was instrumental in the promotion of a $25,000 winner-take-all match race with none other than Seabiscuit and his horse Ligaroti. Well, the connections of 'The Biscuit' found that this invitation was too hard to dismiss, and the great race was scheduled for 12 August 1938.

The race was to be run over 9 furlongs (1800 metres), with Seabiscuit to carry 130 lb (59 kg) and Ligaroti to carry 115 lb (52 kg). George 'The Iceman' Woolf was on Seabiscuit, and Noel 'Spec' Richardson was riding Ligaroti.

Thanks to all the publicity by the press and radio media, more than 20,000 fans turned out to see the event. Would the US champion defeat the Argentinian champ?

Just after they jumped in the race, Seabiscuit worked his way to the rail and took the lead by the barest of margins. At the half mile (800 metres), Ligaroti's rider, Noel Richardson, moved up to be on equal terms with Seabiscuit, and just before the turn took a narrow lead. But on entering the straight, Seabiscuit once again took the lead. Once they straightened up, they were going nose for nose.

The Del Mar Match Race was on. May the best horse win!

In an article appearing in the *Del Mar Times*, Robert Kelley wrote:

All down the stretch, with the crowd roaring, both riders fought tooth and nail. Ligaroti had a reputation of laying in during his races, and did so to Seabiscuit, dangerously crowding him on the running rail. But Seabiscuit's rider, George Woolf, lashed out at Richardson, and they were literally locked together as they crossed the finishing line.

Interviewed after the race, course broadcaster Oscar Watts, who had called the 1938 race for the first time ever on a national radio broadcast, told the media:

> This was as rough a race as I've ever seen in my whole life. They were hitting each other over the head with their whips and Richardson had Woolf in a leg-lock. Never seen so much trouble in one race and there was a helluva stink over it.

On return to scale, both jockeys were in a heated verbal joust. There was quite a bit of pushing and shoving, and both riders had to be restrained by the racing stewards.

The photo finish result, to the cheers of the crowd, showed that Seabiscuit had defeated Ligaroti by a nose. In doing so, he took four seconds off the track record, clocking an amazing 1:49.00 for the journey. Authorities thought that there must have been a malfunction with the official clocker's time and that they could not have possibly gone that fast. However, there were also another three independent clockers there that day and they recorded the same time. Seabiscuit did indeed break the record by four seconds, which meant Ligaroti, just a nose behind, also broke the track record by just less than four seconds.

After the photo result came down, it was no surprise to see Noel Richardson fire in a protest for interference all the way down the straight. At the stewards inquiry, the recording tape showed that Ligaroti's jockey, Noel Richardson, grabbed Seabiscuit's saddle cloth and George Woolf's whip, then locked his leg with Woolf's. Woolf responded by grabbing Ligaroti's bridle just before the finishing line, urging Seabiscuit to win by a nose.

The stewards dismissed the objection and found that Richardson was the instigator, but they fined both jockeys for foul riding and both were suspended.

Historian John Harvey, quoted in the *Del Mar Times*, described the aftermath of the sensational race:

Both jockeys were suspended for the remainder of the meeting for foul riding. According to the testimony of the patrol judges and presiding officials, when Richardson saw that Seabiscuit could not be beaten, he reached over in the home stretch and grabbed Woolf's saddle cloth and then his bridle rein, impeding the horse and making it impossible for him to move away from Ligaroti.

In retaliation, Woolf had used his whip on Richardson to loosen his hold. The horses themselves had committed no fault.

It was doubtless bad judgement to have such a match race in the beginning. The behaviour of both jockeys was reprehensible.

The speed of the race must have done both horses a treat as Seabiscuit, some three months later, trounced the 1937 Triple Crown winner War Admiral in the 'Match Race of the Century', and at his next start, Ligaroti won the Del Mar Handicap.

Oh, the irony of recording tape being Ligaroti's undoing in the appeal. Some years earlier, Ligaroti's owner, Bing Crosby, was one of the driving forces in America of recording on magnetic tape. He was also the man behind the innovation of multi-track recordings.

Seabiscuit went on to greatness, also winning the Hollywood Gold Cup. In 1939, he won the Santa Anita Handicap, which was the race that had eluded him in his earlier years.

However, after a few disappointing runs, Ligaroti was retired to stud. He was regarded as a failure. One day while covering a mare in the breeding barn, he collapsed and died of a massive heart attack.

The mare did foal, and the colt raced under a very appropriate name: Last Bang. We're pleased Ligaroti had the last say.

Miracle at Gilmour's barn
... where a horse did what the surgeons couldn't!

We believe we are in the hands of greater forces in life that in some way determine our journey. We may have a lot of influence in what happens in our lives, but sometimes there are those twists and turns that we never see coming. We have all lost a loved one and we know deep down that all of us harbour a wish just to see or touch that person one more time – it is human nature.

There are some of us who have, unfortunately, through accidents or through natural causes, ended up with a disability of some sort. Through our strength of character and our acceptance that life is what it is, we try to live our life to the full. In many cases, we must take advantage of any opportunities that come our way, because we can't turn back the clock and we often can't improve the cards we have been dealt. Don Karkos felt this way and this is his story.

Don Karkos joined the US Navy just before his seventeenth birthday. He found himself aboard the USS *Rapaden*, whose purpose was to roam the seas during World War II, dodging the German U-boats and refuelling Allied warships. One particular day they were near the English coast when they suffered a direct hit from a U-boat. All hell broke loose on board. It was just twelve months after Karkos enlisted.

The next thing the young Don could recall was waking up in an Icelandic military hospital with some very serious shrapnel wounds to his face, in particular, above his right eye. His fears were answered in good time when he was sympathetically told by the resident doctors and surgeon that he had lost the sight in his right eye.

On returning home there was very little to do except get on with life. Don married and raised a family. He never allowed the loss of sight in one eye to hamper his approach to what he wanted to do, and he decided that he must continue on and live as normal a life as possible. He was always very mindful of the fact that he had to look after his remaining good eye – total blindness was not an option.

Throughout his life, Don Karkos was a frequent visitor to his doctor, always asking about medical science, how it had progressed and if there was any chance at all of reclaiming his eyesight. However, as he was told by the experts, there was nothing that could be done for the sight in his right eye. He became increasingly nervous about his sight as he got older, because over time he needed to have a couple of cataracts removed from his good eye.

Don Karkos was 82 years of age. He had lived a fruitful but careful life, and he had worked for the last sixteen years as a security guard at the Monticello Raceway, in New York, checking in runners before their race and also helping out in the stables.

This one particular morning he was helping John Gilmour in his barn on the course and adjusting the gear on a trotter, My Buddy Chimo, which they co-owned. As anyone who has worked with horses would know, they can be unpredictable. My Buddy Chimo lowered his head, and in a split second he raised his head so quickly that Don could not get his head out of the way in time and *whack*! The horse's head hit him right above his right eye. He was stunned by the head butt, but with his back against the wall, he managed to stay on his feet. For an 82-year-old it was quite a shock. He took himself home later that day to recover.

Still feeling quite unsteady on his feet, he cupped his hand over his right eye and bumped his way down his hallway. He just didn't feel right. In an inexplicable action, he then cupped his hand over his good eye. Lo and behold, he could see out of his right eye!

After all those years – the doctors, the specialists, the many times Don asked about new advances in medical science – it took one nasty bump on the head above his right eye by the little trotter My Buddy Chimo and his full sight was restored.

They called it a miracle.

Don Karkos died within twelve months of the miracle injury, but what happiness he must have had for that year, having his sight restored after losing it more than 60 years before. We believe that Don probably said to himself that he would die a happy man if he could only have his full sight restored – it was thanks to My Buddy Chimo.

Believe it or not!

Malicious, the people's champion
... and how he kept everyone's attention!

The year was 1927. A colt was born in the United States by the sire Omar Khayyam from the mare Ridicule. There must be a cryptic explanation for naming this foal Malicious; nevertheless, his talent kept everyone's attention for a number of reasons.

In American thoroughbred terminology, Malicious was a 'claimer'. He was certainly not a fashionable horse with loads of talent, but more a 'gut-busting' trier that belongs to a kind of racing that is synonymous with the working class. One of the records that was attributed to him was that he began his racing career in California at the age of two years old and retired to the paddock at the age of thirteen. That long career in itself deserves applause, but consider now that his statistics show that he had 185 starts and managed to take first prize 32 times. He was owned by his breeder and trainer, Lonnie Coperhaver, for his entire racing career.

Malicious became the battlers' champion because he always seemed to be on the course trying his heart out. If you consider his 185 starts over eleven years, he must have started on average every three weeks during that whole period of time.

Malicious also managed to solve a major problem that exists even today – and it's a wonder that some race clubs haven't taken a leaf out of the books of the organisers from way back then. How many times as a racegoer have you seen the large crowds slowly make their way out of the course after the main race of the day? By the time the 'lucky last' race is about to start, only the desperates, the drunks, and those trying to get back the rent money on the last are left at the course.

Problem solved. Malicious was such a popular horse with the working class – due to his trademark last-to-first dash, even over 2 miles (3200 metres) and longer – the penny dropped with the race officials and they began to program his race as the last on the race card. The crowds stayed and lived it up all day, just to see their champ go around.

One wonders why it takes so long today for the penny to drop.

Steeplechasing in America
... a far cry from the steeples in England and Ireland

Even before the American Civil War (1861–65), there were recognised steeplechase race meetings in New York, Pennsylvania, Maryland and Virginia. They had been introduced to the country by the migrating English and Irish settlers. The earliest recorded jumping race was held in Washington, DC, in 1834. More jump courses began to be created, and the National Steeplechase and Hunt Association was founded in Maryland in 1895 in order to bring under the one umbrella all jumping enthusiasts and to establish proper rules and codes of conduct for the fast-growing sport.

It did not prove to be an easy road for any form of horse racing in America at that time. The Hart-Agnew Law was passed in New York in 1908, banning gambling, and this made it difficult for any form of racing to prosper.

In an act that is bereft of common sense, New York Governor Charles Evan Hughes, after which the Act was named, sent instructions to his police that they were to arrest men who congregated in groups of more than three, or who were suspected of gambling. Needless to say, the economic ramifications of this short-sightedness sent many businesses bankrupt. It was reported that between 1908 and 1913, more than 1500 American horses were sent to Europe to race. Unfortunately, during that same period of time, the trainers and jockeys in America felt the full brunt of unemployment and despair. These were very hard times indeed.

Steeplechasing was not dependent solely on the betting public for its survival, so jumps race spectacles started to appear. They were accepted as a form of entertainment for all. This was the thin edge of the wedge, however, and gradually politicians saw the error of their ways. Horse racing in general began to reappear on the American horizon. The old-timers and followers of jumps racing in America can proudly state, 'Jumps races saved horse racing in America'.

One English horseman described the distinction between flat and jump racing in the following way: '*Steeplechasing has more glamour and excitement than the flat racing. It has a trace of chivalry, a sense of danger and a refreshing vigour that flat racing lacks. It has an atmosphere that is more open, friendly and at the same time intimate, and gives the impression of really being a sport and not just big business.*'

Jumps races have essentially gone back to their roots in America, and there are now many smaller race meetings in more rural settings. The National Steeplechase Association controls meetings on the East

Coast and has its own circuit and schedules. The season runs from March through to November.

Steeplechase meetings are now held in nine different states and share prize money worth more than $5 million. The *jewels in the crown* are the Breeders' Cup Grand National and the Colonial Cup. This sport is once again thriving in America.

Greats under the Star Spangled Banner
... *America's contribution to thoroughbred folklore!*

Here are the brief resumes of seven of the greatest thoroughbred racehorses ever to grace the tracks in America. This list does not include Secretariat and Seabiscuit; they have been covered elsewhere in this book.

Man o' War

Man o' War's nickname was Big Red. He was retired to stud after his three-year-old season because his owners did not want to tempt fate. Man o' War was born in March 1917 and was owned by August Belmont Jnr. In 1918, the colt was sold to Samuel D Riddle.

August Belmont Jnr was a strange one indeed. At the age of 65, he had volunteered to serve in World War I. While he was at war, the colt was born and his wife decided to name the horse after her absent husband, who was fighting overseas – Man o' War. Years later, the Belmont Stakes was named in honour of August Belmont Jnr.

Man o' War was hugely talented, and he lost only one of the races he contested. This was due to the old method of starting races, where the horses just mingled behind the starting line. Unfortunately Man o' War was facing the other way when the race was started; when the starter said 'Go!', he lost many lengths. However, the big chestnut put in a soul-stirring run to finish a gallant second to the aptly named Upset.

As the season went on, no-one wanted to race him and it wasn't until the running of the Lawrence Realization Stakes that they finally persuaded another horse to participate. His name was Hoodwinked. They all knew what the outcome would be, and it came as no surprise when Man o' War won by 100 lengths and set a new world record.

Retired to stud duties in Lexington, Kentucky, Man o' War had a long and fruitful life, siring some of America's greatest horses. At the age of 30, the great Man o' War died from an apparent heart attack.

War Admiral

War Admiral had impeccable credentials, as his sire was the great Man o' War. Born in Lexington, Kentucky, in 1934, 'The Mighty Atom', as he was affectionately called, was such a dark brown colour most people thought he was black.

War Admiral detested the starting gates, but even this quirk could not stop him from winning races. He was the Triple Crown winner in 1937, and he was racing so well in the 1938 season that his jockey didn't even carry a whip.

Unfortunately, War Admiral is best known for his defeat by Seabiscuit in the 'Match Race of the Century' on 1 November 1938, not for his record of 21 wins and 4 placings from 26 races. Seabiscuit's sire, Hard Tack, was also by Man o' War

After War Admiral's death, he was buried next to the great Man o' War at the Faraway Farm in Kentucky. Years later, his remains were moved to the Kentucky Horse Park.

Citation

Citation's claims to fame were that in 1948 he became the eighth Triple Crown winner in US history and he was the first horse to win prize money in excess of US$1 million.

At his only loss as a two-year-old, Citation ran second to his stablemate Bewitch. Before the start of that race, their trainer had stated that whichever of them was in front at the home turn, he should be allowed to win. Despite his ability, Citation was reined in behind Bewitch and ran second.

Citation retired with an outstanding record of 32 wins and 12 placings from 45 starts, and he was inducted into the US National Museum of Racing and Hall of Fame in 1959.

On his death, he was buried at Calumet Farm in Lexington, Kentucky – but this giant of the turf had one more claim to fame to come. The chairman of the Cessna Aircraft Company chose the name Citation for the new business jet that his company was developing at the time. The Cessna Citation went on to rule the air as well!

Affirmed

Sired by Exclusive Native, a grandson of the famous Native Dancer, Affirmed was the first thoroughbred racehorse in North America to win more than US$2 million during his career. He was also known for his intense rivalry with the ill-fated champion Alydar.

Affirmed won the 1978 Triple Crown and became the eleventh horse in US history to do so. His racing style was double-edged: he could start like a bullet out of a gun, and then remain in front and run the opposition ragged.

The legendary contests with Alydar had to be seen to be believed. They raced head to head on a number of occasions, never giving the other an easy run. This came to a very unfortunate conclusion when, after severe interference caused by Alydar's rider winning the 1978 Travers Stakes, Alydar was disqualified and the race was awarded to the second-placed Affirmed.

History was made in the Marlboro Cup International in 1978, when two Triple Crown winners went head to head for the first time. It was Affirmed versus Seattle Slew, with Affirmed emerging victorious.

Affirmed retired from racing having started on 29 occasions for 22 wins and 6 placings. The only time he was out of a place was in the 1978 Jockey Club Gold Cup, when his saddle slipped and he couldn't be ridden out. He was inducted into the US National Museum of Racing and Hall of Fame in 1980.

Spectacular Bid

Born on 17 February 1976, this horse's nickname was 'The Bid'. His claim to fame came from a remark by the great jockey Bill Shoemaker, who said, 'He is the best horse I have ever ridden.' Racing as a two-year-old, he was often compared to Seattle Slew and Affirmed.

Spectacular Bid raced in the same era as the great Affirmed. Even though he was a little younger, he faced the older horse in 1979 in the running of the Jockey Club Gold Cup; unfortunately he was narrowly beaten by the champ.

Although a heavily backed favourite for the Triple Crown in 1978, Spectacular Bid found trouble in the third leg, the Belmont Stakes, and was unable to win the race. When brought back to the enclosure, a close inspection showed that a safety pin was lodged in his hoof. There was no suggestion of foul play, but it must also be said that his jockey, Ronnie Franklin, and a rival hoop, Angel Cordero, got into a fist fight in the waiting area before the great race.

Spectacular Bid was also a great influence on racing in Australia, where one of his sons, Spectacular Spy, was the sire of Australia's great front-running grey Quick Flick, whose record was 55 starts for sixteen wins, ten seconds and three thirds, winning one Group 1 race, the 1998 George Ryder Stakes, and total prize money of $1,295,789.

Spectacular Bid was retired after 30 starts, including 26 wins; he finished out of the money only once. In 1982, he was inducted into the US National Museum of Racing and Hall of Fame.

Dr. Fager

This magnificent animal, nicknamed 'The Doctor', set a world record over a mile and held it for 20 years. His Hall of Fame trainer, John Nerud, had a bad fall from a pony early in his career and had needed two lifesaving operations. His surgeon was none other than Dr John Fager, a Boston brain surgeon – hence the horse's name.

Here was a very talented horse, but he was also very arrogant and unruly. He won more than US$1 million in prize money from 22 starts, eighteen wins and three placings.

In 1968, Dr. Fager was awarded Horse of the Year, Champion Handicap Horse, Champion Sprinter and Co-Champion Grass Horse. He was the only horse to hold four titles in the one year.

Other racing teams would use his unruly nature to their advantage. They would send out a tear-away in the hope that 'The Doctor' would chase it and tire out. They were successful on a few occasions, but more often than not, it backfired on them. In 1971, he was inducted into the US National Museum of Racing and Hall of Fame. Unfortunately, he died very early, at the age of twelve years old, from a colon obstruction.

Seattle Slew

Born on 15 February 1974, Seattle Slew was sold at auction for $25,000. His new owners, Karen and Mickey Taylor, named him after a city in their state and also the slough (pronounced 'sloo') channels that loggers transported logs along. Karen changed the spelling, as she thought it would be too confusing to use as it was. So instead of being Seattle Slough, he was officially named Seattle Slew.

Seattle Slew won all his races as a two-year-old, and then as a three-year-old he won six consecutive races, including the races of the coveted Triple Crown. He suffered what could have been a couple of career-ending setbacks during his time, but kept on confounding the experts in getting back up, dusting himself off and racing like the wind. Some of those ailments were a collapsed jugular vein, a suspensory ligament problem and a suspect ankle.

As a four-year-old, he battled back into contention and was named the Horse of the Year in 1978. Seattle Slew raced a total of seventeen times, for fourteen wins and two seconds. He earned more than US$1.2 million in prize money.

Seattle Slew was inducted into the US National Museum of Racing and Hall of Fame in 1981. This magnificent champion died on the twenty-fifth anniversary of his Kentucky Derby win.

Memories come flooding back.

Foundation sires of American horse racing
... where it all began

From their humble beginnings, who would have estimated the global contribution these few horses would make?

Diomed

Foaled in England in 1777, Diomed enjoyed a brilliant early career, with his major win being the inaugural English Derby in 1780. Things didn't go as planned after his early successes, however, and the wins soon dried up. Sent to stud, he did not get the opportunities that he deserved in England, and at the age of 21 he was sold to Colonel Hoomes, who took him to America to commence stud duties there.

A stellar stud career blossomed in America, and Diomed built up a great national reputation for siring champions. His greatest son was Sir Archy, who also bred many champions, such as Timeloen, Lady Lightfoot and Sir Charles. The effect that Diomed had on early American horse racing is part of the reason the Byerley Turk was so strong for so long. Duroc, a son of Diomed, came from the Byerley Turk line via Herod.

Messenger

Son of Mambrino, Messenger was an incredibly important sire to the standardbred line of American harness racers, but not quite as important as a breeder of thoroughbreds. His great grandson was Hambletonian, who was the major foundation sire of standardbreds in America.

Medley

Bred by Lord Grosvenor and foaled in 1775, this exceptional horse won eleven Classic races during his four-year-old campaign in England. Sold to Malcolm Hart, he was then sent to stud. During his eight years at stud, he sired such champions as Tayloe's Bellair II, Gimcrack and Tayloe's Quicksilver. Probably his greatest contribution to American thoroughbred racing was the number of quality dams that he sired.

Shark

Shark first saw the light of day in England in 1771, and was shipped off to Virginia, in the United States, in 1786. His most significant contribution was his ability to sire quality and successful mares from the Diomed line.

It's interesting to see where it all began.

CHAPTER 5
Scams and Scandals

The very phrase 'scams and scandals' conjures up a racing world where money and personal gain have the highest priorities, and all kinds of improper practices abound. A scam is usually 'a disgrace and a fraudulent business scheme; a swindle', and a scandal may be 'an action or event that is morally or legally questionable and that causes public outrage' or the outrage and anger caused by such an event. These two words very much describe what we have in store for you in this chapter.

The Black Opal Stakes blunder
... where the earthquake tremors changed the result

Our first book, *Off the Track*, includes the story of the first time a photo-finish camera was used in the Melbourne Cup, in 1948. In a tight finish between the roughie Rimfire (80/1) and the fast-finishing favoured Dark Marne, the nod was given to Rimfire. The bookies were delighted. Jockey Jack Thompson was absolutely certain he had won aboard Dark Marne, and he was one of thousands who demanded to see a copy of this 'photo-finish print'. Yes, it showed Rimfire winning by the smallest of margins.

History books will show that a few months later, it was pointed out to the authorities at Flemington that the camera was not aligned properly. This left in grave doubt the decision made on the 1948 Cup. However, the decision obviously stood.

Well, this may also have happened in Canberra.

It was the inaugural running of the Black Opal Stakes in 1973. In a driving finish to the line, Ted Doon, the rider of Wanted Man, had a Jack Thompson moment and thought that he had won the race. Quite content to sit back waiting for his number to come up, he was dumbfounded when the race was awarded to Rich Reward, ridden by Chris Gwilliam. Doon, too, along with many a racegoer, had a long look at the photo-finish print that day. Yes, it showed Rich Reward winning by the smallest of margins.

Just a few days before the race, the Canberra area had experienced some severe earth tremors. Later, the possibility was raised of the tremors causing movement that affected the alignment of the camera. The Canberra racing authorities took it in their stride, and followed it up and checked. Quietly and without fanfare, the camera angle was readjusted. Oops!

Maybe Ted Doon was right.

The Trodmore Hunt Club sting
... the biggest and best sting in English racing history

It is a long-held belief that the bookies – whether they are on the racecourse, in the betting shop or in the pub – are there to rip the punters off. As hard as the punter tries, the bookies seem to have everything stacked in their favour. So when the chance comes to get one over them, all the punters rush and join the queue.

The setup
Allow me to introduce you to the main players in this theatre of deception:

- the Trodmore Hunt Club
- Mr Martin of St Ives in Cornwall, England
- *The Sportsman* newspaper
- *The Sporting Life* newspaper
- all down-trodden punters.

In July 1898, the London newspaper *The Sportsman* received correspondence from Mr Martin of St Ives, Cornwall, simply stating that:

It has come to my attention that *The Sportsman* is having difficulty in covering the Trodmore Hunt Club race program scheduled for the long weekend Bank Holiday in August of this year. Because of this, I would like to offer my services. I would convey to you at the appropriate times, the fields and the riders of the day, so the paper can print the details thus allowing the punting public to support the paper and the Hunt Club races.

As many would know, whether it was 1894 or 2014, the racing department of any newspaper is a whirlwind of information and activity, with a daily scramble to produce accurate information as far as racing programs are concerned. Newspaper staff have to make sure that the race times, horse numbers, horse names, riders and prices are 100 per cent correct, because their paper is a bible when it comes to the punting public.

Now let us return to 1898. To nominate an agent to review a particular country race meeting for the newspaper was common practice; there were so many racetracks and hunt clubs that it was impossible to have sporting reporters cover them all. The opposition newspaper, *The Sporting Life*, also engaged agents from time to time. Luckily for Mr Martin, *The Sportsman* offered him the going rate of 1 guinea to perform this service for them.

As the information became available, our Mr Martin meticulously communicated the nominations, followed by the horses that would run in each race. Eventually, just before the bank holiday weekend in August, in time for publication, he reported the jockeys engaged and the opening prices of the horses who would run that day at the Trodmore Hunt Club races. The racing reporter at *The Sportsman* had built a trusting relationship with Mr Martin. There was no doubt that if everything went according to plan, Mr Martin would be engaged as an agent in all future races in his area.

Well, that busy bank holiday in August came and went and *The Sportsman* was once more a hive of activity, with checking and rechecking all the race results to be published in the next edition. The information had to be right, because these details were referred to by the bookies, far and wide, to identify the winning horses and their prices so they could pay out to the punters. There were no radio broadcasts of the races then.

The racing reporter was getting quite nervous about the lack of information that was coming in from Mr Martin of the Trodmore Hunt Club. At the eleventh hour, our man in St Ives, Cornwall, came through and communicated the results for publication:

- Race 1: 1st Jim, 5/4
- Race 2: 1st Rosy, 5/1
- Race 3: 1st Spur, 2/1
- Race 4: 1st Reaper, 5/1
- Race 5: 1st Curfew, 6/4
- Race 6: 1st Fairy Bells, 7/4

With every post, Mr Martin made his new-found friend at the news-paper very happy, because he was also supplying a detailed account of any horse, race by race, that he felt was backed with particular certainty. Because there were no big 'shorteners' on the course, Mr Martin reported that:

> ... apart from Reaper in Race 4 being backed from his opening price of 6/1 into 5/1, I feel that the day was conducted to such a level of honesty and integrity, the Trodmore Hunt Club should be very pleased with their organisation and professionalism.

It was just what the reporter wanted to hear. With that, the results for the Trodmore Hunt Club race program were prepared and printed in the next edition. When *The Sporting Life* saw that they had been trumped by an agent working for *The Sportsman*, they hurriedly took the printed information from *The Sportsman*, and the same results appeared in the next edition on the streets of *The Sporting Life*. They did this in such a hurry they made a mistake reporting the winner of race 4. Reaper was quoted in their paper at 5/2 and not 5/1, as was reported by our Mr Martin.

The sting

The first paper to hit the streets was *The Sportsman*, and the bookmakers started to pay out on all race results from the races held over the bank holiday weekend. Because *The Sporting Life* got their results from the printed edition of *The Sportsman*, their second edition – with the misprint on the price of Reaper – was distributed at least a day later.

The bookies took the results in their stride, but they did see a pattern emerging when it came to the winner of race 4 at Trodmore. There were quite a few collects all over the country, and it was also reported that some gentlemen who were paid out in one pub were also seen collecting in another pub in the same area . One particular gentleman was reported to have been seen in no fewer than nine pubs in one county, collecting winnings from bookmakers in each of the pubs – all bets on Reaper at 5/1 and all the same day.

The bookies weren't overly worried; they had seen pub bets before where the punter, having had too much to drink, splashed out on a horse and it had spread like wildfire with others around him. In most cases the horse had worse form than the punter. It happened, and it was just human nature.

It was the second day of the payouts and *The Sporting Life* was now on the streets. Mr Hingeley, a well known and respected bookmaker in the Kensington area of London, had paid out a substantial amount on Reaper once *The Sportsman* had hit the streets. But it was when a 'well-dressed geezer', as Mr Hingeley would later describe him, came in to collect his winnings on Reaper at the pub on his patch, that Hingeley felt the urge to double-check the information published.

The Sportsman showed 5/1, but Hingeley was sure that he could recall that that morning's edition of *The Sporting Life* had reported that Reaper's winning starting price was in fact 5/2. He asked the punter if he could return later in the day, as he wanted to check the starting price. If *The Sporting Life* was right, Mr Hingeley had been the victim of a 'sting' as he had been paying out twice as much as he should have. Before he let go of another pound, he would check with the authorities.

He checked both papers again. Yes, *The Sportsman* had Reaper at 5/1 in race 4 and *The Sporting Life* had him at 5/2. Which one was right? Of course he suspected it was *The Sporting Life* at 5/2.

If in fact the sting was the price on the horse, then it was probably the tip of the iceberg. He reasoned that the authorities must have noticed something on race day to indicate what was going on. If Reaper was such a good thing, what was its real price? Mr Hingeley went to the offices of *The Sportsman* to try to get confirmation from the sporting editor of Reaper's winning price. Had they made the error? If they had published 5/1 instead of 5/2, then someone at the newspaper might be involved in the sting itself.

All of *The Sportsman*'s printed results were as per Mr Martin's detailed and exact list, so the next thing was for Mr Hingeley and the sporting representative of *The Sportsman* to make their way to the opposition's head office to see the reporter's opposite number at *The Sporting Life*. They hastily compared their files and it became painfully obvious that all *The Sporting Life* had to go on was the printed information that they had clipped out from *The Sportsman* that day. Well, at least, they all saw how the mistake was made, and it was an embarrassment all round for the sporting editor of *The Sporting Life*.

Mr Hingeley told the sporting editor of *The Sportsman* that it was now his responsibility to go back to his agent and to double-check all the information and results from the Trodmore Hunt Club. He was satisfied that there had been no sting on the pricing now, but it didn't make him feel entirely happy.

Well, *The Sportsman*'s representative did in fact correspond with Mr Martin of St Ives, Cornwall. Unfortunately for him, and for all of the bookmakers who had paid out on Reaper all over England, they were all victims of one of the biggest stings of all time.

The aftermath

There was no such place as the Trodmore Hunt Club, no such person as Mr Martin of St Ives, Cornwall, and of course, no races at that mythical place of Trodmore, somewhere in England. The aftermath of the sting included a very embarrassed, out-of-work sporting editor of *The Sportsman*.

Our Mr Martin and all of his commission agents were never heard of again. The claim from the bookmaking fraternity was that the sting had cost them hundreds of thousands of pounds – in 1898, it was certainly a king's ransom.

Three weeks after the event, *The Sportsman* newspaper published the following statement.

Trodmore Race Meeting – On August 1, we published the program of a race meeting purporting to be held at Trodmore, Cornwall, and on August 2, a report of the alleged meeting. Both the program and the report were sent to us by a correspondent who signed himself as G. Martin, St. Ives, Cornwall.

Investigation has shown that there is no such place as Trodmore and that no race meeting was held on August 1 in the neighbourhood of St. Ives, Cornwall.

It is obvious therefore, that Martin by himself or in league with others invented the program and reports in question for the purpose of defrauding bookmakers, several of whom have communicated with us.

We are endeavouring to trace the fraud to its source, and meanwhile would recommend agents who receive commission in connection with the meeting to withhold payment and to forward to this office names and addresses of any persons who sent commissions to you.

It appears that our contemporary, *The Sporting Life*, was a victim of the same fraud, as the report results of the fictitious meeting appeared in its column on August 3.

Lesson: don't be lazy, always check your sources.

And the winner is ...

... but he wasn't even in the field!

More than 100 years ago in Melbourne, on 13 July 1906, the sun rose on a somewhat quiet winter's day. By late afternoon, all hell had broken loose.

On the last day of the Grand National meeting at Flemington Racecourse, Victoria, a horse by the name of Blue Jacket was backed in from 15/1 to 6/1 in the Footscray Steeplechase. Back then, there were no on-course or radio broadcasts. The telephone system was still in its infancy, and telephones were deemed unreliable. All communication regarding race results was via telegrams from the Flemington Racecourse to the Universal Press Agency, which then passed on the results to all the Melbourne clubs and betting agencies.

The steeplechase was run and 'correct weight' was announced. The telegram was sent. It declared that Blue Jacket had won the race. The clubs and agencies were in for quite a large payout.

Many of the alert off-course punters, who were in the know, quickly stepped in to claim their winnings from the bookies, who were absolutely stunned by the result. Within minutes, those punters had quickly vacated the premises.

A short time later, a second telegram arrived at all the betting agencies, stating that the winner of the Footscray Steeplechase was Error, a well-performed horse that had run third in the 1905 Grand National Steeple.

That's when 'the proverbial' hit the fan. How was it possible for there to be two telegrams and two different winners?

Officials at the Universal Press Agency had noticed that the telegram clerk responsible for sending race results was not at his station. He couldn't be found, and they did not know at the time if the winner had been sent through. They had then sent the 'winning' wire to all the clubs and agencies. They also found that the scratching of Blue Jacket had not gone through, and that was immediately attended to as well.

That day, the punters who had not already cashed in their 'winning' Blue Jacket tickets were refunded their money because it was declared a scratching.

One could just imagine the turmoil in the betting shops, especially in regards to those original 'losing' bets on Error. It would have been absolute chaos trying to find those real winning tickets, many of which had probably been torn up.

Somehow the sting had come off. It was reported days later that it had cost the off-course bookies and betting shops thousands of pounds.

After a police inquiry, two people – a small-time punter and the telegram clerk – were arrested and charged. It was soon realised that these two did not have the smarts to hatch such a scheme. Further investigation led police to the so-called mastermind, Frederick Green, who lived in the eastern suburb of Hawthorn. Green was nowhere to be found. It was thought that he had done a 'runner' and moved to Queensland.

Green was never seen again. He probably changed his name and decided to ply his craft in Brisbane. Who knows, he may have been a distant relative of one of Brisbane's most flamboyant punters of the 1900s, 'The Butterfly', John Mort Green.

Thank goodness today for TV and early morning scratchings.

A phone box and a fraudster
... the Legend of Yellow Sam

The year was 1975. In Ireland, the Irish had a flying visit by the Canadian prime minister for bilateral talks held at Dublin Castle, and the soccer legend in his own lifetime, George Best, played a League of Ireland match for Cork Celtic against Drogheda.

In County Meath, and more specifically in a village called Bellewstown, the seeds were being planted and the crop was being nurtured for what has become known as the Legend of Yellow Sam. Bellewstown is a village on the Hill of Crockaforth in County Meath. The one important thing to all red-blooded horse lovers was that Bellewstown has a 1 mile and 1 furlong (1800 metre) left-handed racecourse.

The course is basically in the middle of nowhere and is used sparingly for flat and hurdle racing, with the big event being a three-day carnival in the Irish summer. The history of the course spans a couple of centuries. It is written that King George III sponsored a race at Bellewstown in 1780 that was called His Majesty's Plate. Who would have thought?

So here we have a village tucked away from the hustle and bustle of the city life, fully complemented with a primary school, a Catholic church, two pubs, a general store, a field that saw activity from the Gaelic Athletic Association, a golf course and, of course, a racecourse with one telephone booth.

It just so happens that Barney Curley, a professional gambler from Northern Ireland, spied the isolated facilities of the Bellewstown Racecourse and decided that maybe his horse could reap some riches for him. Curley was quite the creative gambler, and he saw opportunities in some circumstances that others would not.

Curley had a hurdler called Yellow Sam. He instructed his trainer that he wanted his horse to be set for a specific race to be held in the middle of nowhere. The trainer scratched his head at the obscure National Hunt race in Bellewstown, but seeing that Barney Curley was paying the bills, it was onwards and upwards. The trainer was also given a list of races that Yellow Sam would run in his lead up to that particular race.

All the lead-up races that had been selected for the horse were unfavourable in some respect. Distances were either too long or too short, he was running against a much better class of jumper than he had previously, there were terrible weather conditions – it was almost as if Curley was willing his horse to fail, and fail he did.

As the trainer was following his brief to the letter, Curley was putting together a plan to have a team standing by in betting shops all over Ireland. Each of the key personnel was instructed to have another group of trusted 'punters', who would work on a commission basis and when told of the 'bet', they would be telephoned and would follow their instructions to the letter. Each of his key commissioners was cashed up by Curley, and in turn their team was cashed up as well. No-one knew the horse in question until before the race. Each of the inner circle had a sealed envelope containing the name of the horse and instructions on when to place the bets; the envelope was only to be opened after a call from Curley on race day – just before the start of the race.

How was it going to work? All of Barney Curley's life savings were going to be invested. All the money would be placed on Yellow Sam with bookmakers off-course; if their exposure was too great, they would simply lay off some bets so that if the horse won, their losses would not be crippling. And, of course, Yellow Sam had to greet the judge.

Here was the key: the on-course bookmakers at Bellewstown determine the starting price of all horses. Because Yellow Sam had been beaten convincingly in all of his lead-up races, his starting price was an unwanted 20/1. If he stayed 'unwanted' by punters on course at Bellewstown, the money could be placed off-course at the 20/1 odds.

One potential problem was that if the bookies off-course over Ireland were hit with lots of money at big odds, then some of those bookies would lay off some of their bets with the on-course bookmakers at Bellewstown. Remember, the on-course bookies determine the price based on the money that is placed on Yellow Sam on course.

Another important element was that this was 1975, before mobile phones, and there was only one phone booth at the racecourse with which to contact the on-course bookmakers.

Barney Curley could not be at the races on the day, because he was known as a punter with a purpose. If they saw him walking around, then the bookies would sense something was amiss and shorten his horse's price.

Race day came and Barney Curley smuggled himself on course through a back entrance, tip-toed his way to the middle of the course and hid himself amongst some thorny green shrubs – with his binoculars, of course. This was a country course so there was plenty of shrubbery he could blend in with. No-one would see him.

Before making his way there, Curley rang his key commissioners with specific instructions, who in turn contacted hundreds of other commissioners across the length and breadth of the land.

Now there still was a phone box, that one source of communication with which the off-course bookmakers would ring to offload some bets with the on-course bookies. As part of Curley's plan, a very good friend, who shall remain nameless, took possession of the phone box and made a call to his 'aunty', who was on the verge of death in hospital.

Everyone outside the booth was taken aback by his outpouring of emotion on the phone. They allowed the gentleman to stay talking and weeping for as long as he liked. He had nothing more to say to his dying aunty, just after Yellow Sam crossed the line, winning by a couple of lengths at 20/1.

No-one had backed Yellow Sam at Bellewstown, and his official winning price on course was 20/1, so the hundreds and possible thousands of bets laid all over the country had to be paid out at 20/1. The bookies hadn't been able to check the price or lay off any of their bets, because the phone booth on course at Bellewstown was occupied at the crucial time of the race and betting.

Barney Curley extracted himself from his thorny thicket and made his way off the course, through the back entrance, unnoticed by anyone at all. There was a great cry throughout the land that the bookies had been the victims of a scam, and many bookmakers refused to pay up. There was a quick investigation and as there were no laws broken, all bookies were advised that they had to pay out on the winning tickets on Yellow Sam at 20/1.

All bets were paid, but as part of a silent protest, the bookies paid up the enormous amounts in single notes that filled to the brim more than 100 bags. It is estimated that Yellow Sam netted his owner the equivalent of around GBP £1.5 million.

Soon afterwards, the rulebook was altered, requiring that all bets of £100 or over be placed at least 30 minutes before the start of a race. Of course, the ordinary punter in Ireland and throughout the world would always see the lighter side of such a scam.

In 2005, 30 years after Yellow Sam's historic win, Barney Curley was invited as a guest of the Bellewstown Racing Club to view and present the winner's sash to the winner of the Seamus Murphy Yellow Sam 30th Anniversary Hurdle, believe it or not.

Don't you just love an inventive mind!

Andrew Lloyd Webber's new musical
... the phantom interference at the Prix Vermeille

As our world continues to spin through history, there seem to be attitudes and practices in some countries of the world that are as unchangeable as our own DNA. In this case, I have to ask, 'What is it between the French and the British?' There always seems to be a hatred – could that be too strong a word? – or perhaps an intense dislike between the two nations. When in Paris, the British will say that the French have unmatched arrogance and then display it very openly towards them, and the French will say exactly the same thing when they venture onto English soil. So I ask, 'What is it with them?'

Could it be that back in 1066 at the Battle of Hastings, the Norman French gave the British a hiding? Or is it because Germany invaded France in World War II and the French people were finally liberated by armies including the British, so that the good English Generals and their people think that the French should be forever grateful? Whatever the reason, they say still waters run deep. With this little tale, we will let you be the judge ... and jury.

The Prix Vermeille was inaugurated in 1897. It is run at Longchamp racecourse, home to the Prix de l'Arc de Triomphe, on the banks of the Seine, in Paris, France, every September. It is run over 2400 metres and is open to fillies and mares three years old and up. Three-year-olds are weighted at 54.5 kg and older mares at 58 kg. In 2013, the prize money was equivalent to AUD$600,000. The Prix Vermeille is considered the third leg of France's Fillies Triple Crown. It is run three weeks before the Prix de l'Arc de Triomphe and it is used as a guide as to who is highly regarded as a chance in that great race. Based on those facts alone, the Prix Vermeille is one of France's premier races.

In 2009, British composer Andrew Lloyd Webber, of 'The Phantom of the Opera' musical fame, owned a very good filly by the name of Dar Re Mi. She was English-owned, trained in England by John Gosden, and ridden by the Irish jockey Jimmy Fortune.

Dar Re Mi was going for a Group 1 hat trick, after previously winning the Pretty Polly Stakes at the Curragh and the Yorkshire Oaks. However, her main opposition in the Prix Vermeille was the European-owned and French-trained and French-ridden Stacelita, who was going for her sixth successive win. Stacelita was trained by Jean-Claude Rouget, and she also had a stablemate running in the race called Volver. Stacelita was being ridden by Christophe Lemaire and Volver's jockey was Ioritz Mendizabal.

It was clear that Volver was going to be Stacelita's pace-maker in the race, a practice that is not accepted as a legitimate tactic in many countries. As the race unfolded, Volver was doing the job for her stablemate, out front with Stacelita travelling comfortably on the inside behind the leader. To make the finish all the more interesting, Dar Re Mi was tracking up behind Stacelita, not letting her out of sight.

At the business end of the race, Volver's jockey was seen having a look over his shoulder and then moving off the fence to allow Stacelita to turn for home with a handy lead. Dar Re Mi, with the ever-alert Jimmy Fortune taking up the challenge, saw the gap that Volver had left for the stablemate and, around 300 metres from home, he took advantage of the open gate left by Volver as well.

You must watch the race on YouTube to see how Dar Re Mi responded over the last 200 metres: she simply went up to Stacelita and 'gave her a cold' as she went past to win easily. Andrew Lloyd Webber and his wife and all connections were ecstatic with the win. Stacelita had started at even money, and the winner at 2/1.

To everyone's amazement, a protest was called.

The majority of people on and off course that day were simply stunned when a protest was lodged by an unplaced horse, the German filly Soberania, for 'interference towards the inside rail at the 300-metre mark'. While the deliberation continued in the stewards rooms, it is fair to say that the great majority of owners and trainers would put their hands up if their horse or jockey caused any interference that would alter the outcome of any race. There did not appear to be any interference whatsoever, but we come back to that question about the French and the British again ...

The result of the protest was that Dar Re Mi was relegated to fifth place and Stacelita took out the 2009 Prix Vermeille, her sixth win and a triumph for the French horse, trained by a Frenchman and ridden by a Frenchman. It is an understatement to say that the crowd on and off the course were stunned, especially Lloyd Webber, his wife and everyone in their camp. The next day the newspapers on both sides of the Channel were headlining the 'hometown decision'. Looking at the race, you would certainly have to question the ruling that was handed down.

As Andrew Lloyd Webber's wife said, if there was interference caused to another horse at a crucial time by her horse, she would accept the decision – but there was no interference.

After viewing the race, a couple of betting agencies – in fairness to all concerned – paid out on equal winners: Dar Re Mi and Stacelita.

The British and the French: don't go there!

The remote-controlled horse
... but what will happen to the jockey?

One Saturday in August 1969, the stewards at Rosehill Racecourse, Sydney, suspected that there may be a possibility that a battery would be used in race 3. They conducted a thorough search of all the jockeys and their equipment, then confiscated the saddle of popular young jockey Sammy Mezzasalma. He was to ride the heavily backed Smashing Blonde.

The saddle contained quite a sophisticated battery, the likes of which had never been seen before. After quite a lengthy stewards and police inquiry, Mezzasalma and three other men were disqualified for life and warned off all racecourses.

During the inquiry, a Sydney electronics expert stated that he was approached and asked to perfect a remote-controlled battery-saddle, which would be used to administer an electrical shock to the horse's back, to frighten the horse and spur it on to run faster. He replied that he could, but added that the jockey would have no control over the horse.

Obviously the syndicate members weren't interested in jockey and horse safety, and they went ahead and had the saddle adjusted. 'This is absolutely perfect. No need to let the jockey know how dangerous it could be for him.' If Mezzasalma knew this, one doubts if he would have agreed to ride Smashing Blonde.

The racing gods must have been smiling on Sammy Mezzasalma, because his ban was later reduced to four years. He was eventually allowed to get a strapper's licence, but not a jockey's licence.

A few months after being granted his strapper's licence, Sammy had his first 'winner' in a race when he led in Sylvania Girl at Canterbury. The mare drifted from 7/1 to 20/1 – so different to that day back in August 1969, when Smashing Blonde was backed for a small fortune.

Lesson well and truly learnt.

Sorry to hear about that, old chap!
... no bones about it

The 1866 AJC Champagne Stakes was brilliantly won by the Victorian colt Fishhook. The result may have been different but for the unfortunate scratching of his chief rival, Angler.

The day before the Champagne Stakes, the VRC St Leger winner,

Angler, had been backed by his owner at the good odds of 4/1, wagering £3000 pounds to win £12,000, and thus the horse was firmed into favouritism. Both Angler and Fishhook were promising young stayers, being by the English import Fisherman.

However, that night someone broke into the property where Angler was stabled and drove a large piece of sharpened bone into the hoof of the unfortunate animal, crippling him. Come morning, seeing the horse in such a distressed state, his owner had only one option and that was to notify the racing club that Angler had to be scratched.

Fishhook took his place in the field and won brilliantly from Blue Light and Blondin. Later in 1867, he went on to win the AJC St Leger, Sydney Cup, VRC St Leger and VRC Champion Stakes. Angler never raced again.

Now, the names of the two gentlemen whose horses were the topic of conversation back then?

- Fishhook, owned by Mr Hurtle Fisher
- Angler, owned by Mr Charles Brown (CB) Fisher

And their relationship: they were brothers. Was it part of a family feud? It makes you wonder.

Scandal, scandal, read all about it!

One hamburger and chips, please
... but hold the horses!

There is nothing like a good old beef burger with plenty of lettuce, onion and sauce. It's the staple diet of many a young person on the run or when they frequent their favourite fast food outlet. However, there would be one thing that would make you think twice about your favourite 'meal on the run', and that would be if you found that there was a little something extra between the layers of your burger that wasn't supposed to be in the mix. We're talking about an ingredient that is quite acceptable in some parts of the world, but definitely not in others.

There are a lot of foods processed throughout the world for human consumption. Medication, vitamins and processed food in general are all subject to strict controls to ensure that what we are putting into our bodies is exactly what is listed on the label, on the packet, on any other ingredient list or as advertised.

In terms of meat and meat mixes, these strict controls sometimes include DNA testing to check that a product is what it is advertised to be – for example, that food that is advertised as beef has no other contaminants within it, just graded beef, spices and acceptable fillers, preservatives, etc.

During January 2013, it came to light that all was not what it was supposed to be. Beef burgers sold in many English and Irish supermarkets were found to contain DNA traces of horse meat. Even though eating horse meat is quite acceptable in many countries in Europe, that is not the case in England and Ireland.

Worse still, many of these products were also found to contain traces of pork. This sent a shockwave through Muslim and Jewish communities, as pork is considered a taboo food in these religions.

If nothing else, this debacle brought to light a major problem with food products and the traceability of their food chains. It would appear that our beloved racehorses had entered a food chain that was not designed for them, and nor for us. The source of the contamination was difficult to locate; the investigation is ongoing and samples of horse meat in other meat products have been found in many other European countries as well.

A whole new set of standards and safeguards of traceability of products has now been put in place. Now when we order a beef burger, we know it is what it is supposed to be, as stated in the ingredients printed on the packet or as stated in food standards rules and regulations.

Many racehorses are treated with the drug phenylbutazone, which is an anti-inflammatory that is not approved for human consumption. So if your partner is a big beefburger eater, and he or she starts to nuzzle into you and 'neighs' every now and then, maybe it is time to change their diet and make the move away from burgers.

Just hold your horses.

The luckless Craganour

... he was dudded in two Classic races of the Triple Crown

In this yarn, we are not talking about two ordinary races: we are talking about the 2000 Guineas and the Epsom Derby, the very top of the tree in England in 1913. Craganour was seen to be first past the post in both races, yet the establishment apparently found a way to mete out their own justice through disqualification. You are the judge.

The 1913 2000 Guineas

Craganour was a brilliant two-year-old and so his connections set their sights on the big two races for a three-year-old: the 2000 Guineas and the English Derby. He was trained by Jack Robinson at Foxhill and owned by Bower Ismay.

In the 2000 Guineas, Craganour was the 6/4 clear favourite. The 2000 Guineas is a Group 1 horse race on the flat, open to all three-year-old colts and fillies. It is run at the Rowley Mile at Newmarket over the mile (1600 metres), and it is run in either late April or early May each year. It is the opening leg of Britain's Triple Crown and is one of the five Classic races run in Britain each year.

The race was a torridly run affair in 1913, with the field spreading out from the inside fence to the outside fence. The sole adjudicating judge sat in the stand with his assistant and called the places from there. He noted to his assistant as the horses crossed the line that Louvois was first past the post, and he named other horses as running second and third. The assistant then hurriedly remarked to the judge, 'Didn't you see Craganour tucked in beside the fence, right under our noses? He has beaten Louvois by a length.'

The judge was the sole decision-maker. While he did not change the winner, he did relinquish the fact that Craganour may have run the place and announced that decision accordingly – second. The punters were in an uproar, but as there was no replay or camera to go to, the howls of disgust soon lost themselves to the running of the next race and the end of the program.

Louvois was declared the winner and Craganour was cheated out of his 2000 Guineas win by a not-so-alert judge. Soon after that debacle, the judge was asked to consider a retirement plan. It was the doozy of all decisions.

The 1913 Epsom Derby

This race is the second leg of the British Triple Crown, and it is run in the first week of June. Craganour's connections had been bitterly disappointed following the shocking result in the 2000 Guineas, but Bower Ismay, the owner, and Jack Robinson, the trainer, did not cry over spilt milk. The turned their attention to the Epsom Derby, the most prestigious race on the racing calendar.

The 1913 Derby is probably best known for the suffragette Emily Davison's death on the track at Tattenham Corner. After another exhibition of quality, Craganour was the first past the post in the Derby. While the sensational news of the death of Emily Davison was playing out on the course, there were also sensational decisions being made in the stewards room.

At the finishing line it had ended up a blanket finish by five horses: Craganour, Aboyeur, Day Comet, Shogun and Louvois. The margins between first, second and third were given as a head and a neck. Craganour had beaten them all – again.

As there was quite a bit of rough riding, the stewards called an inquiry into the running of the race. Most of the attention centred on Aboyeur as he was a cantankerous brute of a horse. Irrespective of the inquiry, the cheers of the crowd erupted as number 5 was put into the winner's frame: Craganour.

Aboyeur had originally been in the lead and then had moved away from the fence quite some distance, which allowed Craganour to scoot up along the inside. Seeing there was still a gap there, Shogun's rider had taken that advantage as well.

This is what really happened at this point. After Craganour had made his move when Aboyeur shifted his ground, Shogun also went through the gap. The brute Aboyeur took a dislike to Shogun on his inside and pummelled into him, putting Shogun effectively out of the race. Aboyeur's attention then turned to Craganour and, closing in on him, he took a great bite out of the winner. His bite mark was very evident on Craganour's neck.

The stewards, in their wisdom, decided to disqualify Craganour for his interference with Aboyeur. The race was awarded to Aboyeur at 100/1. Needless to say, the crowd erupted in disbelief as they had clearly witnessed Aboyeur savage Craganour in the straight and up to the finishing line. But the stewards were unmoved and the decision stood.

Now, here are some points to consider – rightly or wrongly – that may give weight to the argument that a bum decision was made on the day.

- Aboyeur's connections raised no objection after the race. The objections were made by the stewards.
- No reprimand was issued to Craganour's jockey after the disqualification.
- Interestingly, one of the three stewards, Major Eustace Loder, had bred Craganour and it was suggested at the time that he was unhappy at having sold the horse to Bower Ismay.
- It was also stated at the time that Major Loder, the steward, despised Ismay because of an affair Ismay had had with Loder's sister-in-law.

And the interesting points keep on coming.

- Bower Ismay, the owner of Craganour, was part of the family that owned the White Star Line, owners of the ill-fated *Titanic*. The family was very unpopular in many circles because of the ship's disastrous maiden voyage the previous year.
- One of the main witnesses called by the stewards was William Saxby, the jockey who rode Louvois. That would appear straightforward, but it was William Saxby who was sacked after what was described as 'his less than vigorous' ride on Craganour in the 2000 Guineas, even though the judge's assistant and many people on course had seen Craganour as the clear winner on the day. William Saxby's statements could certainly have been clouded by those events.

The outcome of all the injustice that came Craganour's way in both the 2000 Guineas and the Derby was that he was then sold to Argentinian interests and had a very fruitful stud career. One of the conditions of sale was that he never race again, and he didn't.

Aboyeur, on the other hand, failed in his next two starts and was then sold to interested parties in Russia. The last sighting of the 1913 Epsom Derby winner was of him pulling a cart after the 1917 Russian Revolution.

Justice served?

But, sir, I couldn't help myself
... ah, the age of innocence

The 1924 Victoria Steeplechase, on VRC Derby day, was won by King's High, from Wooloo and Swordbin. When the riders brought their horses back to scale to weigh in, however, all hell broke loose.

First, King's High: weight's right.

Second, Wooloo: weight's right.

Third, Swordbin: 'What?'

When Swordbin's jockey stepped onto the scales, the Chief Steward said, 'What's this? Hold on, you're not Tommy Butler! You're not the horse's jockey!'

'No, sir, I'm Sean Murphy.'

Apparently, Swordfish had fallen at the back of the course during the first lap, losing his jockey, Tommy Butler. The horse picked himself up and wandered over to the fence where a keen young bystander, Sean Murphy, jumped the fence, mounted the horse and took off after the field to run a very courageous third behind King's High.

Swordfish was disqualified, and Murphy was heavily fined for trying to mislead the racing stewards. It seems that young Sean had been waiting for the right day for this to happen.

The following day, *The Age* newspaper ran the headline, 'Racing stewards quick to avoid possible scandal.'

Well, boys will do what boys will do.

A hometown decision
... or was it the stewards who knew better?

On Caulfield Cup Day in 1948, Sydney jockey 'Demon' Darby Munro was on board the brilliant Sydney colt and 5/1 second-favourite

Vagabond in the Burwood Handicap, the second-last race of the day. In a close finish, Vagabond was beaten by Ellerslie.

Stewards immediately opened an inquiry, to be adjourned until after the last race. Munro then claimed he had given the three-year-old the best possible run in transit, ridden it right out to the line and was beaten by a better horse on the day.

This was confirmed at the inquiry by Melbourne radio's 3AW race caller Fred Tupper. Tupper said that Munro was using his whip from the home turn to the winning post. Both trainer Dan Lewis and owner Frank Spurway stated that they were satisfied with Munro's handling of Vagabond, and that the horse was something of a rogue and did not handle Melbourne's anti-clockwise way of racing.

Not according to the stewards. It came as a complete shock to everyone when Munro, Lewis and Spurway were all disqualified for two years. The reason? For not having tried to win on Vagabond, and for not allowing the horse to run on its merit.

The racing public was stunned. The outcry from Sydney was that it was a hometown decision.

At a subsequent nine-hour hearing, the VRC Committee upheld the appeals of both Lewis and Spurway, but Munro's two-year disqualification stood. In retrospect, maybe the stewards misread his handling, in the straight, of a horse that could do no more.

At the end of the two years, Munro applied to the AJC to have his licence renewed. He resumed riding in Sydney in October 1950, and it wasn't long before winners came thick and fast. It was Munro's dream to eventually ride in the United Kingdom, and in 1953, he applied for a licence to ride in England. The application was denied, but a licence was granted to ride in France and California, in the United States.

Maybe not being allowed to ride in England was due to something that was published in *The Argus* newspaper in Melbourne while Munro was disqualified.

Back in the 1946 Epsom Handicap, Munro's mount, the short-priced favourite Shannon, hopelessly missed the start by a half furlong (100 metres), but flashed home to be beaten by a neck by Blue Legend. Angry backers of the favourite were in shock and demanded a 'no-race' result. They vented their anger at Munro. However, the jockey was cleared of any wrongdoing concerning the horse missing the start by such a big margin. The starter, Mr Gaxieu, took full responsibility for the debacle.

But what had Munro revealed to *The Argus* in 1949 while under disqualification? Days before the 1946 Epsom Handicap, Munro had been offered £15,000 to 'pull' Shannon. He said he did not accept the bribe.

For some reason, at that 1946 inquiry relating to the Shannon starting fiasco, Munro forgot to mention the bribe attempt to the AJC stewards. Or did he?

Payback. Maybe the stewards had long memories.

The Great Turf Scandal

... Scotland Yard detectives had fingers in the cookie jar

It is fair to say, and we hear it often enough in our modern lives, 'if a deal sounds too good to be true, then it generally is'. We have all been involved with horse racing at some time or another, and even if you haven't, you would remember plenty of two-person contests where the favourite gets rolled. It happens, and it just goes to prove there is nothing factual about a 'sure bet', a 'good thing' or an 'absolute certainty'.

In both years gone by and in the modern era, there have been cases where criminals have worked in the background to affect a particular racing outcome. Few schemes have worked, and many have ended up in the courts, with the criminals convicted and many people in tears. However, as long as there is an attraction for winning money on a 'sure thing', there will always be those who offer up certainty and those who – blinded by the call of more money – will offer what they can on a gamble to fill their coffers.

In 1877, in England, a couple of fraudsters by the names of Harry Benson and William Kurr cooked up their own get-rich scheme. They had a few brains between them and decided that there were plenty of mugs out there who were willing to part with their money on a 'certainty' at the races. The only trouble for Benson and Kurr was that they needed patsies who knew little or nothing about English racing. They figured that if they could attract some 'foreigners' into their scheme, then the adage 'a fool and his money is soon parted' would be their just reward.

This story is not so much about the many hundreds of people who fell into their trap, but more about the one punter who put a stop to their scam.

Benson and Kurr thought that the best way to advertise investment in a racing 'sure thing' was to advertise across the channel in France, and to see what French fish they could lure into their net. They were making a very lucrative living from their advertising, when one day a woman who lived the high life in Paris, Madame de Goncourt, saw their advertisement in her local French paper and applied to invest her money on horse racing in England. As the villains stated in their advertisement, 'their close contacts with stables and trainers allows their system to operate at such a high level of success, all investors will be very much satisfied.'

Madame de Goncourt was certainly a lady of means. Her first 'investment' with Harry Benson and William Kurr was the equal to £10,000 then; in today's currency she parted with around £650,000 (around AUD$1 million) first up on this 'certainty'.

These guys knew a sucker when they saw one, so after one of the races in question, they communicated back to her that her horse had just missed out but, not to worry, they had a certain winner for her next bet. They asked her for another £30,000 for her next wager, to make up for the bad luck that she had on her first bet. This was no small change and is the equivalent today of £1.86 million (around AUD$3 million).

They were going for a big payday.

The Parisian punter started to smell a very expensive rat. She enjoyed making money, and easy money was even better, but losing money was hard to take. She contacted a solicitor in London with all of the information she had about these two characters, their get-rich scheme and where they could be found. As there would be some translation difficulties dealing with the French Madame de Goncourt, Scotland Yard were brought in. They had a young chief inspector, Nathaniel Druscovitch, who could speak French and handle the investigation.

Try as they might, whenever Scotland Yard obtained an address for the whereabouts of Harry or Bill, they would raid the establishment but would find that the birds had already flown the coop. They even had tips that one or both were in the Netherlands, but try as the Chief Inspector might, he was always too late.

Superintendent Williamson of Scotland Yard thought that his investigators were dragging the chain a little, so on his own bat, he sent some wanted posters of Benson and Kurr to the Dutch police, without telling any of the investigating team.

Well, well, well. Harry Benson was soon arrested by the Dutch police. Williamson thought that was a little too easy – he had expected his team to have done this kind of basic police work. Soon after, working on his own initiative, he tracked down Mr William Kurr, who was holed up in London. They were both caught.

When the Super had both villains in the 'nick', he noticed a certain edginess about Chief Inspector Druscovitch and his trusted co-investigators, Inspector Meicklejohn and Inspector Palmer. It appeared to Superintendent Williamson that things were not on the 'up and up' with his investigative team. Acting on legal advice, he had the three men questioned – the game was up.

All three men were found to be on the take from Harry Benson and William Kurr and had been so for a couple of years. They were paid to let Benson and Kurr know if there was any suspicion surrounding their scheme and if any arrests or warrants were imminent. It now made sense how Benson and Kurr had stayed ahead of the law in England and in Holland. But as they say in the classics, 'Scotland Yard always gets their man'.

Chief Inspector Druscovitch, Inspector Meicklejohn and Inspector Palmer were all convicted of corruption and each lost their job and received a two-year sentence as guests of His Majesty's Prison. Madame de Goncourt – along with hundreds of other small French fish – lost her initial investment but her persistence brought down this little earner for Harry and William. Harry Benson and William Kurr were both sentenced in the Old Bailey to lengthy prison terms for their part in the Great Turf fraud. Being an inmate of the local prisons in the late 1800s was a sentence of hardship in itself. After Druscovitch's two-year term, he succumbed to tuberculosis and died at the age of 39.

This whole nasty business certainly cast a very dark shadow over Scotland Yard and its operations, so the Detective Branch – of which Druscovitch, Meiklejohn and Palmer were involved – was restructured into what is known today as the Crime Investigation Department (CID).

A woman scorned, for love or money, is a very dangerous person.

I'm going home to America
... and I may never come back!

In 1950, top American jockey Johnny Longden accepted an invitation to do a short-riding stint in Australia. At Caulfield Racecourse on 8 April, Longden had five rides, but the best he could do was to finish with one second placing.

Some four days later, it was off to Sydney to ride at the Randwick Autumn Carnival. He was unsuccessful in his first three rides, but finally had a winner when the 12/1 shot, The Groom, romped home in the Group 1 All Aged Stakes. The crowd gave Longden a huge reception when he brought the horse back to the enclosure, and the cheering continued right up until 'correct weight' was announced.

The following day, all hell broke loose when Sydney's *Daily Telegraph* ran an article with words to this effect: 'The age of chivalry is not dead. Yesterday, there was a possible gracious gesture by fellow jockeys to allow American jockey Johnny Longden to win on The Groom and leave our shores with at least one win.'

The six other jockeys who rode in the race – Sydney's Billy Cook, Neville Sellwood, George Moore and Arthur Ward, and Victorian riders Bill Williamson and Vic Hartney – bitterly denied any suggestion that the race was rigged.

George Moore commented: 'It is an insult to everyone. I wanted so badly to win on my horse, De La Salle, the favourite. I am a friend of Longden, but the friendship stops there in a race.'

Neville Sellwood commented: 'It is ridiculous and stupid to say that the race was put on for Longden. My horse, Lord Moss, was trying his heart out but was no match for The Groom at weight-for-age.'

The AJC totally agreed and stated that it was irresponsible for the *Daily Telegraph* to publish such an article.

Further to the newspaper's comments, each of the six jockeys sued Consolidated Press Limited, publishers of the *Sydney Daily Telegraph,* for a total of £10,000 each. The case was settled out of court.

When interviewed at the airport awaiting his flight back to the United States, Johnny Longden said that he might never ride in Australia again.

Enough said!

Hands up, drop your whips!

... *otherwise someone will die*

For generations, the Hoysted family has been a household name in horse racing circles in Victoria. But in February 1966, the family could have done without the sensational headlines that unfolded at the start of the Fullham Hurdle at Flemington Racecourse.

Apparently, former jockey William Hoysted, son of the famous trainer 'Father' Fred Hoysted, had walked onto the racecourse with a concealed weapon, a double-barrelled shotgun. He made his way down to the start of the hurdle race, bailed up the starter with the shotgun and was protesting against the whipping of horses in races. His demands included that no whips were to be used in the hurdle race, and that all jockeys should drop their whips. He demonstrated his seriousness by discharging the shotgun. Horses and riders took fright, but thankfully no-one was injured.

The police arrived. To calm Hoysted down, they agreed to his demand that whips would be banned. William Hoysted surrendered, and was quickly taken off course. He was later sentenced to one month's jail.

When the Fullham Hurdle field finally got under way on that Saturday, the pledge to ban whips was not honoured.

The police are mightier than the sword.

Rules were rules for Prince of Dance
... wouldn't you think someone would have noticed?

Here is a yarn in which even the best in the business got it wrong. The horse in question was Prince of Dance. He was a son of the great racehorse and sire Sadler's Wells. Sadler's Wells dominated breeding, and during the 1990s he was the leading sire in France, Ireland, Canada and the rest of North America, Asia, Dubai and Great Britain. He is said to have been the greatest sire Europe has ever seen.

In 1986 Sadler's Wells sired a dashing young colt out of the Oaks-winning mare Sun Princess. This star of the future was named Prince of Dance. The young colt was owned by Sir Michael Sobel, a very successful businessman and a serious philanthropist, who spent much of his life involved in his great love, racing and breeding thoroughbred racehorses.

Prince of Dance was taking all before him in his two-year-old year, and one of the races he contested was the Dewhurst Stakes, a Group 1 flat race over 7 furlongs (1400 metres), which was open to colts and fillies. The Dewhurst was run over the Rowley Mile at Newmarket in October each year, and the winners usually figure in the Classic races as three-year-olds. He did not disappoint his owner, but he dead-heated for first place and had to share the spoils with Scenic, owned by Sheikh Mohammed.

However, all the attention and disappointment had been in his run prior to the Dewhurst Stakes, the listed Washington Singer Stakes run at Newbury in August. This had been Prince of Dance's lead up to the Dewhurst, with the Washington Singer run over 7 furlongs (1400 metres). He toyed with his opposition and won as a good two-year-old does.

He was the winner. There was no interference. There was no protest. His jockey weighed in correctly. But much later, Prince of Dance was disqualified.

Someone pointed out to the officials that all runners in the Washington Singer Stakes had to be sired by horses who had won at least 1 mile and a half (2400 metres). As Sadler's Wells had never won beyond 10 furlongs (2000 metres), Prince of Dance was disqualified.

It was one of those rare moments on the turf when everyone missed the blatantly obvious. The racing authorities associated with the race club, the trainer, the stable personnel and, of course, the experienced owner, Sir Michael Sobell – they all missed it. Always read the fine print.

However, the disappointment didn't stop there for the connections.

A classy young colt sired by Alhaarth was entered to run in the 2003 Washington Singer Stakes. The precocious colt was named Haafhd. However, the racing authorities involved in the Washington Singer had learnt a very painful lesson back in 1988. Alhaarth's longest victory was in the 1997 Prix Dollar run at Longchamp, over 1 mile 1 furlong and 165 yards, way short of the mile and a half (2400 metres) required to be eligible to run.

Haafhd's entry was rejected by officials, which spurred his owners and connections on to officially have the race's criteria questioned. It was then revealed after much scrutiny by the club that they had got the interpretation wrong all those years before. The Washington Singer Stakes was open to two-year-olds whose sire had won over 1 mile and about 2 furlongs or over (1800 metres). As Alhaarth's longest winning distance was only 55 yards (50 metres) short of the newly interpreted criteria, Haafhd was allowed to take his place in the field. He duly won at a canter by five lengths.

Remember, Sadler's Wells had won over 2000 metres. If only Prince of Dance's connections had insisted.

The Year of the 'Roid'

... will 2013 create a question mark on the integrity of racing?

'Roid' (steroid): also known as candy, juice or gear.

The basic premise of our racing game is that sponsors pour money into events, the racing administration – along with trainers, owners, horses, jockeys and stablehands – all meet a criteria that is deemed fair and reasonable for the races to take place, and after all that, the punters fill the stands and the bookies' bags with their attendance. Once there is 'correct weight' announced after each race, the punters lose some money or win some. Prize money is distributed, along with any prestigious silverware, and everyone is happy.

The racing industry will always have those who operate in the 'grey area', trying for any advantage they can get, but in the main, horse racing all over the world is a very clean operation and a correctly run enterprise.

But then comes 2013. It certainly leaves you with a nasty aftertaste when it comes to pushing the limits.

One difficulty that racing ruling bodies have is keeping abreast of the many drugs and derivatives that are classed as 'banned substances'. Trainers and other trusted personnel need to be fully aware of the substances, too. It may be getting to a stage where you will need a person with a degree in chemistry to be attached to all stables to ensure that what is being administered to the racehorses is legal and above board.

This is how 2013 unravelled.

20 February 2013: The British Horseracing Authority (BHA) had cause to go to the stables of Gerard Butler at Newmarket and take samples from several horses. While this investigation was quietly going through its motions, the following event caused the BHA to choke on its racing integrity issues.

9 April 2013: Samples were taken from several thoroughbred racehorses at Moulton Paddocks, the pre-training yard under the control of Saeed bin Suroor, the long-standing trainer for the Godolphin Group, owned by the ruler of Dubai, Sheikh Mohammed bin Rashid Al Maktoum. Mahmood Al Zarooni worked under the head trainer, so it was a shock to all to hear the test findings in April.

21 April 2013: The test results were published by the BHA, and after questioning Al Zarooni, he issued a statement that he had used banned anabolic steroids on some of the horses under his care.

25 April 2013: Al Zarooni was banned by the BHA for eight years. The BHA also placed a ban on the fifteen Godolphin horses that were involved, for a period of six months.

29 April 2013: Just four days later, the results of the February tests on the Gerard Butler horses surfaced. Due process took some time to come to fruition, but Butler was sanctioned in December.

4 December 2013: Gerard Butler was banned from racing and from holding a trainer's license for a period of five years.

The charges relating to both Al Zarooni and Gerard Butler refer to the administration of either Sungate or Rexogin. Sungate contains traces of the steroid stanozolol, and Rexogin, manufactured for use in humans, also contains the same steroid.

Both trainers expressed their sincere apologies for their 'disastrous lapse of judgment'. They are certainly paying a very hefty price for that lapse, as innocent as some may believe it was. Sungate was supposed to have come recommended by some veterinary surgeons.

In their statement, the British Horseracing Authority made mention of the 'actions of these trainers being seriously prejudicial to the integrity and conduct of their sport'. While both men could only offer their sincere apologies to all bodies involved, their time on the sideline will be punishment enough. There is no doubt that more scrutiny and testing needs to become a part of the Sport of Kings, perhaps equalling the level of scrutiny that we read all about in our Commonwealth and Olympic Games.

Lessons learnt the hard way.

Who controls the controller?

... the 2002 Breeders' Cup Race Day betting scandal

Remember the good old days at university? You tend to make friendships and bond for life. What days they were ... especially for three young men who found each other's company at Drexel University, which is a private research university that has its main campus located in Philadelphia, in Pennsylvania, the United States.

Drexel University is rather unique in many ways. There are many opportunities available to those who attend, because the university has networked with many corporate and government institutions to offer the full-time students a program designed for a future beyond university.

This is where three young men – Chris Harn, Derrick Davis and Glen Da Silva – forged a friendship that would take them on a journey that wasn't what they had wished for.

Chris Harn found his niche in computer programming, and he was eventually employed as the senior programmer at Autotote, the online betting company that handles more than 60 per cent of North America's horseracing 'investments'. It was in this world, in the ebb and flow of millions of dollars, that Chris stumbled across the value of unclaimed tickets.

Most online and offline betting agencies accumulate many unclaimed tickets on their balance sheets. We know we have been guilty of this ourselves on many occasions, when after a day on the 'punt' at home, there is that odd ticket that just isn't worth the trip to the agency to pick up the few winning cents.

Unclaimed tickets also include cases where the unlucky punter has destroyed a good ticket by accident or where he has just lost it in the frenzy of a 'beer and bet' afternoon with mates. Because of the paperwork trail and the details required to authenticate your winnings without the original ticket, it just isn't worth the effort.

Being a senior computer programmer and a high-level security employee of Autotote, Chris was unable to place bets. One day though, as he was scanning through the betting program that he had helped to develop, he noticed huge amounts of money in a pool of 'unclaimed betting tickets'.

Autotote carried bets on most races held in North America, so the pool was enormous. We all know what temptation is and where it can lead; unfortunately it got the better of Chris. He did something that a lot of us may have considered – after all, the unclaimed monies would probably eventually go into the government coffers, and we give them enough as it is, don't we?

Using his access as a senior programmer, Chris printed out the unclaimed tickets that represented hundreds of thousands of unclaimed monies. As an Autotote employee, his contract restricted him from making any wagers himself. Enter Derrick Davis and Glen Da Silva, great friends from good old Drexel.

As Chris would have been easily recognised on the racetrack due to his position at Autotote, he enlisted his mates to take the tickets and do the rounds at racetracks in New Jersey, New York and many other places, cashing in the tickets at the payout windows. The three of them split the winnings. This was easy money and there was lots of it. I just wonder how many of us reading this would have had a go as well – after all, the boys at Capitol Hill have plenty.

Chris realised that if they kept up their little scheme, someone would get wise to it. They had a taste for easy money, and the fact that Chris could get in there and manipulate certain facts and figures to his own advantage got them all thinking of a bigger payday.

It was decided that they would collectively go after some bigger fish. Both Derrick Davis and Glen Da Silva opened betting accounts at the Catskill Off-Track Betting Corporation in Pomona, New York. Catskill was chosen because of Harn's knowledge of their computer system, the low-level security, and the lack of betting volume compared to Autotote. It was much easier to open an account with them online as well.

Their plan was about to be put into motion. This is what they wagered and what they won – but the 'how' we will explain later.

There are different types of bets all over the world, and one type that accumulates the bigger payout is the 'Pick 4' and the 'Pick 6'. In other words, you pick the four winners in races that are nominated by the betting agency, or six winners in the six races that are nominated. The 'Pick 4' and 'Pick 6' were always at one nominated track in the program.

3 October: At the harness races at Belmont Park, Glen Da Silva successfully picked the 'Pick 4' on the program and netted the group $80,000. Good pick up.

5 October: Belmont Park again, and Da Silva wagered a 'Pick 6'. It was extraordinary good luck, and another $100,000 jumped into the kitty.

26 October: It was Breeders' Cup Day. It seemed the 'lucky touch' had been picked up by Derrick Davis, and he placed a 'Pick 6' on the Breeders' Cup Day program. Well, what do you know? Along the fence, in the straight in the final race of the 'Pick 6' program, the

50/1-outsider Volponi put six lengths on the field. Davis netted a cool total pick up of $3,100,000. Wow.

Had the favourite or a more fancied horse won the last leg, there may have been a greater number of winners to share the pool. As it was, there was only one winning ticket and some alarm bells started to ring. Most bets in a 'Pick 6', for example, carry a couple of selections in each leg. However, this particular winning coupon clearly nominated the first four winners before nominating the entire field in the fifth leg and the entire field in the sixth leg.

Suspicions were being raised because the large payout was through such a small betting agency as Catskill and, of course, because of the way the bet was put together, with four clean winners and then all the field in the following two races. Immediately, the New York Racing Association asked the Wagering Board to delay the massive payout. They just wanted to make sure all was okay.

They then found another two interesting bets at the beginning of the month that used the same type of selection process. On 3 October, a 'Pick 4' at the Belmont Park Harness Meeting picked the first two clear winners, with the entire fields in the following two legs. Then on 5 October, just two days later, there was a 'Pick 6' at Belmont Park with the first four clear winners and the entire fields picked in the remaining two races.

It was almost exactly same betting spread as the one under investigation on Breeders' Cup Day, and the first 'Pick 4' and the first 'Pick 6' had been placed through the same account at Catskill. The 'bonanza' bet on Breeders' Cup Day was placed by a different account holder at Catskill.

The State Police and the FBI joined the investigation. Everyone involved was starting to feel a little sick but, nevertheless, they stuck to their stories. Then the investigation took a turn that would change the lives of Harn, Davis and Da Silva forever.

How did they do it?

Harn had found out through his computer program work that the off-track betting establishments only forwarded their take and the number of remaining live bets to Autotote after the first two races had been run and won in a 'Pick 4' and after the first four races had been run and won in a 'Pick 6'. Harn also knew that after the first two wins of a 'Pick 4' and the four wins of a 'Pick 6', there was a 30-minute window before the live wagers were sent through to the main computer.

It was in this 30-minute window of opportunity that Harn was able to manipulate the system on site, search out the ticket that they had placed on a 'Pick 4' earlier, change the first four selections, and then take the entire fields in both race 5 and race 6. He was able to alter a losing ticket that Derrick Davis had placed earlier in the day, changing both the selections and the amount invested. During that 30-minute window, the ticket was made a live ticket with no chance of losing.

Had the winner of the sixth leg on Breeders' Cup Day been a little shorter in price, then there could have been other winners of the 'Pick 6' and their win may have gone through unnoticed.

Although feeling the pressure, Derrick Davis went to the press as bold as brass and protested his innocence, stating that his win was 'fair and square'.

The FBI and other investigators began their inquiry based on the premise that it was more than likely that this was an 'inside job'. Autotote also started their own inquiry and they questioned all staff in the proximity of the track and with computer access. It soon became apparent that Harn was not scheduled to work on Breeders' Cup Day, but he had been in the office at that time anyway. Harn maintained his innocence, but Autotote sacked him and handed their investigation over to State and Federal officials. The law was closing in.

The link was soon made between Harn and Davis and Da Silva, the two betting account holders. Authorities discovered the similar betting pattern used by Da Silva in his two dry runs of the first 'Pick 4' and then the first 'Pick 6' in early October. After a forensic investigation of Autotote's computer, it was discovered that Harn had been able to access the computer and change the bets after the first two and first four winners were established.

Phone records showed that on Breeders' Cup Day, there were a number of phone conversations between Davis and Harn, while the latter was busy manipulating bets using the computer system from Autotote's office.

The three men were arrested and each was charged with wire fraud. On 20 March 2003, each pleaded guilty and were given the following sentences.

- Chris Harn: sentenced to one year and one day in a Federal prison
- Glen Da Silva: sentenced to two years' imprisonment
- Derrick Davis: sentenced to three years and one month

There was a silver lining for the people who had their own 'Pick 6' that day. There were 78 punters who had picked five of the six winners legitimately. Recalculating the payout after the mens' fraudulent win was taken from them, each of the 78 punters received a payout of around $44,000.

If only the favourite had won the last leg, then we would have been none the wiser, and Harn, Da Silva and Davis may still be enjoying 'sweet little fish'.

Volponi, the long shot they didn't need.

Studying the form guide

... after all, the papers have the right facts, haven't they?

For those who religiously look to race day as their day of rest, a day to have a few quiet ones and study the form guide in an endeavour to retrieve some of your hard-earned money previously lost to the betting agencies or bookies, this may come as a bit of a shock. Thousands of punters all over the world put in hours of their time perusing the race fields, looking for that 'special' that is going to lead them to great riches. Some form readers do their homework and even study the times that the horses do in training runs and in trials. Some punters weave their statistical magic to try to find that horse that might have a few lengths on the field according to their form guide.

On the other hand, you should also understand that in some sections of the crowd at the races, the bookmakers spend the same amount of time looking for the loser, and not necessarily the winner.

Such is the racing game.

The following events were uncovered in late 2013 at Penn National Racecourse in Grantville, Pennsylvania. The Penn Racecourse also has the Hollywood Casino on its grounds, which offers all sorts of gambling. What better way to celebrate a winning day at the races than to try for more at their casino? Wishful thinking, we say.

The racetrack opened in August 1972. It consists of a one-mile (1600-metre) dirt track and a 7-furlong (1400-metre) turf track. It is owned and operated by Penn National Gambling.

On the racetrack in the early morning, there are hundreds of thoroughbreds who come out to train, six days a week. In all sorts of weather, you will find a trackrider aboard a stable's horse, working under the instructions of the trainer. There could be at least twenty trainers at a time, so you can imagine how busy and frantic it can be.

One of the most important people on the track early in morning is the qualified 'clocker'. His expertise and experience in identifying horses – because there are no jockey colours to guide him – is a specialist talent in itself. The official clocker employed by Penn Racecourse was Danny Robertson. Using his experience and knowledge, he would identify different horses, watch their official workouts, note the distance and accurately record the time taken. His job was to then compile all of the morning's records and pass them on to the racing officials so that information could be included, when required, in the racing program.

Danny Robertson also sent the same information electronically to Equibase, a company based in Kentucky that provides millions of punters with the same statistics to complete their form guides. As long as the information collected and sent is accurate, then everybody benefits – but it wasn't.

As said at the outset, it may not be about picking the winner on the course, because some are looking for the loser. Some of the track times as reported were manipulated by Robertson, so that a true form line was not attainable. It is still a matter for the law courts, but it is said that some horses were recorded, with times and distances, when they weren't even at the track so that the serious punter would be thrown off the scent of a winner, or in some bookies' cases, a loser.

Over time, a few discrepancies had been reported to the club. It wasn't long before the Pennsylvania police and the FBI were involved in a criminal investigation.

One of the most frowned upon blue-collar crimes in America is wire fraud. Because Danny Robertson had sent the manipulated information electronically for someone else's gain, even if not for his own, then he faced this most serious charge.

Indictments and arrests followed and three trainers, Patricia Rogers, Sam Webb and David Wells, in company with Danny Robertson, were charged with dozens of offences. They included manipulation of races, offshore gambling, wire fraud and embezzlement. The four have been suspended indefinitely pending the outcome of the cases against them.

So we suppose the lesson learnt is that while the printed word should report something exactly as it happened, there are sometimes mistakes made. It just may be that the 'sure thing' that you have recognised, and that you think will get you out of a hole, isn't doing the times the form guide leads to you think. Please, please take the time to consider what could happen, and keep your 'house' in your pocket. It may not be an honest misprint.

Punters are always up against it.

Greyhound Lucy's Light
... and the part she played in the biggest of all stings!

To understand how this sting came about, you have to understand how some bookies calculate their odds or pay out on winners. Some bookies will cover all races – dogs, trots and gallops – so instead of studying form and trying to be expert in all fields, they just accept the TAB pools and starting prices and pay as they are announced.

That sounds all very good and easy and as it should be. However, there were a couple of gentlemen who found that they could manipulate this system to their advantage. A loose control on starting odds and payouts by a bookie is now well and truly a thing of the past, but in 2005, it remained a very careless practice.

Two gentlemen – well-known Sydney brothel owner Eddie Hanson and professional punter Steve Fletcher – found that they could manipulate the UNiTAB, the weakest of the Australian Betting Corporations, to their advantage. The action was centred on a Gold Coast greyhound race in December 2005. The bookie was Adelaide bookmaker Curly Seal, who always paid the equivalent of the TAB odds regardless of how much was bet.

Now the action. The favourite in this greyhound field of six was Lucy's Light, which was paying a fraction over $1.00 for every dollar invested. You would have to agree it was a very short-priced favourite, which was odds-on to win. The pool on these sorts of greyhound races is not very big at all, probably around $2000, so any substantial investment on any dog in the race would make a significant difference to the odds on the TAB.

Literally seconds before they jumped, these two punters placed $16,000 on each of the five runners apart from Lucy's Light on the UNiTAB. With the size of the pool, the prices on these five dogs shortened dramatically and the price on Lucy's Light went from an unbackable favourite to $13.00 per win. It was a very simple case of mathematics.

One doesn't have to be a rocket scientist to work out what happened next. As soon as the new price showed for Lucy's Light at $13.00 on UNiTAB, and again with only seconds to spare, the two punters plonked $60,000 to win on her with bookmaker Curly Seal, who always pays on starting prices of winners on the UNiTAB. Bad move, Curly.

Lucy's Light won the race and the two punters collected a cool $780,000. Considering their original outlay of $80,000 across the other five dogs and the winning stake on Lucy's Light, they walked away with a very substantial profit of around $640,000.

Good to his word and not totally sure as to whether the legality of the actions could be tested in a court of law, this honest bookie took nearly two years to settle the bet.

Just another way to sting a bookie ... big time!

CHAPTER 6
Bits and Bridles

How spoonerisms have their way
... even in the Sport of Kings

We can thank the clergy for some of our race callers having to tiptoe through a race call on occasion – race callers know that the old 'spoonerism' can come into play anywhere and at any time, but especially in a race call. Most people have been guilty of this kind of play on words sometime during their life. We can thank William Archibald Spooner, a well-known cleric and scholar early in the twentieth century, for his addition to the English language and for the embarrassment that he brought upon himself from time to time.

The word spoonerism can be defined as 'a transposition of the sounds of two or more words, especially one that creates a humorous or ludicrous effect'. An example of a spoonerism attributed to William Spooner is saying, 'Let me sew you to your sheet', instead of saying, 'Let me show you to your seat.'

Before we get on to spoonerisms in horse racing, here are a few spoonerisms that dear Archibald was said to have made in some of his sermons.

- 'The Lord is a shoving leopard' (maybe 'a loving shepherd')
- 'He was killed by a blushing crow' (would you believe 'a crushing blow'?)
- 'It is kisstomary to cuss the bride' (maybe a little 'kiss' instead of a 'cuss')

So now we come to our poor, poor race caller. Just as an example of how fraught with danger race calling can be, have a good look through the guide to the last race meeting and look at all the names of the horses. There would have to be some traps of spoonerisms amongst them all.

Well the year may give it away, but the circumstances were set for an 'oopsie' moment. This poor race caller had it all in the one race and as you would have heard in golfing terms, if you hit it in the rough, you generally stay in the rough. Well, the same can be said for spoonerisms in a race call because once this bloke started, he couldn't help but fall at the second as well. It just so happens there were two horses in the same race that attracted all of his attention. Yes, there was Fanny Tucks, and down the outside came Ned's Ripples.

Believe it or not.

Only in America
... believe it or not!

When writing about apprentice jockeys in Australia, New Zealand, Canada or the United Kingdom, we seem to do things as simply as possible so that people can understand. The jockeys are referred to simply as apprentice jockeys, with or without their allowances.

However, this is not so in the United States. There they are known not as apprentice jockeys, but as bugs or bug boys, and here is the explanation.

A 'bug' or 'bug boy' is an apprentice jockey, so-called because of the 'bug' or asterisk (*) beside his name in the official program that denotes that the weight carried includes the apprentice allowance.

'Bug waive' is when one of those bug boys is replaced by a journeyman (senior rider). In this case the weight concession extended to the apprentice or bug boy is relinquished, hence the bug is waived.

Well, I'll be bugg-ed!

Biscuits and pork crackling!
... and that sweet taste of defeat

The Americans had Seabiscuit; the Australians had Tea Biscuit.

We all know about Seabiscuit, the people's champ, and his 'Match of the Century' race in 1938, when he defeated War Admiral. In Australia, a very capable stayer of the 1960s, Tea Biscuit, was no slouch either. The son of Dalray, Tea Biscuit competed at the highest level in all the major staying races.

Here are some of his major race results:

- 1st: Moonee Valley Gold Cup, 1966
- 2nd: Hotham Handicap, 1965
- 2nd: Brisbane Cup, 1966
- 3rd: Metropolitan Handicap, 1966
- 3rd: PJ O'Shea Stakes, 1966

On the morning of the 1966 Melbourne Cup, Tea Biscuit's trainer, Pat Murray, was so confident in his horse winning the Cup, that he went to his local butcher and purchased a 20 kilogram suckling pig in anticipation of a victory celebration. If he didn't win, then there was always 'Plan B'.

Unfortunately for the Murray camp, Tea Biscuit ran sixth, behind the winner Galilee. The connections celebrated the wake long into the night.

Pork and bikkies anyone?

What's in a name?
... Where a change is as good as a holiday!

Throughout racing history, there have been some horses that have a name change and never win another race. However, this can also sometimes work in reverse. Change the horse's name and things start to happen.

Take the case of a horse by the name of Rothschild. As a young horse he was quite successful, winning the 1880 South Australia Derby and was placed as runner-up in the 1881 Adelaide Cup.

Obviously the owner thought that by changing the horse's name, he just might go on to bigger and better things. Out with Rothschild and in with The Assyrian – a name that sounded more assertive.

History shows us that the horse racing as The Assyrian won the Duke Handicap, the Hobart Cup, the Derwent Plate, the AJC Autumn Stakes and the biggest prize of all, the 1882 Melbourne Cup.

So, what's in a name? Quite a lot, apparently!

The punter saved his bookie from drowning
... but did he have second thoughts?

Over the years, Australia has had quite a few flamboyant punters: Rufe Naylor, Eric Connolly, Mick 'Melbourne Mick' Bartley, Bob 'The Baron' Skelton, 'Hollywood' George Edser, John 'The Butterfly' Mort Green and, of course, Perc Galea.

One day in 1961, Perc Galea was having a bit of a shocker on the punt. At day's end, he owed leading bookmaker TB 'Sharkey' Dwyer, £1700.

Perc arranged to meet Dwyer the following day around 4.30 pm at the Clovelly Surf Club. When he arrived at the surf club, Dwyer was nowhere in sight. Perc turned to look at the surf, and spotted a swimmer in difficulty.

He took a running leap down the surf club stairs, tripped and banged his face heavily on the steps, landing face first in the sand. With his head and face throbbing, Perc took off, battling the surf. When he got to the struggling swimmer, he soon realised it was Sharkey Dwyer, on the point of drowning.

It took five to ten minutes of struggling in the surf for Perc to get Dwyer back to the beach. Both men collapsed from sheer exhaustion.

Sharkey Dwyer certainly owed his life to Perc Galea and said to him, 'Perc, if you had kept me in the water for one more minute, I would have wiped out that £1700 debt that you owed me.'

With that, Dwyer got up, headed back to his car, turned and yelled, 'I'll see you at tomorrow's settling, Perc.'

One wonders what was going through Perc Galea's head at that stage – something like 'Christ, I should have let the bastard drown.'

Bookies with a heart? Don't think so!

The Adelaide Cup

... *a concept by the entrepreneur Mr Edward Bagot*

Edward Meade Bagot – 'Ned' to his friends – had such a vision of a great race that he nearly toppled the Melbourne Cup by his promotion of the Adelaide Cup.

In 1840, at the age of 18, Bagot had come to South Australia with his family from Scotland. As a pastoralist and agent, it was fair to say that he had a flair for new ventures, and he ended up being a very successful businessman in his own right, with interests and businesses spread far and wide in South Australia.

At the age of 42, Edward Bagot found great joy working with the newly formed South Australian Jockey Club in efforts to present a feature race that would rival anything of its type in Australia. He had a vision of a state fair or carnival atmosphere in Adelaide, with visitors and participants coming from all over Australia to enjoy the racing environment that would surround the running of the newly nominated great race. Some say that Ned Bagot was 100 years ahead of his time with what he envisaged for South Australian racing.

On 21 April 1864, the running of the inaugural Adelaide Cup was to be held, with a similar purse to that other great race, the Melbourne Cup. The Adelaide Cup prize money was £500, which compared very capably with the Melbourne Cup's purse of £754.

It would go down in history that the first Adelaide Cup was won by Falcon, contested over 13 furlongs (2600 metres). The youngster Roebuck ran a courageous second place, with a dead-heat for third between Little John and the heavily backed favourite at even money, Musidora.

Not content to rest on his laurels, nor those of the South Australian Jockey Club, Bagot was then instrumental in upping the ante on the prize money for the second running of the Adelaide Cup the following year to approximately £1000.

In the third running of the Adelaide Cup in 1866, it is fitting that Cowra was first past the post, owned by the man who put South Australia's great race on the map, Bagot. As was his habit of achieving things in life, the Bagot-owned Cowra went on to win the Adelaide Cup the following year in 1867 as well.

Edward Bagot moved on to other ventures and, unfortunately for the club, that all too familiar loss of collective enthusiasm started to happen. When you have a person taking ownership of something important and driving an event to success after success, year after year, and then that person is suddenly not as prominent, a certain slowdown always seems to occur.

The great race in Adelaide was not held in 1870 and 1871 because the unthinkable happened: the Jockey Club went bankrupt. Following this unfortunate event, and almost as an omen, a horse called Totalisator won the Adelaide Cup in 1881. Why was it an omen of an impending catastrophe?

With the *Totalisator Repeal Act 1885*, the South Australian Government introduced a bill that banned all forms of gambling on horses. The Adelaide Cup was cancelled in the years 1886, 1887 and 1888.

A group of stalwart followers of racing in South Australia explored all avenues to return their race to the calendar. After much deliberation, they accepted a kind invitation from the Victorian Racing Club and had the 1885 Adelaide Cup run at Flemington Racecourse.

The irony of this was not lost. Even though there was a very strong contingent of Victorian horses – as it was being held at Flemington, in Victoria – the race was won by the Adelaide-owned Lord Wilton.

The race was finally reintroduced into the South Australian racing calendar at Morphettville in 1889 when the Government finally saw the light and totalisator betting was reintroduced.

There has been only one triple winner in the history of the Adelaide Cup and that was Lord Reims, who won it in the consecutive years of 1987, 1988 and 1989. There have been four horses that have won the Cup twice: Cowra, owned by Edward Bagot (1866, 1867), Eyeglass (1911, 1912), Peerless Fox (1950, 1951) and Our Pompeii (1993, 1994).

So that is the early history of the Adelaide Cup, plus some modern-day record holders. There is no doubt that Edward Bagot and his vision for a great race in Adelaide was way ahead of his time.

The Adelaide Cup being run at Flemington – amazing!

Jim Houlahan
... the grand old man of jumps racing in Australia!

Some people in their late fifties start looking forward to retirement in their mid-sixties, but not so the legendary Jim Houlahan, the doyen of Australian jumps racing trainers.

At the age of 57, Jim Houlahan decided to give up his job as a successful building contractor and have a go at horse training full-time. Some 45 years later, at the young age of 92, Jim decided to give the game away and enjoy what he called 'his retirement years'.

On his ninety-first birthday, Jim trained Fidel to win a flat race at Werribee. He also trained Bellzevir to win the 1997 Group 1 Goodwood Handicap, South Australia's premier sprint race.

But it was as a jumps trainer that JJ Houlahan made his mark on Australian racing. Here are just some of his major wins:

- 8 wins, Australian Hurdles
- 2 wins, Australian Steeplechases
- 7 wins, Grand National Hurdles
- 1 win, Grand National Steeplechase
- 4 wins, AV Hiskens Steeplechase
- 4 wins, Grand Annual Steeplechases
- 3 wins, Great Eastern Steeplechases

The legacy of Jim Houlahan's contribution to the Australian racing industry is the $2.26 million JJ Houlahan Jumps Championship, which encompasses eighteen premier hurdle and steeplechase events in Victoria and South Australia, held between March and July each year. Also, the Jim Houlahan Medal is awarded each year to the outstanding jumps jockey achiever of the week during the Warrnambool jumps carnival.

On the night in 2004 when 91-year-old Jim Houlahan was inducted into the Racing Hall of Fame, there was not a dry eye in the room. He was also the recipient of the OAM, the Medal of the Order of Australia.

The legendary trainer passed away in April 2007, aged of 93.

JJ Houlahan, one of the all-time greats!

They had Lots Of Time
... *when the stars came out to play*

The brilliant Lots Of Time was one of Australia's most controversial hurdlers. He is famous for setting an Australian record of nine jumps race wins in a row, back in 1969, but it all came apart in the 1969 Grand National Hurdle.

Lots Of Time made his amazing sequence of wins in world record time, over thirteen weeks between 12 March and 21 June 1969. He certainly had an incredible constitution, but there was always colour and innuendo surrounding his ownership. Lots Of Time was owned by television and radio star Jimmy Hannan, high-class callgirl Sally Wood, and her partner, George Eccles. He was trained by Norm Creighton.

Around early June 1969, Sally Wood began a relationship with star North Melbourne footballer Sam Kekovitch. (Yes, the same Sam who we know as the Australian Lamb Ambassador.)

Just prior to the running of the 1969 Grand National Hurdle, the stewards were not happy about the horse's ownership, which resulted in a number of inquiries. Lots Of Time was finally cleared to run and was to be ridden by George Costello. This is where things started to get a bit hairy.

Lots Of Time was going for his tenth consecutive win. One of the part-owners doubted Costello's ability as a rider, and the arguments began to fly thick and fast. However, cool heads prevailed and Lots Of Time took his place in the field with Costello retained as his jockey. Unfortunately, they could only run second to Brother Bart in the Grand National.

The following Tuesday, front-page newspaper headlines claimed Costello had been sacked because of his ride. Had George Costello become the sacrificial lamb? George Eccles claimed that Costello had pulled Lots Of Time. Costello has vigorously denied that claim for decades.

So, there we have it. Some horses are mostly remembered for controversial issues, not for all the right things. Nine wins in a row: we would all like that as owners.

Lamb anyone?

These half-brothers were Bent

... but couldn't they jump

Some Are Bent

A lot of thought goes into the naming of a racehorse, and this one ranks as one of the very best names. He is Some Are Bent, foaled in 2001, a son of Distorted Humour – we need say no more.

However, there was nothing humorous about him on the racetrack, and by retirement in 2010, he had won $1,023,523. Of that, $950,488 was won contesting jumps races, winning twelve.

Although a winner over 1100 metres as a young horse, it was the distance races that brought out the best in Some Are Bent. On the racetrack he was easily recognised in the pale blue livery of the Robert Smerdon stable, and once he was introduced to jumps racing, it wasn't long before the Australian public was in awe of his ability.

The champion chaser won on all types of going but was clearly at his best when the tracks were slow and heavy, winning eleven and placing ten from 28 starts. His winning distances ranged from 1100 metres to 4300 metres.

Here are Some Are Bent's major wins:
- Grand National Hurdle: 2007 (68 kg)
- Galleywood Hurdle: 2007 (65 kg)
- Macdonald Steeple: 2007 (69 kg)
- JJ Houlahan Steeplechase: 2007 (66.5 kg)
- AJ Hiskens Steeplechase: 2008 (67 kg)
- JJ Houlahan Steeplechase: 2008 (67 kg)

Trainer Robert Smerdon rated Some Are Bent better than his 2002 Grand National Hurdle winner, Zabenz, who later in his career was very successful in the United States. He said, 'Early in Some Are Bent's career, he was a scrappy jumper, but did become quite proficient as time went on. Records are records, and his record says he was the best.' Prize money of $1,023,523 would certainly say he was right!

Black And Bent

Foaled in 2005, Black And Bent is the younger half-brother to Some Are Bent and is by the renowned sire of wet-track stayers, the UK sire and Group 1 winner Black Hawk, son of the legendary Nureyev.

Since his racing career began over the hurdles, Black And Bent has been one of Australia's most dynamic jumpers. One thing that endears him to the Australian public is that he can also compete at the highest level in handicap flat races. This was borne out by his brilliant win on 9 July 2011, when he won the final of the Banjo Paterson Winter Series over 2600 metres, ridden by Melbourne Cup winning jockey Michael Rodd.

Now, back to his earlier days as a hurdler. One of his wins was the 2009 LV Lachlan Hurdle, just two days after his fourth birthday. Black And Bent was then mixing his flat races with hurdle races, but it was now time to see if he could compete with the best over the jumps.

In 2010, he put paid to Grizz in the Galleywood Hurdle at Warrnambool. However, while being set for the Grand National Hurdle, Black And Bent succumbed to a severe tendon injury. Through patience and good old TLC, trainer Robert Smerdon had him back on the training track soon. In his sights was the 2011 Grand National Hurdle.

Black And Bent did not let the stable down, and under the urging of Steve Pateman, he cruised to an amazing eleven length victory. Two weeks after that memorable win, he took his earnings past $500,000 when he won the JJ Houlahan Hurdle.

Still only a young horse, but a seasoned one, was it possible for Black And Bent to be competitive with the best of the handicappers on the flat? Robert Smerdon mapped out a program for the horse with the ultimate goal being a start in the Melbourne Cup. However, after a mediocre effort in the Bart Cummings Handicap over 2600 metres, it was back to what the horse did best: winning hurdle races.

The 2012 jumps season was now back on the agenda. Lots Of Time's record of nine wins in succession was now in Robert Smerdon's sights. Well, the champion jumper did his part when Black And Bent brilliantly won his second Galleywood Hurdle. Could he now set an Australian record of ten successive hurdle wins?

Sadly, Black And Bent reinjured his tendon, and everything was put on hold. Maybe this was it. Maybe he would be denied his chance at history.

Once again, good old TLC and plenty of solid work brought Black And Bent back to peak fitness, and that elusive record was again well in the sights of Robert Smerdon. Could the horse achieve their goal, after breaking down with those two severe tendon injuries in 2010 and 2012?

On 5 May 2013, a crisp, chilly and sunlit morning dawned at Sandown Park. Later in the day, Black And Bent, brilliantly ridden by Steve Pateman, defeated Xaar in the Jack Dow Memorial Hurdle to set an Australian record of ten successive hurdle wins.

Unfortunately the champion jumper missed out on eleven in a row, but he finished his 2013 season in magnificent style by winning his second Grand National Hurdle, carrying 72 kg, the highest weight since Cheery Jack's 73 kg in 1940.

At that point of time, in 2013, Black And Bent had had 56 starts, with 20 wins and ten placings. His jumps-only CV reads as 21 starts, with thirteen wins and five placings. He has won from distances of 1600 metres to 4300 metres and taken $1,013,216 in prize money.

Here are Black And Bent's ten consecutive hurdle wins:
- Lakeside Hurdle: 2010 (68 kg)
- Galleywood Hurdle: 2010 (67 kg)
- Australian Hurdle: 2010 (66 kg)
- Morphetville Parks Hurdle: 2011 (73.5 kg)
- Warrnambool Hurdle: 2011 (68 kg)
- Grand National Hurdle: 2011 (69 kg)
- JJ Houlahan Hurdle: 2011 (69 kg)
- Sandown Hurdle: 2012 (70 kg)
- Galleywood Hurdle: 2012 (68 kg)
- Jack Dow Memorial Hurdle: 2013 (69 kg)

One could just imagine what Black And Bent could have done to any records had he remained a sound horse. Following are the remarks of both jockey and trainer after his record-breaking ten consecutive jumps wins.

Jockey Steve Pateman said, 'It was great to create history. I think he is going better than ever, and a lot of credit definitely goes to Robert Smerdon.'

Trainer Robert Smerdon said, 'I had a few butterflies throughout the run. He's come off the canvas, not once but twice – what a champion'.

He was simply the best!

What's in a name?
... let's think about it!

When it is time to submit thoroughbred names to the Registrar of Racehorses, many people put a lot of thought into the names they select. This can take up quite a lot of time. It can take hours and hours of marrying up the sire's and dam's name just to get it right.

However, some people want to avoid that sort of brain damage and just want to name their horse something easy – possibly just after somewhere on the map. Here are a handful of horses that have been registered and raced in Australia and Tasmania and other Far Away Places. Yes, these were racehorse names as well.

Here are just a handful of similarly well-thought-out names. We can start with the first culprit, the 1861 AJC Derby winner, Kyogle.

Melbourne, Moe, Wangaratta, Packenham, Portsea, Cobram, Donald, Kosciusko, Sydney, Mossman, Grafton, Tenterfield, Ballina, Dubbo, Wellington, Brisbane, Laidley, Tangalooma, Dalby, Mackay, Gladstone, Theodore, Cunnamulla, Chinchilla, Port Douglas, Darwin, Alice Springs, Perth, York, Geraldton, Fremantle, Marble Bar, Adelaide, Mildura, Kangaroo Island, Gippsland, Hobart, Launceston, Devonport.

Last, but not least, there's Surfers Paradise.

Yes, the Aussies and Kiwis can be an inventive lot. Maybe the selection of these names was done with that time-honoured method ... using a dart or pin.

You want to name him after a lolly?

... why not name him after something in the air?

At the 1950 Sydney Easter yearling sales, well-known racehorse owner Ernie Williams spotted trainer Ted Hush in the crowd. Now, Hush was famous for always sucking on his favourite sweet, Minties.

Williams sidled up to Hush and asked if he could have one of his Minties, to which Hush replied, 'Why the hell should I give you one? You only buy horses and give them to TJ Smith to train.'

'Okay, if you give me a Mintie, you can buy me a horse, and I will give it to you to train.'

Well, Hush probably thought that one way to pay back Williams for never letting him train a horse for him was to buy one that cost a small fortune. Ernie Williams was not happy when Hush paid 3200 guineas for the colt by Delville Wood from Sweet Sound. Once over the shock of the price, Williams told Hush he was going to apply for the name of Minties because of Ted Hush's love for the sweet.

However, the name was rejected. Under the accepted name, Hydrogen, the horse won 26 races between 1951 and 1955, and he won the equivalent of seven Group 1 races, including the Cox Plate in 1952 and 1953. His prize money of £60,000 was second only to the great Phar Lap's £66,000 won in the early 1930s (approximately $13 million and $15 million respectively today).

One wonders: if the horse had been named Minties, maybe Hydrogen would not have climbed to such great heights.

How sweet it is!

The difference was 72 years

... but they still managed to keep it in the family

Bill McLachlan was one of few jockeys to have multiple wins in the Melbourne Cup. His three winners were Prince Foote (1909), Comedy King (1910) and Westburn (1917).

Lee Freedman has trained five Melbourne Cup winners: Tawrrific (1989), Subzero (1992), Doriemus (1995) and Makybe Diva (2004 and 2005).

What is the significance of the 72 years' difference between

McLachlan's last winner in 1917, and Freedman's first winner in 1989?

Family ... It was a long time between drinks. Bill McLachlan was the great grandfather of Lee Freedman.

There was something else that was shared by the jockey and trainer: both were associated with winners bred overseas. Both Comedy King, for McLachlan, and Makybe Diva, for Freedman, were bred in England.

Yes, keeping it in the family.

Is this the first time in the world?
... or did they just need an extended break!

Many horses win a race, then for some inexplicable reason – with fitness not being an issue – they cannot rediscover their winning form until twelve months later. Some horses reproduce their best in the spring, in the summer or even when the tracks are at their heaviest, in the winter. Two examples of this are Zipping and Think Big.

Zipping won three Group 2 Sandown Classics, in 2007, 2008 and 2009. He competed in the highest of company and was a multiple place-getter in many Group 1 races during that period of time, but he could not record a win until the month of November in each of those three years. Zipping won the 2010 Sandown Classic, and recorded two Group 1 wins between his 2009 and 2010 victories.

Think Big won two Group 1 Melbourne Cups, in 1974 and 1975, and he too could not win a race in between. Once again, he only produced his best in the month of November. That is some record: winning a Group 1 race and your very next win is the same Group 1 race some twelve months later.

The same could be said about Black Piranha, who won the 2009 and 2010 Group 1 Stradbroke Handicap in Brisbane ... a non-winner as well in between.

However, has there been any horse in history – in Australia or overseas – that has done what Sniper's Bullet did?

As a three-year-old, Sniper's Bullet brilliantly won the Group 1 Stradbroke Handicap in June 2007. Big things were expected in the future for this colt trained by Tracey Bartley. But with all his might, Sniper's Bullet could not break through for a win anywhere. He consistently ran places in Group races, but not once did he see the winner's circle.

Two years passed and still no more wins. Bartley knew there was nothing wrong with his little horse, and it was just a matter of time … or was it a sign to retire the son of Bite the Bullet?

After a winter's spell, the now six-year-old Sniper's Bullet was put back into work with his main objectives being the 2009 Melbourne Spring Carnival and the Perth Summer Carnival. Once again, to the horse's credit, he performed well in the Group races in Melbourne, but he still remained winless.

Immediately after the Melbourne carnival, it was off to Perth for the summer racing carnival with his main priority now the $1 million Group 1 Railway Stakes, over 1600 metres. 'In for a penny, in for a pound', so to speak.

Then it finally happened. Brilliantly ridden by Nash Rawiller, Sniper's Bullet won the Railway Stakes – nearly 2.5 years after his previous win, which also happened to be a Group 1 race. To add icing to the cake, two weeks later he won the Group 1 Kingston Town Classic over 1800 metres. This took his earnings to $2.43 million, which was a very healthy bank balance.

Take a bow, Tracey Bartley: old Tommy Woodcock would have been proud of you for your sheer persistence and your faith in your horse.

There you have it. One Group 1 win, then a 2.5 year drought; then your next win happens to be a Group 1 win, and two weeks later another Group 1 win into the bag!.

Some record!

The author tells the tale!
… he finds another way to lose a fortune

One Saturday afternoon in August 1975, I put my bets on at the local TAB, then headed off to the local footie club. Being just a 'five-bob' punter, my punting outlays were quite minimal.

During the course of the afternoon, with the discussion getting around to my bets, my mate Frank Pearson said, 'So, Baz, you took the Melbourne Daily Double of Taras Regent and Stainvita for $10. I know the odds-on pop Stainvita is a super wet tracker and is by Staincross, but how the bloody hell did you come up with Taras Regent? It's 50/1 in the form guide.'

'Just on breeding, Frank, just on breeding.'

Well, being a lover of breeding, I explained that Taras Regent was the year younger half-brother to Taras Bulba, who had won the Rosehill Guineas and the AJC Derby on a wet track the previous year. I figured that his younger brother would also handle the wet.

Yes, Taras Regent was a bolter, but he did win and paid $66 in Queensland, and the double with Stainvita was paying approximately $140. How good was that? Smiles all round!

When they crossed to Sandown for the second leg of the double, I kept thinking about the wet track form of Stainvita, who had developed a cult following all around Australia for his incredible wins on wet tracks in Melbourne by very large margins. Yes, that $1400 collect was looking better and better as the field jumped.

Things were going to plan as Stainvita moved up to the leaders on the turn; within a short space of time, he had put lengths on the field. He was six lengths clear with 50 metres to go and I thought, 'How bloody good is this!'

And then it happened. To this day, I can still hear Bert Bryant's call of that race:

'Oh my God! Stainvita has stumbled and broken his leg – can you believe it?'

Yes, Stainvita had put his foot in a hole and snapped his leg. Frank just looked at me and shook his head and said, 'Mate, you just found another way of going from the penthouse to the s**thouse.'

I'm living peacefully between the two houses these days.

Our Australian Hall of Famer
... Ron Hall Snr, that is!

It must run in the blood being a jockey. Ron Hall Snr is no longer with us but his spirit and his great legacy continued on through his son, Melbourne Cup winning jockey Greg Hall (now retired). Today we are thrilled by the exploits of Ron's grandson Nick Hall, who shows us that the gift that his dad and his granddad had lives on through him.

While Ron Hall Snr also rode on the flat, he was best known for his jumps rides and more especially the rides he had on the magnificent jumps champion Crisp before that horse went overseas. Ron just wanted to be a jockey like his dad before him. When asked the best racehorse he had ever witnessed he replied, 'Tobin Bronze'.

He was asked what was the most amusing experience he had ever had in racing, to which he replied, 'Having ridden the winner of a hurdle race by the length of the straight after several horses had fallen during the course of the run, I returned to the jockey's room the victor when one of the riders of the fallen brigade said to me, "You're a lucky bastard." So I asked why. He said to me, "I was fair dinkum trotting mate when my horse fell." I said well where did you fall? To which he replied, "At the first."'

Thank you, Ron Hall Snr, for your jumping humour.

Mighty Malua
... Bagot, who became Mr Versatility!

The great trainer Bart Cummings once stated that champions should never be compared, just recognised. This champion became one of our immortals of the turf.

Foaled in 1879 in Tasmania, Bagot was raced by his owner Mr Thomas Reiby, the former Premier of Tasmania. After Reiby's horse Stockwell ran a disappointing second in the 1882 Melbourne Cup, he was so disillusioned with racing that he sold all of his horses, including Bagot, to Mr JO Inglis of Victoria for 500 guineas. When the horse arrived in Victoria, Mr Inglis decided to change its name to Malua.

Malua's versatility was such that he won at distances ranging from 6 furlongs (1200 metres), to 3 miles (4800 metres). Here are Malua's major successes in Melbourne:

- Melbourne Cup (1884) – 2 miles (3200 metres)
- Newmarket Handicap (1884) – 6 furlongs (1200 metres)
- Melbourne Stakes (1884) – 10 furlongs (2000 metres)
- Adelaide Cup (1884) – 2 miles (3200 metres)
- Oakleigh Plate (1884) – 6 furlongs (1200 metres; the distance of the first ever running)
- Australian Cup (1886) – 18 furlongs (3600 metres)
- Grand National Hurdle (1889) – 3 miles (4800 metres)

In the 1884 Newmarket Handicap – what we know today as the 'straight 6' at Flemington – Malua's jockey set somewhat of a precedent by taking the horse to the Grandstand side of the track for his win. For many years after that, this part of the course was known as Malua's track.

When he won the 1884 Melbourne Cup, Malua carried 9 stone 8 lb (61 kg). His versatility was such that two days after winning the Melbourne Cup, he won the Flying Stakes at weight-for-age.

On retirement, Malua had recorded 47 starts, with twelve wins, ten seconds and three thirds, and his prize money was equivalent to around $6 million today. He then went on to have a very successful stud career. His son Malvolio won the 1891 Melbourne Cup, while another son, Ingliston, won the 1900 Caulfield Cup.

When Malua won the Grand National Hurdle in 1889, he was ridden by his owner JO Inglis. In those early days it was not unusual for owners to ride their horses in jumps races.

What's in a name? A lot, apparently.

The undisputed country champion
... and the winner is *Robert Thompson*

This definitely has to be a world record. On 2 July 2013, Robert Thompson, riding Youthful King, won his ninth Jungle Juice Cup. The Jungle Juice Cup is usually held at Cessnock, New South Wales, but due to very heavy rain, it was transferred to Scone.

Winning the race in 2012 for the eighth time, Thompson had ridden General Sniper to victory, defeating Never Doubt Me and Better Not Doubt, and in doing so he had made it a great family day. Ron Godbolt was the trainer of the second and third place-getters. He is the father of Alison, who married Robert's son Simon, who just happens to be Godbolt's stable foreman. Yes, the racing gods were definitely smiling on the family that day!

Thompson, who goes by the nickname 'DOB', recalled the day that he was riding a heavily backed favourite on a very heavy track at Wyong, New South Wales. The going was so bad against the running rail that he took his horse to the outside fence trying to search for better going. However, the track happened to be just as bad out there, and his horse ran unplaced.

When he brought his mount back to the enclosure, Steward John Haigh informed him that he had just received a phone call in the stewards room and had been told, 'If Thompson rides in the next race, I will bloody well shoot him.' It was obvious that this bloke had just backed Thommo's mount in the previous race.

John Haigh said to Thompson, 'Are you prepared to ride in the next race?' To which Thompson replied, 'Look, I'm not worried and will take the ride.'

To that, Haigh said, 'You might get shot – let's hope this bloke is a bad shot.'

Thompson's mount ran unplaced, and no, not a shot was heard.

At Newcastle on 3 May 2014, Robert Thompson made history in race six when he drove Lay Down The Law through a narrow gap to give him another winner, and thus became Australasia's 'winningest' jockey – the first to ride 4000 winners.

Take a bow, sir.

By the left, quick march
... and move out NOW!

During both World War I and World War II, many racecourses throughout Australia were taken over by the Army. Townsville in northern Queensland was one that was occupied during World War II.

But did that stop the racing on Saturdays? No! The authorities regarded racing as important to the entertainment of both civilians and servicemen, so the massive concentration of troops moved out from the racetrack each Saturday morning so that the race meetings could go ahead.

Ah, where sensibility prevails!

Tasmania's humble beginnings
... and the way they did it way back then!

So often we take it for granted that racing just evolved in the outposts as well as in the capital cities. We assume that there are always crowds to cheer the horses on, proper racecourses to run on, betting facilities to challenge the punters and an organisation behind it all that has all of the answers. Not so!

This is the story of how the Taswegians managed to pull together and contribute ever so slowly to the great racing scene that now thrives in Australasia. Tassie has produced many champions through their breeding program, including Beer Street (the winner of the 1970 Caulfield Cup), Piping Lane, (winner of the 1972 Melbourne Cup) and the great Tasmanian-bred Sydeston, who was the best flat-race performer since the mighty Tasmanian Malua, who won the Oakleigh Plate (1884), the Melbourne Cup (1885), the Grand National Hurdle (1888) and many other top races.

Early races in Tassie did not consist of a large field of horses. They were generally contests between two runners that were not bred for horse racing.

The first recorded race was at New Town in 1813. The grey mare Whyena, owned by Mr John Inglis, went up against the Hobart paymaster's black filly, Sally. In the early days, to extend the interest in a race, there would usually be three heats, each over a 2-mile (3200-metre) course. The purse was self-contained, as the loser paid the winner an amount of about 20 guineas. These were very popular events in Hobart and Launceston. The thoroughbred involvement evolved only after the 1820s, when genuine racehorses began to be imported from England.

Hobart and Launceston tried to establish racing in those early days, and some success was earned by the Cornwall Turf Club when they made a serious attempt at racing in Launceston in 1830. After short-lived attempts to start elsewhere, in places such as Newnham and Invermay, Tasmanian racing finally found its home at Mowbray. The Tasmanian Turf Club had been formed in 1826, but it wasn't until 1865 that it came of age with the inaugural running of the Launceston Cup at Mowbray.

From 1927, Sandy Bay Beach had been the early site for racing in Hobart. A site was developed at Moonah, but when railway plans decided a track would go straight through the middle of the course, a group of the Tasmanian Turf Club members bought a parcel of land at Elwick Farm and established the present-day course. The first Hobart Cup was run in 1875 at Elwick Racecourse, and Elwick and Mowbray continue to be Tasmania's principal horse racing venues. The progress that is achieved in the very early days of anything often comes down to a person or a small group of people with deep pockets.

In an amazing feat of breeding in the Apple Isle, Mr John Field of Cressy and Mr John Lord of Hobart both bred two winners each of the Melbourne Cup. Lord started the trend by breeding Nimblefoot, who won the 1870 Melbourne Cup; he waited two years before he tasted success again with his horse The Quack winning in 1872. Field bred Malua, who won the Cup in 1884; in the following year, Sheet Anchor won it again for him.

In the late 1800s, those with deep pockets – the wealthy supporters of racing and breeding in Tasmania – became very thin on the ground. Unfortunately Tasmania's thoroughbred industry began a period of mediocrity and stagnancy that would last for nearly 70 years.

The arrival of the Irish-bred stallion Lanesborough in 1964 changed the landscape of racing in Tassie. He was the shot in the arm that sparked interest again in all things racing in the Apple Isle. It didn't take too long for Lanesborough to leave his mark. In 1970, his son Beer Street won the Caulfield Cup and that was followed by Piping Lane winning the Melbourne Cup in 1972. Tasmanians must have been jumping for joy over those two wins and the resurgence of racing.

Three years after Piping Lane's win, a most significant event took place that would ensure the viability of racing and its associated industries in Tasmania for a long, long time to come. The Totalisator Agency Board (TAB) came into being, and this would give racing a strong financial base for the future. A high standard of racing is now experienced at Elwick and Mowbray, with each club holding about 30 meetings per year. A smaller number of meetings are allocated to Devonport in the north-west of Tasmania.

Tasmania has produced some great jockeys too. In 1972, Geoff Prouse became the first jockey to ride a seven-race card at an Australian metropolitan meeting. From 1970 to 1984, Max Baker won every major Tasmanian race except for the Hobart Cup; at Elwick on Anzac Day in 1981, he rode every winner on the five-race card.

Beverley Buckingham became the first and, at the time, the only woman to win a senior jockey's premiership. She rode 906 winners, including three Hobart Cup winners and a Launceston Cup winner, but her career was cut short by a serious race fall at Elwick in 1998.

What a great contribution from the Apple Isle.

When you're hot, you're hot!
… one is a professional, the other a battler.

Saturday 26 June 1976 was just another Saturday for Australians having a punt at their local TAB. Well, it was not just an ordinary day for flamboyant Sydney professional punter Mick 'Melbourne Mick' Bartley, who decided that he would let loose on the jackpot tote on the Canberra TAB.

The journey of 290 km from Sydney to Canberra certainly paid dividends for Mick, because he was the only punter to have the winning combination that paid a record of $419,453. After the TAB commission of $62,918 was deducted, it left him with a very healthy $357,535 win. Yes, it was a very satisfying trip back to Sydney.

Not to be outdone, on 4 October 1980, Saturday afternoon 'five-bob-punter' John Moore struck gold when holidaying at

Queensland's Gold Coast. At the time, trifecta-betting was not available in Queensland, but it was just a short walk over the border to Tweed Heads to have a quiet punt on the Epsom Handicap. His trifecta selection won, with Bold Diplomat first, Ariva second and Prince Pherozshah third, and paid a very healthy $68,144. Having it three times meant Johnny's collect was $204,432.

Yes, a quiet 290-km journey and a 100-metre stroll certainly reaped rewards for these two punters.

It's great when you're hot to trot.

The Jockey Club is on the lookout for the angle
... because we hide the truth in the names

In the 1920s, Australia had an English stallion imported to its shores. His name was The Bastard. His connections were advised to change his name, and so he was registered as The Buzzard – imagine, horses sired by The Bastard would have left the gates open for some very undesirable horse names.

In the early 2000s, we had two horses running around with the names Kennelle and Kenoath. One does not have to be a literary genius to work out what their names were possibly shortened from.

One US horse owner was not going to change his horse's name without a fight, so he took his case to the courts in September 2005. US District Senior Judge Karl Forester dismissed the lawsuit and told owner Garrett Redmond that his argument 'that the denial deprived him of his rights under the US Constitution' would not stand.

What was Garrett Redmond's horse's name that upset so many people and that the US Jockey Club rejected? Sally Hemings. History shows that Sally Hemings was a colonial slave reputed to be the mistress of the third US President, Thomas Jefferson.

Now the breeding of the filly? Sally Hemings, by the sire Colonial Affair, from the dam Jefferson's Secret.

Yes, a lot of thought had been put into that name, but maybe the horse should have been named 'Don't Tell 'Em' or maybe something from that era, 'Well I Never'.

The names some people play.

CHAPTER 7
Around the World

The secret of Waikikamukau
... or should we say 'Why kick a moo cow'?

Horse names lead us up some very strange garden paths. This horse name makes you think and you just have to know the origins.

First of all it must be said that there is a vegetarian cafe in Bristol, Sussex, England, called Wai Kika Moo Kau cafe; there must have been some New Zealand influence on its origins. But our Waikikamukau (pronounced by Aussies exactly the same way as the English cafe) was a very handy thoroughbred that raced in the 1990s here in Australia. He was by the American stallion Clear Choice and his Australian dam was Empress Koyro. He ran in 68 races, for six wins, nine seconds and eight thirds. So, all in all, in one-third of the races he ran in, he gave some sort of return to the owners.

But the name ...

The name Waikikamukau was supposed to have derived from a real town in New Zealand called Waipukurau, situated on the North Island. *Wai* is Maori for water and it is used a lot as a prefix in the names of New Zealand landmarks. It is said that during World War II, some American soldiers were stationed near the town and had a lot of difficulty pronouncing it. What was Waipukurau became known as Waikikamukau by the American soldiers, and that is how it all began.

So began the legend of the name. In much the same way as Aussies say 'behind the Black Stump' or going to 'Timbuctoo', Waikikamukau became that New Zealand place that is far away and impossible to locate.

What's in a name, they say ...

The 18th Duke of Alburquerque
... *he was desperate to win that big race at Aintree*

He was a Spanish aristocrat known as the 'Iron Duke', but the comfort of his home country could not keep him away from his obsession of riding the winner of the Grand National at Aintree in England. His real name was Beltran Alfonso Osorio and, apart from having many other titles, he rode under his aristocratic moniker of the Duke of Alburquerque.

The name in itself must have been strange enough to the English racing public. Instead of a horse being ridden by Billy Bloggs or Peter Deacon, they had to get their tongues around his full title.

How did the Iron Duke's obsession begin? We are afraid that we can blame Tipperary Tim for that.

As part of his eighth birthday celebrations, the young duke was shown a film of the 1928 Grand National. That race stuck with him. It developed into more than just an interest, but a lifelong obsession to win that great race. Maybe what appealed to him was the luck of the race. In 1928, Tipperary Tim, unwanted by the punting public at 100/1, managed to stay upright throughout the race; it was one of those rare times when only two horses with riders finished the race – all of the others fell or were pulled up.

The Duke had a pony from a young age, so the goal of becoming an accomplished rider was a natural progression. He became an experienced amateur steeplechase jockey and eventually rode around the world, honing his skills – but, unfortunately, he was not good enough for Aintree yet.

In 1952, he accomplished his childhood dream and had his very first ride in the Grand National. He fell from his charge, Brown Jack III, and woke up in hospital nursing a cracked vertebra. He went back to Spain to sharpen his skills over the next decade, waiting for his opportunity to come again. He secured a ride in 1963, but unfortunately, his horse collapsed on him mid-race, and as a consequence, the Iron Duke broke his leg.

You could never call the Duke a quitter. It took another decade before he would be able to secure another ride in the great race. In a ride earlier that same year, in another country, he received another broken leg and needed to have screws inserted so it would heal properly. Just after having the screws removed, he commenced his training regime to once again prepare for the Grand National.

While in training, the Duke managed to fall from his mount and break his collarbone. The Duke was not to be deterred and he took his place in the 1974 field wearing a plaster cast – the Duke of Alburquerque was not the kind of person to give up easily! After three attempts, the strangest thing happened to him and his mount – they actually finished the race.

The Iron Duke finished in eighth and last place on Nereo, and there is an anecdote from the race that has found its way into Grand National folklore. There was another rider participating that day, Ron Barry, and the following exchange is supposed to have happened. Both riders and their horses were approaching the Canal Turn, when the Duke's mount barged into Ron Barry's mount.

Ron Barry: 'What in the f*** do you think you are doing?'

The Duke of Alburquerque: 'I have no idea, my friend. I have never been on this part of the course before.'

The 1974 race was the Duke's watershed moment. There was no holding our man back when he managed once more to get a ride in the great race, in 1976. Unfortunately, yet again and true to his form, he fell and was trampled by other horses. This time he suffered broken ribs, broken vertebrae, a broken wrist and thighbone, and severe concussion. He was in a coma for a number of days.

The racing authorities responsible for the running of the Grand National performed the unenviable task of revoking his riding licence – for his own safety.

This colourful and much loved figure died peacefully on 7 February 1994 in his beloved Madrid. He never fulfilled his dream of winning the Grand National at Aintree, but he entertained generations with his brave efforts to do so.

The Iron Duke rides again.

Update on the elite
... the top 10 undefeated of all time

Since our very first list of the most wins by undefeated horses in the history of racing, there has been one notable change of position on the list – that of the horse from the Land Down Under. The mighty mare Black Caviar retired in April 2013, with 25 wins in a row without a loss.

Here is an update of the top 10 horses in the history of horse racing.

- 1. Kincsem – Hungary-foaled 1874 – 54 wins from 54 starts
- 2. Black Caviar – Australia-foaled, 2006 – 25 wins from 25 starts
- 3. Peppers Pride – United-States-foaled, 2003 – 19 wins from 19 starts
- 4. Eclipse – Great-Britain-foaled, 1764 – 18 wins from 18 starts
- 5. Karavel – Turkey-foaled, 1970 – 18 wins from 18 starts
- 6. Ormonde – Great-Britain-foaled, 1883 – 16 wins from 16 starts
- 7. Prestige – France-foaled, 1903 – 16 wins from 16 starts
- 8. Ribot – Great-Britain-foaled, 1952 – 16 wins from 16 starts
- 9. Colin – United-States-foaled, 1905 – 15 wins from 15 starts
- 10. Macon – Argentina-foaled, 1922 – 15 wins from 15 starts.

What are the odds that any horse could get close to the record set by Kincsem? It would take a super horse, that's for sure.

The luck of the Irish
... Conor Murphy shows how it is done

What has Saint Patrick's Day, a stable lad by the name of Conor Murphy and the Cheltenham Festival, in the United Kingdom, got in common? They are the stars in this true tale of a gamble that paid off. It just so happened that these stars were all aligned at one time and they combined to give us this story of the Irish and their 'luck'.

It was just before Christmas in December 2011 on a very, very cold winter's evening in Lambourn, county of Berkshire. Conor Murphy was just filling in time before hitting the sack so that he could be up nice and early for work in Henderson's stables as the lead stable boy. It was bitterly cold. There was not much a stable boy could do except think about his horses and have a dream for them, as well as for himself. 'I know what I can do. I can pick a few winners from our stable for the Cheltenham Festival to be held in March.' It was not a hard task, because the races were only four months down the track.

The Cheltenham Festival is a National Hunt racing event held over four days in March every year. It is second only to the Grand National in prize money. It is the home of the great British steeplechase event the Gold Cup. The festival is held around St Patrick's Day (17 March) and as you could imagine, it is very popular with Irish punters and horse lovers.

It is fair to say that Conor really had no idea four months out if any of his selections from Nicky Henderson's stable would make the grade, let alone all race at the Cheltenham Festival. He kept the bet to himself so as not to attract any ridicule, and quietly 'invested' his £50 on an accumulator bet. His picks in the Cheltenham Festival in March and the results are:

- Tuesday 13 March 2012: Sprinter Sacre – won the Arkle Challenge trophy at 10/1
- Wednesday 14 March 2012: Simonsig – won the Baring Bingham Novices' Hurdle at 14/1
- Wednesday 14 March 2012: Bobs Worth – won the RSA Chase at 10/1
- Wednesday 14 March 2012: Finian's Rainbow – won the Queen Mother Champion Chase at 8/1
- Thursday 15 March 2012: Riverside Theatre – won the Ryanair Chase at 9/1

Conor Murphy's win that day netted him £1 million.

Because Conor's bet was placed months before, the prices that he got did not reflect the prices that were on offer on the day. The odds would have been far higher because the betting agency, like Conor, had no guarantee that the five horses he chose would even end up running in the races at the festival.

Before the maths boffins reach for their calculators to tell us what he should have won, let's crunch the numbers ourselves. Let us take the prices on race day and not what Conor would have been offered in December, and then multiply them out on the winning prices.

£50 × 10/1, all up × 14/1, all up × 10/1, all up × 8/1 and finally all up × 9/1. The calculator – overloaded as it may have been calculating the maths – should come out at a figure in the vicinity of £5,040,000 (around AUD$8 million).

So the question remains, why did Conor Murphy only receive £1 million from the betting agency? The fine print on the terms and conditions on accumulator tickets explains that 'the maximum payout can only be £1,000,000 and no more'.

The bookies have got you no matter what. Well done, Conor Murphy.

Pulling the wrong reins
... it happened to the best of them

Finding that right combination of horse and rider is everything. Think back through the history books. You will see that Luke Nolan knew Black Caviar better than anyone and it got to a point where he knew when the great mare was hurting. We also have the great Jim Pike and the relationship he showed winning all of those Classic races on the wonder horse of his time, Phar Lap. Included in these 'marriages' would have to be Malcolm 'Miracle' Johnston and his exploits aboard the inimitable Kingston Town.

All in all, many horses and riders fit well together; like that comfortable pair of old slippers, it just feels right. With the cut and thrust of racing as it has evolved over more recent times, jockeys now have managers and the managers do all of the work in chasing rides. On occasion, owners or trainers will contact managers offering rides, and others go directly to the jockeys. Some jockeys have choices that others envy.

So it happens, with all the to-and-fro, that mistakes are bound to happen. When that happens in a big race or, worse still, on the world stage, we tend to hear about it and we remember the argy-bargy before it all went wrong.

Ron Hutchinson – In the 1959 Melbourne Cup, Australia's jewel in the crown, Ron Hutchinson was like a kid in a candy store. It was an embarrassment of riches. Some jockeys wait all their lives to have a mount in the Cup, but Ron was blessed with choice. He was booked to ride Macdougal, but just before race day, he decided to jump ship and ride Trellios, trained by Bart Cummings.

Result: 1959 Melbourne Cup: Macdougal, first – Pat Glennon; Trellios, fifth – Ron Hutchinson.

George Moore – Now take old 'Cotton Fingers' himself, so named because of his light gossamer touch, riding the best of the best. George rode all over the world after a very successful career in Australia; he won many Classic races in Australia and on the world stage. He was at the top of his game in Australia, winning many premierships.

On retirement from riding, he took up horse training in Hong Kong; between the years 1973 and 1985, he won the trainer's premiership there a remarkable eleven times.

But of all the wins he had in his career, he could have added two more Classic wins to his already impressive list. He was offered and rejected the rides on El Gordo in the 1966 AJC Derby and on Royal Parma in the 1968 Golden Slipper. Neil Campton must have enjoyed hanging around old Cotton Fingers.

Result: 1966 AJC Derby: El Gordo, first – Neil Campton.

Result: 1968 Golden Slipper: Royal Parma, first – Neil Campton.

Jack Purtell – Jack made his mark on the Australian racing scene and was a very popular and experienced rider in the 1940s and 1950s, winning seven jockey premierships before enjoying success riding in Europe in the 1960s. He rode the winners of the Irish Oaks and the English Oaks before returning to Australia where he began a career as a steward, so highly was his reputation regarded.

Jack rode the champion Comic Court in nineteen of his wins. In 1950, Jack was offered the ride on Comic Court in the Melbourne Cup. He waited to make his decision until after the running of the Caulfield Cup, and because Comic Court ran unplaced in that race, he opted to let the mount go and ride Alister in the Cup for a rival trainer.

Result: 1950 Melbourne Cup: Comic Court, first – Pat Glennon; Alister, eighth – Jack Purtell.

Robert Heffernan – The Melbourne Cup has many a hard luck story, but many of these are self-inflicted by the jockeys themselves, and some even take place before the race is run. Here we have the story of Robert Heffernan, who was regarded as a 'gun' Victorian jockey and who was well regarded by his peers.

In 1982, Heffernan was the regular rider on Noble Comment, trained by George Hanlon. Unfortunately he finished third, behind Gurner's Lane ridden by Mick Dittman, in that year's Melbourne Cup.

In 1983 the team of Heffernan and Hanlon were on song again, and they had another go at the Cup. They went one better this year, and Noble Comment, ridden by Heffernan, ran second to Kiwi, ridden by Jim Cassidy.

Surely 1984 was going to be their year. George Hanlon had patiently brought along the talented Black Knight, son of the 1971 Melbourne Cup winner Silver Knight. The stars were aligned.

Heffernan was Black Knight's regular rider, but for some reason known only to Robert himself, he jumped ship before the great race and opted to ride Martian's Son. He was determined not to let blind faith stand in his way of winning his first Melbourne Cup. Only four days before the great race, Peter Cook was booked to ride Black Knight.

Result: 1984 Melbourne Cup: Black Knight, first – Peter Cook, trained by George Hanlon; Martian's Son, seventeenth – Robert Heffernan.

Brent Thompson – It was the late 1970s when Australia was introduced to Brent 'The Babe' Thompson, otherwise known in his native New Zealand as the 'Wanganui Whiz Kid'. When he arrived in Australia as a seventeen-year-old, he made an immediate impact. He guided home Fury's Order in the 1975 WS Cox Plate, a race regarded as second only to the Melbourne Cup.

Brent became the regular stable jockey for one of the greatest and most loved horse trainers in Australian racing history, Colin Hayes. Being the top stable jockey, he had the choice of any of the four horses that were going to compete in Hayes' colours in the 1980 Melbourne Cup. The options were Belldale Ball, owned by Robert Sangster;

Yashmak, the surprise winner of the 1980 Coongy Handicap at Caulfield; Bohemian Grove; or the roughie Gay Tribo. The win by Yashmak in the Coongy Handicap, even though he had not ridden the horse, had captured Brent's eye so he was set – Yashmak, it would be.

Result: 1980 Melbourne Cup: Belldale Ball, first – John Letts; Yashmak, eleventh – Brent Thompson.

Lester Piggott – Australian jockeys are not the only ones to 'pull the wrong rein'. It can be contagious, and it can come back to bite even the best in the business on the world stage. The great English jockey Lester 'Stoneface' Piggott was regarded as one of the very best of all time, yet the inimitable Piggott had a horror selection in the 1967 English Derby. He was given the opportunity to ride Royal Palace in the great race, but he chose Ribocco instead. Sometimes, you just can't keep your mouth shut. Piggott was so scathing about Royal Palace's chances that he uttered these very words, which would come back to beat him over the head for years: 'Royal Palace does not have the guts to win.'

Result: 1967 English Derby: Royal Palace, first – George Moore; Ribocco, second – Lester Piggott.

Olivier Peslier – To finish with more international flavour, here is the tale of Olivier Peslier, one of the great French jockeys of his time, four-time winner of the classic Prix de l'Arc de Triomphe. In the 1997 English Derby, Olivier was offered the ride on Benny The Dip but he passed that up to take the ride on Cloudings.

Result: 1997 English Derby: Benny The Dip, first – Willie Ryan; Cloudings, tenth – Olivier Peslier.

It was reported that Olivier did not take the win of Benny The Dip too well. It was probably best that the English punting public could not understand French, because apparently what was said by Olivier Peslier about the winner after dismounting wasn't very complimentary.

Sometimes it just pays to keep your mouth shut.

Riot on the racecourse

... call the police, there's an angry mob after the jockey!

Visiting English jockey Martin Dwyer probably thought that 17 February 2013 would be just a normal day of racing in India. WRONG!

Dwyer had ridden Sir Percy to victory in the 2006 English Derby. He was currently engaged to ride the 6/4 favourite, Ice Age, in the final event at Mahalaxmi Racecourse in Mumbai, India.

The field jumped as one, and Ice Age settled off the pace. However, in the run home, she continued to duck in badly behind the leaders from the 100-metre line to the winning post, and she eventually ran third.

On returning to scale, Dwyer found out what all jockeys fear when beaten on a hot favourite in the Indian subcontinent. He was chased by angry punters, and the punting public started rioting and demanded that the racing stewards declare the race null and void.

The next day, the *Mumbai Mirror* reported:

> Jockey Martin Dwyer was in fear of his life when returning to scale, and was chased by a very angry crowd. The Royal Western India Turf Club guards managed to shield Dwyer from an extremely large mob, and it was well into the night before some type of order was installed.

Chief Steward Pradyumma Singh issued a statement that declared:

> Martin Dwyer's riding, prima facie, appeared doubtful following which the stewards declared Ice Age a non-starter and all bets on this horse were refunded.

The result of a delayed inquiry said, 'Today, the stewards of the Royal Western India Turf Club have suspended jockey Martin Dwyer for 8 weeks.' They did not give much weight to the fact that Ice Age had bled during the race.

Dwyer appealed the eight week suspension, and his hearing was held on 14 August 2013. The result of the appeal read, 'Ladies and gentlemen, jockey Martin Dwyer's appeal has been thrown out, and his suspension has been increased to 8 months.'

Racing in India – so, so different!

The man who would be king!
... he was trustworthy, through and through

His funeral in mid-August 1894 was reputed to be the largest the city of Melbourne has seen. As the cortege travelled from his home in Caulfield to the general cemetery in Melbourne town, thousands lined the streets.

The following day, *The Age* newspaper reported that Swanston Street was 'one mass of humanity' and that road traffic had been suspended for three hours. Flags flew at half-mast, and shops closed for the day. The procession to the cemetery was reported to be over 2 miles (3.2 km) long. Grown men, women, dignitaries, children: all had a tear in their eyes.

Who was this man? Who could bring a city to a standstill?

He was Tommy Corrigan, the Irish lad who became an Australian legend.

Born in 1851 in County Meath, Ireland, Tommy and his parents migrated to Victoria in 1864. As a lad who seemed to have no fear of riding or jumping fallen trees and broken fences, it did not take him long to gain recognition at the local picnic races.

At the age of 14, riding his own mare, Juliet, young Tommy won the hack steeplechase at the Woodford publican's purse race meeting. First prize was a saddle, and thus the career and legend of Tommy Corrigan began.

In 1865 Tommy persuaded his father to allow him to leave home and serve his apprenticeship with the stable of Tozer and Moran in Warrnambool, in south-west Victoria.

Not being a heavy jockey, he was able to ride with great success in both jumps and flat races. Riding at 7 stone 11 lb (49.5 kg), he rode Emblem to be unplaced behind The Quack in the 1872 Melbourne Cup.

In total, Corrigan rode in 788 races, for 238 wins and 230 placings. That gave him an incredible winning strike rate of 1 in every 3.5 rides. However, it was in jumps races that Tommy was the absolute champion. Amongst his wins were a total of seven Grand National Steeplechase races. Such was his following, the first thing that many people on course asked was, 'What's Corrigan riding?'

Then came that fateful day of 11 August 1894. Tommy Corrigan's mount, Waiter, fell in the Caulfield Grand National Steeplechase. The champion jockey suffered a fatal head injury, and passed away the following day, leaving a young widow, Robena, and two young children. Thought once to be worth £15,000, Corrigan died poor. So popular was this man, a fund was set up to help his young family.

At the time, Corrigan was considered to be the most popular and best cross-country rider in Australia. Many of the colonials doubted whether England could boast a superior horseman.

The Age newspaper, which often reported at the time that racing was 'morally dubious', stated: 'Tommy Corrigan was a model of fair dealing and unquestionable integrity.'

At his funeral, the statement made by his close friend and fellow jockey Douglas Lower said it all: 'He was the straightest jockey who ever breathed.'

Each year, the Tommy Corrigan Medal is awarded to the leading jumps rider of the season. In 2013, Steven Pateman won it for the sixth time.

Long live the King!

The handicapper's lament!
... here's one for you and one for me

He was regarded as the 'Father of Racehorse Handicapping', but who was this man?

Born in 1795, John Henry Rous was the second son of John Rous, the first Earl of Stradbroke. He was educated at Westminster School and later at Dr Burney's Naval Academy in Portsmouth, England.

He joined the Royal Navy in 1808 and served as a midshipman during the unsuccessful Walcheren campaign in the Netherlands in 1809. He was then appointed to HMS *Bacchante* and received medals for bravery on various expeditions. He was later appointed Admiral in charge of HMS *Pique*.

Admiral Rous had quite a distinguished career. On one trip to Australia in 1827, he was commander of the HMS *Rainbow*. One of his duties was to organise Sydney's first regatta. Later, travelling along the eastern coast of Australia, Rous sailed into Moreton Bay where he dropped anchor. It was there that he named the Rous Channel, Dunwich and Stradbroke Island. Admiral Rous was also an influencing figure in the naming of the now city of Ipswich.

Now to Admiral John Rous's legacy of horse racing handicapping.

The first Earl of Stradbroke owned a stud farm in county Suffolk. One of his horses was Tigris, who as a three-year-old in 1815 had won the 2000 Guineas. The Earl was hoping that his second son would someday become stud squire.

Although a great lover of thoroughbreds, young Rous did not follow in his father's footsteps; instead, he followed the path of administration, and in 1838, he was appointed as a steward of The Jockey Club. In 1855 he was appointed racing's first public handicapper. He held the position of steward until his death in 1877, at 82 years old.

Admiral Rous is credited as being the man who first set out the weight-for-age scale. This is the basis for race handicapping today.

Many archival newspapers, books, and magazines describe Admiral Rous as having a keen wit. 'On the subject of handicapping', Rous once said, 'there is nothing so easy as to find fault; it is a capacious field for the scribblers on Racing topics.'

Rous was once asked to describe the qualifications one needed to be a handicapper. 'A public Handicapper', replied Rous, 'should be a man of independent circumstances, in every sense of the word; and beyond suspicion of accepting illicit compensation for favours received. Attached to no stable; a good judge of the condition of the horse; but with a more intimate knowledge of the disposition of both owners and trainer; he should be a spectator of every race of importance; and his station should be at the distance post where horses are pulled, not at the winning post where they are extended; he should never make a bet; and he should treat all remarks that may be made about his handicaps with the utmost indifference.'

SUCH A MAN IS NOT TO BE FOUND!

So, there we have it. Many thanks to Admiral Rous in the mid 1800s.

Monsieur!
... *your dog, please!*

Famous French trainer Andre Fabre has trained a record seven Prix de l'Arc de Triomphe winners, the first being Trempolino (1987). However, even today, he refuses to speak with certain French journalists.

As he said many years ago, 'I refuse to speak to the *Paris-Turf* newspaper. I give them as much respect as my dog Basil does for the trees of Chantilly.' Sounds like Basil had a dingo's breakfast – a p**s and a good look around!

Andre had a way with words, as well as horses.

Group 1 glory for an adopted Kiwi!
... *and the only one to do it*

Question: Who is the only horse to win a Group 1 race in New Zealand, Queensland, New South Wales and Victoria?

Answer: Rough Habit.

Foaled in New Zealand in November 1986, the son of Roughcast and Ashabit showed nothing of note in his two-year-old and early three-year-old career. In May 1990, John Wheeler ventured to Queensland, Australia, to get a gauge of the horse's ability. The Winter Carnival is the last major meeting of the racing season, where many three-year-olds start putting their galloping abilities together in preparation for the upcoming Spring campaigns in Melbourne.

After a sound performance running second to Stargazer in the 2200-metre Grand Prix Stakes, Rough Habit was sent out third favourite behind the two other Kiwis, Ray's Hope and Castletown, in the 2400-metre Queensland Derby.

That Queensland Derby day in June 1990 set the scene for what was to become known as 'Rough Habit's Winter Group 1s'. Not only did he win the Derby, but over the next four years the 'honorary Queenslander' won five more Group 1 races. At his final start in

Australia in 1995, he sensationally won the Group 2 O'Shea Stakes over 2400 metres in the brilliant time of 2:26.7.

Following are his eleven Group 1 wins:

- Queensland Derby, 2400 metres (1990)
- Stradbroke Handicap, 1400 metres (1991, 1992)
- Doomben Cup, 2020 metres (1991, 1992, 1993)
- All Aged Stakes, 1600 metres (1992, 1993)
- AJC Queen Elizabeth Stakes, 2000 metres (1992)
- Caulfield Stakes, 2000 metres (1994)
- Captain Cook Stakes (NZ), 1600 metres (1992)

Rough Habit also ran second to the New Zealander Solvit in the 1994 WS Cox Plate.

Rough Habit's second Stradbroke Handicap win in 1992 will go down in history as one of the all-time great winning efforts. Back near last as they turned into the straight, the gallant 'Roughie' just seemed to weave his way through a wall of horses. At the 200-metre mark he was still giving the leaders an enormous start, but unleashing a powerful finish, he got up in the last few strides.

The noise of the crowd was deafening as Jimmy 'The Pumper' Cassidy brought the great horse back to the enclosure to thunderous applause. When interviewed by the press, Cassidy said that all the credit should go to the horse, not him – 'He just grabbed the bit, weaved and steered his way through the field, and I just went along for the ride. He's a bloody beauty!'

Now back to that 1990 Queensland Derby. The third place-getter that day, Castletown, went on to become one of New Zealand's all-time great stayers. During his career, he won a New Zealand Derby, Auckland Cup and two Wellington Cups.

In 1994, the then-BATC honoured Rough Habit, the winner of three Doomben Cups, by naming a race and a bar after him. The Rough Habit Plate is run over 2020 metres, and many a yarn can be recalled in the Rough Habit Bar.

Rough Habit was named New Zealand Horse of the Year in 1992 and 1995. 'Roughie' was definitely one of the all-time greats of the Australian Winter Carnival!

Moifaa from NZ wins great race in the UK
... *after being shipwrecked and swimming 50 miles*

When you are telling a yarn, in some cases, the truth is kidnapped but there is a damn good tale at the end of it all. Let us tell you about a very famous New Zealand horse that was shipped to England to compete in the 1904 Grand National at Aintree. The truth is that a number of horses were shipped from their home country at that time in 1901, and one of the boats was shipwrecked on the way to England, off the Cape of Good Hope. The Cape of Good Hope is a rocky outcrop on the Atlantic Ocean side of Cape Peninsula, South Africa.

One of the miracle survivors of the catastrophe was the horse that was reportedly found by locals on a small island close to shore a few days after the shipwreck. Legend has it that the horse had swum around 50 miles (80 km) to shore. Even if that distance sounds a bit of a stretch, it is a wonder in itself that a terrified racehorse in a massive swirling ocean could find land under those circumstances at all.

Locals found the exhausted racehorse the day after the wreck and managed to care for him. At the same time they advised the proper authorities, and the trainer was contacted and given the good news. After thinking that all was lost, the trainer was delighted to be reunited with his brave and lucky steed and they continued on their way to England. The New Zealand–bred horse went on to win the Grand National – but in real terms 'he missed by that much', as Maxwell Smart would say.

Moifaa was an imposing horse standing in excess of 17 hands high. When you consider the average thoroughbred height is between 15 and 16 hands, then you can see that this bloke was a monster. He was a gelding and was by the sire Natator; his dam was Denbigh. He wasn't the prettiest horse by any stretch of the imagination, and in some quarters they made reference to his size and his looks as that of a camel.

In any case, his owners thought a lot of their big 'oaf' and schooled him over fences in New Zealand because of his size, and he didn't let them down. He won nine of his thirteen races and his last win in NZ was a 3½ mile chase (5635 metres), carrying 13 stone (82.5 kg). He was then sold to a Mr Gollan who had over the years sent a number of horses to England. Besides his family coming from Scotland, Gollan had a desire to win that most famous of all jumps races, the Grand National at Aintree in Liverpool, England.

The other main character in this story is a thoroughbred horse named Kiora, who was also targeting the 1904 Grand National.

In the early days of transporting horses, there was quite a lengthy period allowed for 'conditioning' before a horse raced after landing. If these horses were going to travel so far, having to survive months at sea as well as storms and possible shipwrecks, then the plans for racing on the other side of the world must be counted in years, not months.

Along with other horses, Moifaa and Kiora left at the same time in 1901 but from different ports, both with the express goal of competing in the 1904 Grand National at Aintree. It took a couple of years in recovery and adjustment, but they were both eventually ready for their task. Arthur Burch, a local, was engaged to take the mount on Moifaa, and Mitch Neal was booked for the ride on Kiora.

As Moifaa had not taken to the English style of racing and had been unplaced in his three races prior to the Grand National, it was no wonder that the punting public had no liking for him and he was sent out 'unloved' at 30/1. Kiora had fared a little better and was a bit shorter in the market.

They were off in the 1904 Grand National, a race that would take horse and rider over 4 miles 3½ furlongs (7140 metres), consisting of two circuits of the Aintree course, with a total of 30 fences challenging them along the way before horse and rider head for home, with a 2¼-furlong (490-metre) torturous uphill stretch to the winning post.

Moifaa, unlike the smaller Kiora, relished the big jumps as his 17-hand frame just took each one in its stride. The other 25 competitors on the day could not get near him, and Moifaa went on to win by eight lengths, with Kirkland running second and The Gunner taking third. Unfortunately the other Australasian-based runner, Kiora, was unplaced.

The details of the win, the shipwreck and other facts about the race were sent to all major newspapers throughout the world. The year was 1904, though, so the movement of that information was slow and sometimes not easily – or accurately – communicated.

By the time the newsworthy details had reached the desk of an American newspaper and had been interpreted as only a journalist can – in combination, and a little loosely –the legend and the myth was born.

'Amazing tale of survival – shipwrecked horse wins Grand National'.

The New Zealand horse Moifaa did leave the shores of his home country in January 1901 on a transport vessel headed for England. On the same day, Kiora left on a transport vessel out of Melbourne, Australia, with the destination being England. It was in fact Kiora's ship that had been wrecked off the Cape of Good Hope, and it was Kiora that had swum for his life and found his way to a small piece of land in a turbulent ocean. Moifaa's ship travelled without incident to England.

Everything else about the horse's subsequent rescue by locals and the trainer being advised is absolutely true – but it was Kiora. He did compete in the 1904 Grand National at Aintree, although he finished unplaced.

The truth about Moifaa? 'He missed the shipwreck by that much.'

How fast was that?

... champions for life and one remembered in song!

As punters, many of us have a fascination with times recorded by horses in races. Any edge that one can get when having a bet helps us in our vital selection. What time did he run? What did he run his first 800 in? What did he run his last 600 in?

When Hurricane Sky won the 1994 Blue Diamond Stakes at Caulfield, he ran 1:08.1 for the 1200 metres, considered then to be a world record for a two-year-old racehorse. Young Australian stallion Keep The Faith, on a trip to North America in the mid-2000s, clocked an incredible 1:06.58 for 6 furlongs (1200 metres).

Todman

The benchmark for speed was possibly set way back in early 1957, by a very special young galloper: Todman

In 1956, trainer Maurice McCarten's precocious two-year-old colt by Star Kingdom was reported to be one right out of the box. The racing fraternity was keenly waiting to see if this trackwork flyer could produce his form on race day. He did not let them down.

Todman won by ten lengths on his debut at Randwick in December 1956. He ran the 5 furlongs (1000 metres) in the blistering Australasian record time of 57.8. No horse of any age had ever run that sort of time before in Australia or New Zealand.

During the four weeks of that 1957 Sydney Autumn Carnival, the brilliant two-year-old was to stamp himself as one of the fastest thoroughbreds this country has ever seen. He won the inaugural Golden Slipper by eight lengths, and defeated the mighty Tulloch by six lengths in the Champagne Stakes. Both races were over 6 furlongs (1200 metres). Sandwiched between those two races, he was to suffer his only defeat as a two-year-old, by Tulloch in the Sires Produce Stakes over 7 furlongs (1400 metres).

At the end of his two-year-old career, Todman defeated older horses in a 6-furlong (1200-metre) welter race at Rosehill. The only time he missed a place in his races was when he broke down in the Hill Stakes as a three-year-old. He ran unplaced that day behind the great Redcraze. Unraced as a four-year-old due to injury, the great horse was retired as an undefeated five-year-old after winning the 1960 VRC Lightning Handicap and the VATC Futurity Stakes.

On retirement, Todman had raced twelve times for ten wins and one second, and had run an astonishing one Australasian record, one Australian record and five course and race records in those ten wins.

At stud, he went on to become one of the great champion sires of the Australian turf, siring 30 Stakes winners with 63 Stakes wins. Two of his speedsters were Golden Slipper winners Eskimo Prince and Sweet Embrace. Other great offspring were champion gallopers Blazing Saddles, New Gleam, Imposing, Ricochet and Crewman.

However, should the benchmark for speed belong to the year of 1946, some eleven years before Todman?

Shannon

After winning the 1945 Epsom Handicap with 8 stone 9 lb (55 kg), Shannon was allotted 9 stone 8 lb (61 kg) in the 1946 Epsom. Back then there were no starting barriers as we know them today, only the strand system where jockeys would walk their horses up to the strands, and once in line, the starter would let them go.

Unfortunately, when the field jumped in the 1946 Epsom Handicap and had gone approximately 100 yards (90 metres), no-one could see Shannon, the short-priced favourite. He had missed the start.

In one of the most stirring rides of his career, 'Demon' Darby Munro took off after the field and failed only by a short half-head in catching the winner, Blue Legend. The starter of the race, Mr Gaxieu, took full responsibility for what happened and said that he just did not see Shannon standing so far back behind the field in the shadow of the trees, and he declared Darby Munro was in no way to blame for the debacle. Punters were not happy!

Blue Legend's time for the 1 mile (1600 metres) was 1:36.2. Allowing for the short half-head defeat, the fast-finishing Shannon's time was also a probable 1:36.2. By time calculations, if we allow approximately the 5.5 seconds for the 90 metres Shannon had lost at the start, his actual time for the 1600 metres that day may have been in the vicinity of 1:31.0. This was a world record performance.

As at the end of 2013, no horse in Australia has broken 1:32.0 for the 1600 metres, the next fastest being 1:32.66 by Drack's Back in 2005. So how good was Shannon? Well, the Yanks were about to find out.

In 1948, Shannon was sold and taken to America. William Molter took over from Australian trainer Peter Riddle to condition the horse for his first campaign on American soil.

At his first start in the summer of June 1948, Shannon won the Argonaut Handicap at Hollywood Park, followed by a brilliant win in one of America's most prestigious races, the Hollywood Gold Cup.

On 17 October 1948, Shannon equalled the world record of 1:47.6 for 9 furlongs (1800 metres) in the Forty Niner Handicap Stakes. Just one week later, he equalled the world record of 1:59.8 by winning the Golden Gate Handicap over 10 furlongs (2000 metres).

Sold to a breeding syndicate for US$300,000, Shannon, the son of Midstream, was retired to stud in America. In his short career overseas, the brilliant Aussie champion had equalled two world records and had set two track records. Allowing for his probable 1:31.00 in that sensational Epsom Handicap in 1946, one must say that he indeed may have been the benchmark for future speedsters.

On retirement, Shannon's record was 44 starts for 20 wins, eight seconds, and seven thirds. The great horse definitely passed his speed genes on to many of his offspring, such as Clem, who defeated the great Round Table in the Washington Park Handicap in course record time. Another of his progeny was the Citation Handicap winner, Sea o'Erin, who at retirement had won eighteen other races and prize money of US$407,259.

When Shannon's progeny made it to the sales, it was certainly a time of great interest. With his second crop in the sales ring this particular day, there was a striking filly by Shannon, out of the very good mare Doah. It was reported that day that people could clearly remember the famous American actor Jimmy Stewart rising from his seat as the filly was paraded, arms outstretched, bursting into song with –

'Shannon Doah,
I love your daughter
Away yon rolling river,
For her I'd cross your roaming waters
Away, I'm bound away,
cross the wide Missouri.'
Believe it or not – well, probably not.

The origin of our species
... and where it all began for the thoroughbred

Charles Darwin has had his say and so have the good people in Sunday School who introduced us to Adam and Eve, but have you ever considered where the racing thoroughbred breed got its start, or did you think that they were always there? Somewhere in history, there was a starting point and it is quite remarkable that we can trace virtually all of our thoroughbred ancestry back to three horses. Two were by choice and one by accident.

These three foundation sires gave us the second generation of sires, which we can trace more easily. The second generation sires were Eclipse, Herod and Matchem.

As you will see from the details below, foundation sires were generally imported warhorses – which is not what you would expect to hear. The three horses were the Darley Arabian, the Byerley Turk and the Godolphin Arabian. In general terms, these foundation sires started thoroughbred racing lines in England and Europe, while many years later their generational offspring gave the Americas their thoroughbred line that we know today. Stallions that started it all for the Americans were Diomed, Messenger, Shark and Medley.

Here is a brief history of our three foundation sires.

The Darley Arabian

Bought in Syria by Thomas Darley in 1704, this horse was 15 hands tall and considered a very handsome horse. While standing at Aldby Park Stud, he was responsible for siring many successful horses of that time. With such a dominant bloodline, it is estimated that an incredible 95 per cent of male thoroughbreds trace their line back to the Darley Arabian.

Easily the greatest achievement of this horse was that his offspring led to the existence of the champion Eclipse, who was the most important of the second generation sires in terms of achievements in both racing and breeding. The Darley Arabian's introduction by Thomas Darley was a planned move to improve and create a thoroughbred horse for racing.

It is believed the modern Arabian horse dates back some 4500 years to the Arabian Peninsula.

The Byerley Turk

This horse was the earliest of the foundation sires. He was brought to Britain after Captain Robert Byerley captured him at the Battle of Buda in 1686. The Battle of Buda was fought between the Holy League and

Ottoman Turkey as part of the campaign in Hungary after the Battle of Vienna. The Holy League captured Buda after a long siege.

The Byerley Turk was a warhorse, and as such, served his master throughout the campaign, including the Battle of the Boyne. Incredibly the Turk survived the fighting and Robert Byerley retired from military life and introduced the Turk to stud, where he became a very influential foundation sire.

While his line almost became non-existent in the eighteenth century, the success of his descendant Herod brought it all back on track. Modern thoroughbreds rarely trace their sire-lines back to the Byerley Turk, but he had a massive influence on thoroughbred racing, especially considering his prolific descendants. Herod was the grandsire of the first English Derby winner, Diomed, who is also one of America's foundation sires.

The Godolphin Arabian

The Godolphin Arabian, often called the Godolphin Barb, was named after its famous owner, the Earl of Godolphin. Many of the American foundation sires had a strong connection to the Godolphin Arabian line. While more horses can trace their lineage back to the Darley Arabian, the Godolphin Arabian is commonly found in the dam lines of the modern thoroughbred. Surprisingly, the Godolphin Arabian was not the Earl's first choice to play such an important part in our thoroughbred history.

The story goes that the Godolphin Arabian was only used for breeding purposes after the Earl's other prized stallion failed at his stud duties. When the Godolphin Arabian started to produce champion thoroughbreds, his potential and importance was soon realised. This founding sire is particularly important to American racing, as Messenger was descended from his sire line and basically became the foundation sire for the standardbred harness racing breed.

Great foundations for racing.

Trickie Dickie and the Caulfield Cup
...*from starting gate to Watergate!*

In the early 1950s, a future President of the United States of America was a guest of the Victorian Amateur Turf Club (VATC) and witnessed the running of the 1953 Caulfield Cup. The guest was none other than Richard Nixon, and maybe the name of the winning horse put the mocker on the future President? The winning horse was My Hero.

Probably not an omen bet.

What a ride!
... *the North versus the South*

In January 2008, Brazilian jockey Jorge Ricardo rode his 10,000th winner. Just one month later, US jockey Russell Baze also rode his 10,000th winner.

The race was now on to see who could get to the next milestone of 11,000 winners. Once again, in June 2010, Ricardo was the winner, pipping Baze at the post by one month.

Now who would be the first to ride 12,000 winners? Once again, in May 2013, it was Jorge Ricardo, when he steered Scoop to victory at the Hipodromo Argentino de Palermo Racecourse in Buenos Aires, Argentina.

Not to be outdone, in July 2013, Russell Baze rode his 12,000th winner, Handful of Pearls, to victory at the Alameda Racecourse in Alameda, California. This 54-year-old jockey started his riding career in February 1974. What makes the 12,000 winners for this jockey quite incredible is that he did it from a total of 50,328 rides, over a period of 39 years. This makes his winning percentage at 1 win in every 4.2 rides. Astonishing! Russell Baze was inducted into the US Racing Hall of Fame in 1999.

One wonders who will be the first to ride 13,000 winners, Ricardo or Baze? Only time will tell.

Two very tough jockeys, two very tough posteriors!

CHAPTER 8

Champions from the Vault

Apache Cat

... *looked like he was straight out of a Western movie*

Once you laid eyes on him, there is no doubt that you would never forget him. Just the mere mention of his name drew people to the races or towards their racing TV channels. If you backed him, and most people did at some time, there was no wondering where he was in the race he was competing in, you just looked out for his big white head.

Apache Cat was by the US shuttle stallion Lion Cavern with his dam being Tennessee Blaze. He was a chestnut gelding born and bred at Chatswood Stud in Victoria in 2002.

On his retirement in 2008, his race record was 43 starts for nineteen wins, four seconds and seven thirds, for total prize money of $4.53 million. Of his nineteen wins, eight of those were Group 1 victories and he also ran the place on eleven other occasions in Group 1 races. His versatility was such that he won Group 1 races in Victoria, New South Wales and Queensland.

He was easy to recognise, and in fact, when he was racing he was the most recognisable horse in the world. It was as if someone had placed a stark white cloth over his head – he just stood out in the crowd. From a romantic's point of view, he looked as though he would not have been out of place being ridden by Geronimo.

We can talk about Apache Cat in the same breath as Tulloch as far as one record was concerned. He equalled Tulloch's feat of winning five Group 1 races in succession. Here are the races that Apache Cat won with jockey Corey Brown on board.

- Lightning Stakes: 2008
- Australia Stakes: 2008
- TJ Smith Stakes: 2008
- BTC Cup: 2008
- Doomben 10,000: 2008

Here are other major Group 1 races that he won during his career:

- Australian Guineas: 2006
- William Reid Stakes: 2009
- Doomben 10,000: 2009

To add to his overall success, his record was four Group 2 races, four Group 3 races and two Listed races. He was retired in December 2009 after sustaining a leg fracture during the running of the 2009 Cathay Pacific Hong Kong Sprint at Sha Tin Racecourse in Hong Kong. He was retired to the Living Legends Horse Retirement Home in Melbourne and keeps company with other greats like Might and Power, Better Loosen Up and Fields of Omagh.

He would turn heads, that's for sure.

Northerly blew into town
... and what an impression he left

There are some stories in racing that are extra special, not so much in what the horse ends up achieving, but more to the point that he or she should never have lived and achieved at all. Such was the case with the little colt born on 17 October 1996 at Oakland Park Stud in North Jindong, Western Australia.

Expectations were high because this little bloke was by the sire Serheed, a son of the great Nijinsky II. His dam was North Bell, with the dam's sire being the French stallion Bellewater. There was only one little problem: when the colt was born, he wasn't breathing. His quick-thinking owner-breeder Neville Duncan quickly started to massage the colt's heart area and before too long the colt was breathing normally and up on four wobbly legs. Northerly had hit the ground. It would have been a tragic outcome if there had been no-one around at the time of his birth.

Northerly was to team up with the trainer Fred Kersley, a very interesting individual, too, because his background was harness racing. Fred was a born-and-bred West Aussie boy and he was the very first Western Australian to obtain a dual license to train in the worlds of harness racing and thoroughbred horse racing. During a remarkable career as a driver, training pacers and trotters, he was head of Perth's driver's list seventeen times and also number one harness trainer on no less than fourteen occasions.

In 1989 he made the bold move to train thoroughbred racehorses, and he didn't have to wait too long for his first winner, Little Hero, at Belmont Park on 19 July, directly after being granted his training license. Even though his home base was Western Australia, Fred and Northerly made many raids to the east coast and took home some of the best silverware the Classic Group 1 races had to offer.

Northerly's record ended up being 37 starts for nineteen wins, seven seconds and two thirds with a total prize money of $9,341,850. His trainer and connections never forgot where it started, because even after the most torrid and successful campaigns in Sydney or Melbourne against some of the best horses in the world at the time, Northerly and Fred always came back to WA. Before a spell, he would thrill the Perth racing public by running in one of their major races – normally winning – so they were able to enjoy him as much as the rest of Australia.

He had such a courageous fighting spirit, and even though some great champions like Sunline would head him, he fought like a tiger and never gave up. It was appropriate that his nickname was the 'Fighting Tiger'.

In 2013, Greg Carpenter, Racing Victoria's General Manager of Racing, said that Fred Kersley and Northerly 'revitalised' racing in Western Australia.

Northerly won a total of nine Group 1 races, and just to make sure he placed himself in elite company, he won a few of them twice. Here is Northerly's great record of major race wins:

- Australian Cup: 2001, 2003

- WS Cox Plate: 2001, 2002
- Underwood Stakes: 2001, 2002
- Caulfield Cup: 2002
- Yalumba Stakes: 2001
- Railway Stakes: 2000

He was also given the following awards:

- Australian Middle Distance Champion: 2002, 2003
- Australian Champion Racehorse of the Year: 2003

During his racing career, it has been said by many who raced against him that at some stage they felt they had Northerly's measure in the straight, only to see him coming again, beating them on the line. Such was his never-say-die fighting spirit. In some of his major races, the public on course would have the same feeling when other horses headed him, but he just dug as deep as any horse could and proved them all wrong. He was a fighter, a real fighter.

During the 2004–05 racing season, Northerly was coming back from a torn tendon from 2003 and they once again made the trek east to contest the major Group races. As an eight-year-old, his performances in the Underwood and Turnbull Stakes prompted Fred to talk to connections and retire the great champion.

Sadly, on 10 May 2012, at sixteen years old and at his breeder's property in Busselton, Western Australia, the great Northerly had to be euthanised after a severe bout of colic.

Northerly blew in from the west and blew the opposition away.

He was the one and only Vain
… the yardstick by which all sprinters are judged

Here is a thoroughbred to which all other sprinters at some stage in their career are compared. Some would say he was 'simply the best', but the words of our legend of the track, the inimitable Bart Cummings, echo for us: 'Champions should never be compared, just appreciated'.

Vain was born on 5 September 1966. The proud owner-breeders were brothers Walter, Fred and George Johnson. His sire was Wilkes, a son of Court Martial. Vain's dam was Elated, a daughter of the great Orgoglio. A chestnut, he remained an entire and was trained throughout his career by Jim Moloney. His career record was fourteen starts for twelve firsts and two seconds, with prize money on his retirement in 1969 of $148,485, which now equates to just in excess of $5.4 million.

Vain dominated spring racing through 1968, 1969 and 1970. Looking at his breeding, it just shows that you never know where your next champ is coming from. His sire, Wilkes, won only two races in France with prize money equivalent to $2750. John Kelly took a punt and bought Wilkes in 1956 for £5000. Brought to Australia, he had immediate success in his first year, with his first crop producing nine winners. In his later years, he was to produce the champion mare Wenona Girl and three winners of the Golden Slipper, Vain (1969), John's Hope (1972) and Vivarchi (1976).

Vain's dam was Elated, and although she won ten races and produced a number of foals, he was her only Stakes winner – and what a winner he was. As a two-year-old he was unbeaten in Melbourne, and when sent to Sydney for the Two-Year-Old Triple Crown of 1969, he brilliantly won the Golden Slipper Stakes by four lengths, ran second in the Sires Produce Stakes to Beau Babylon, and finished his Sydney campaign with a brilliant ten length victory in the Champagne Stakes.

When he won the AJC Champagne Stakes in 1:09.2, it was considered to be the fastest time ever recorded for a two-year-old over 6 furlongs (1200 metres). In many of his races, his regular rider, Pat Hyland, could not hold him back to the field, and he was just as eye-catching in his three-year-old wins, winning many races with ridiculous ease, some by twelve lengths.

Here are some of Vain's major race wins and their Group status now.

- Maribyrnong Plate (1968), Group 3
- VRC Sires Produce Stakes (1969), Group 2
- Golden Slipper Stakes (1969), Group 1
- Champagne Stakes (1969), Group 1
- Freeway Stakes (1969), Group 1
- Ascot Vale Stakes (1969), Group 1

- Caulfield Guineas (1969), Group 1
- Craven A Stakes (1969), Group 1
- Linlithgow Stakes (1969), Group 2
- George Adams Handicap (1969), Group 1

Vain retired to Widden Stud at the end of his three-year-old season after sustaining an injury during a track gallop. He was extremely successful as a stallion, siring more than 370 winners, including two winners of the Golden Slipper, Sir Dapper (1983) and Inspired (1984).

Vain also received the following awards during his career:

- Australian Champion Racehorse of the Year (1968, 1969, 1970)
- Leading Sire in Australia (1983, 1984)
- Australian Racing Hall of Fame inductee (2003)

Along with Todman, Vain was considered the benchmark for all Australian sprinters – that is, until the great Black Caviar came on the scene. For the purists, there is a link between Black Caviar, the best sprinter in the world, retired in 2013, and Vain, who was the best sprinter in the world in 1969.

Vain is the great, great grandsire of Black Caviar on her dam's side, being the sire of the mare Song of Norway, foaled in 1982. Song of Norway was the dam of Scandinavia, who is the dam of Helsinge, who in turn is the dam of Black Caviar. Vain was the sire of Bespoken, who, when mated with Royal Academy, produced Bel Esprit, the sire of Black Caviar.

The champion sprinter died on 25 December 1991 at the age of 25 years. He certainly didn't die in vain.

Chatham, the Prince of Strides

… how good was this golden oldie?

While our memories fade over time, the ink in the record books doesn't and thank goodness for that. Here is one remarkable champion thoroughbred racehorse, a term we do not use loosely. We will illustrate his greatness by just telling you a simple fact about the WS Cox Plate – but first a little more about Chatham, the horse.

Chatham was born at Kia Ora Stud, Scone, in the Hunter region of

New South Wales in 1928, and was owned by a Mr EA Blair. Chatham's sire was the mighty Windbag (winner of the 1925 Melbourne Cup) and his grandsire was Magpie. His dam was Myosotis, a daughter of The Welkin (GB), who was by the 1899 English Triple Crown winner, Flying Fox. So being wise in hindsight, with a Melbourne Cup winner and an English Triple Crown winner running through his veins, maybe the writing was on the wall for this horse.

Chatham found himself at the 1930 Sydney yearling sales where he was sold for a little over 600 Guineas to trainer Ike Foulsham. His record shows that he had 45 starts for 23½ wins, 6½ seconds and ran one third on the one occasion. His prize money in the early 1930s amounted to £18,095. You will realise at the end of his achievements that on today's scale, he would have been a multimillionaire many times over.

Australia's WS Cox Plate is a Group 1 race held in Melbourne every year as part of the Spring Racing Carnival. It is run at the Moonee Valley Race Club in October. It is for three-year-olds and older and the race is considered to be the Weight for Age Championship for Australasia. The race is run over 2040 metres and, in 2013, the total prize money exceeded $3 million.

In 1999, the Cox Plate was added as part of the Emirates World Series Racing Championship, which is global testimony and acceptance of this race amongst some of the elite races throughout the world. The races in the 1999 world series races were:

- King George VI Stakes and Queen Elizabeth Stakes (UK)
- Japan Cup (Japan)
- Dubai World Cup (Dubai)
- Hong Kong Cup (Hong Kong)
- Canadian International Stakes (Canada)
- Irish Champion Stakes (Ireland)
- Breeders' Cup Turf and Breeders' Cup Classic (USA)
- WS Cox Plate (Australia)

No doubt, it is in very exclusive company.

Now back to Chatham and why he is regarded so highly. When we look back at the record of multiple winners of the Cox Plate, there is one standout, Kingston Town, who won the race on three occasions, in 1980, 1981 and 1982. We would concede that he would have to be the World Champion as far as Cox Plates go, but look at what Chatham achieved in the three Cox Plates he contested.

In those three Cox Plates, he ran second in 1931, won in 1932 and won again in 1934. Two out of three isn't bad, just one short of Kingston Town. Unfortunately for Chatham in 1931, he ran second to a horse that is regarded as The Best. Yes, he ran 2½ lengths behind the mighty Phar Lap. If there were no Phar Laps around in 1931 to contest the race with Chatham, we would be talking about him in exactly the same breath as Kingston Town.

Here is the list of Chatham's major wins.

- Craven Plate (1931, 1933, 1934)
- Linlithgow Stakes (1931, 1932, 1933)
- WS Cox Plate (1932, 1934)
- Epsom Handicap (1932, 1933)
- Canterbury Stakes (1933)
- Caulfield Stakes (1933)
- Hill Stakes (1933, 1934)
- Warwick Stakes (1933, 1934)
- All Aged Stakes (1934)
- Doncaster Handicap (1934)

Based on his wins listed above, there is no doubt that Chatham dominated racing in Australia in the early 1930s. In 2005, he was inducted into the Australian Racing Hall of Fame.

Chatham was retired to stud in 1935 in New South Wales and later to South Australia, where he was a leading sire. The great Chatham sired sixteen Stakes winners, who won 36 Stakes races between them.

He was the Prince of Strides.

Sydeston, the Tasmanian raider
... the Tassie champion!

When we talk about raiders from the Apple Isle, one horse that springs to mind is the great Sydeston. He certainly kept the flag flying for Tasmania, following in the footsteps of the 1970 Caulfield Cup winner,

Beer Street, and the 1972 Melbourne Cup winner, Piping Lane. Foaled in 1985, he was by the imported English sire St. Briavels, out of the mare Convatrice.

As a two-year-old in his first preparation, the 1000-metre races were definitely far too short for him, as he could not keep pace with the speedsters. However, in his second preparation, and stepping up in distance, the rangy little colt soon found his feet and won a 1200-metre event by four lengths.

Following wins in a couple of races in his second preparation and after running a place in a listed race, connections thought it best to put him away again to see if the improvement continued – and improve he did. First up in November 1988, Sydeston won a three-year-old handicap, and the decision was then made to further step up his distances and classes to see if he could cope. The connections were not disappointed.

After running third of seventeen in the Tasmanian Guineas over 1600 metres, he then won a restricted class handicap. Taking on the older horses as a three-year-old in the Devonport Cup, he ran second, and then was runner up to Bar Landy in the Tasmanian Derby over 2400 metres, followed by wins in a 2000-metre open welter and the Tasmanian St Leger. By this time, his connections were confident enough to make the trip to the mainland and take some rich pickings from Victorian racing.

After the successful campaign in his home state, Sydeston was transferred to the stables of Bon Hoystead in Melbourne in mid-1989. This very plain-looking gelding was about to show the doubters on the mainland what Tassie horses were all about.

Here are a few of Sydeston's classic wins:
- Moonee Valley Gold Cup (1989)
- Sandown Cup (1989)
- Mercedes Classic (1990)
- AJC Queen Elizabeth Stakes (1990)
- Liston Stakes (1990)
- Caulfield Stakes (1990)
- Caulfield Cup (1990)
- St George Stakes (1991)

Starting at 11/2, Sydeston's greatest victory was in the 1990 Caulfield Cup. Ridden by Mick Dittman, he delivered a barnstorming run and won in effortless style, defeating Water Boatman and Shuzohra.

In the autumn of 1991, Sydeston stormed home to beat Savage Toss and Kingston Rule in the 1800 metre St George Stakes. Following this win, he ran into such formidable opponents as Dr. Grace, Shaftsbury Avenue, Super Impose (again) and Surfer's Paradise. Not enjoying the success he had in previous campaigns, one would have to acknowledge that his third behind Surfer's Paradise in the 1991 WS Cox Plate was exceptional indeed.

As a seven-year-old, Sydeston returned in the spring. After two unplaced runs, he lined up in the 1992 WS Cox Plate; the leader, Palace Reign, fell, resulting in both Sydeston and Naturalism (the favourite) crashing to the turf. Neither horse was injured but connections thought it wise to give him another break.

In three runs as an eight-year-old, the old warrior failed to find his form and the decision was made to retire him. The brilliant son of St Briavels had given his connections a ride that they never thought possible. Sydeston started on 65 occasions for nineteen wins, seven seconds and ten thirds, for total prize money of $3.1 million.

What an amazing contribution by the Tassie raider.

Kindergarten
... there was certainly no playing around for him!

This giant of the New Zealand turf was foaled in New Zealand in 1937 and did most of his racing during the 1940s. Kindergarten was bred, owned and trained by EN Fitzgerald. What was unusual about the colt was that his sire, Klincardine, just happened to be a rig. A rig is explained as a male horse that has either one or both testes undescended and retained, or a male horse that has been improperly castrated. They can also display stallion tendencies, especially around mares.

During a career of 35 starts, Kindergarten had 25 wins, three seconds and three thirds, earning prize money of £16,000, which was a very healthy sum of money back then.

Kindergarten won many of New Zealand's major races. In his one and only trip to Australia, the champion galloper was allocated a prohibitive weight and dead-heated for third in the Warwick Stakes behind two great Australian champions in High Caste and Freckles. After the race, he became extremely unsettled, and so as not to risk any injury, his owner returned him to New Zealand.

When weights were announced for the Melbourne Cup, the Australian race handicappers thought so highly of the wins and weights that Kindergarten carried, he was given top weight in three consecutive years: 1942, 1943 and 1944.

Here are the eight highest weights allotted in the Melbourne Cup. As you can see, only five other horses have ever been given more weight than Kindergarten for our great race. Of all these horses, only two started in the Cup and both ran unplaced. One can see that Kindergarten was way up there with the best.

- Archer, 1863: 11 stone 4 lb (71.5 kg) – did not start (DNS)
- The Barb, 1869: 11 stone 7 lb (73 kg) – DNS
- Carbine, 1891: 10 stone 12 lb (69 kg) – DNS
- Eurythmic, 1921: 10 stone 5 lb (65.5 kg) – 24th
- Phar Lap, 1931: 10 stone 10 lb (68 kg) – 8th
- Peter Pan, 1935: 10 stone 5 lb (65.5 kg) – DNS
- Kindergarten, 1943: 10 stone 6 lb (66 kg) – DNS
- Bernborough, 1946: 10 stone 9 lb (67.5 kg) – DNS

As is the case with some champions, Kindergarten had a rather low-key start to his racing. His first three starts were three minor places but then he hit his straps by winning his next ten in a row. Among his victories as a three-year-old were the Great Northern Derby and the Wellington Cup. In the first of his two victories in the Easter Handicap, Kindergarten carried 9 stone 11 lb (62 kg), which was the highest weight ever carried by a three-year-old in that race.

His Auckland Cup victory in 1943 was regarded as his greatest performance. He carried 10 stone 2 lb (64.5 kg), which was 17 lb (7.5 kg) over weight-for-age, and still beat the quality field by five lengths in a then-record time of 3 minutes 22 seconds for the

2 miles (3200 metres). Due to his race and weight record, he is today regarded as the greatest horse ever to have raced in New Zealand.

Here are Kindergarten's major wins:

- Awapuni Gold Cup (1941)
- Wellington Cup (1941)
- Great Northern Derby (1941)
- Easter Handicap (1941, 1942)
- Auckland Cup (1942)

Kindergarten was one of five inaugural inductees into the New Zealand Racing Hall of Fame in 2006, alongside such other turf immortals as Carbine, Gloaming, Phar Lap and Sunline. Very good company indeed!

Here's to Mainbrace!

... giving new meaning to 'splice the mainbrace'

This thoroughbred is what dreams are made of. A chestnut colt by Admiral's Luck (GB), Mainbrace was foaled in New Zealand in 1947, and he was owned and bred by T Fraser. He had 25 starts for 23 wins and two seconds, and in the early 1950s he amassed prize money of nearly £29,000, an amount of money that could have bought a street full of suburban houses at the time.

When Mainbrace won his seventeenth race in succession, he didn't have it all his own way. The going was extremely soft, and in a large field he got up right on the line in the Harcourt Stakes.

Mainbrace broke down after winning that seventeenth race, and he was immediately retired. One wonders whether, if he had remained sound, he may have broken Gloaming's and Desert Gold's Australasian record of nineteen wins in a row. On eight occasions, Mainbrace either broke or equalled race records.

He remains one of the New Zealand's all-time great champions. Just to show how good he was, here are some of Mainbrace's top class wins:

- Great Northern Guineas (1950)
- Great Northern Derby (1951)
- New Zealand St Leger (1951)
- Awapuni Gold Cup (1951)

- North Island Challenge Stakes (1951)

Retired to stud in 1953, Mainbrace was very disappointing as a sire – as can be the case with some outstanding individuals. His best progeny would have been Forebrace. In 2008, Mainbrace was inducted into the New Zealand Racing Hall of Fame.

A great racehorse from the Land of the Long White Cloud.

Freeing Emancipation
... bought as a broodmare, but could she race?

The dictionaries will tell us that her name means 'an act of being freed or liberated'. I think she certainly set free copious amounts of money from the bookmakers' bags. To understand how Emancipation started on a racetrack, and why she was probably lucky to do so, let us have a look at her breeding.

Her breeder was Mark Hough of New South Wales, who bought her mum, Ammo Girl, from the late great TJ Smith when he found that she had issues with her body and bone structure and her sire was not setting the world on fire in the breeding barn. The sire of her dam, Ammo Girl, was none other than the 'Goondiwindi Grey', the great Gunsynd. Of course we remember Gunsynd being grey, and his daughter Ammo Girl was grey, so it was no surprise that Emancipation was a grey as well when she was born on 15 October 1979.

Is it any wonder that Mark had her earmarked as a broodmare? But her sire was the great Bletchingly, a son of Biscay, an absolute flyer. At least on the sire's side there was a reason to get excited, but there was not a lot on the dam's side, except for Gunsynd, and he wasn't proving to be a sire equal to expectations.

When Emancipation was of age, Mark offered her to trainer Neville Begg and recommended that he try and find someone to lease her and race her. She ended up not racing as a two-year-old, and in the next two years her record amounted to 28 starts for nineteen wins and one second. When she retired in 1984, she had amassed prize money to the tune of $550,510, which was a massive sum at the time. The year that she retired she was given the distinction of being named Australian Champion Racehorse of the Year.

Emancipation won six Group 1 races and they all happened to be in Sydney. In her first year racing as a three-year-old, Emancipation won ten of her thirteen starts and beat some pretty good horses along the way, including the great Manikato. As a four-year-old, she won nine of her fifteen starts.

Here are her most important victories:

- STC George Ryder Stakes (1983)
- AJC Doncaster Handicap (1983)
- AJC George Main Stakes (1983)
- STC Rosemount Classic (1984)
- STC George Ryder Stakes (1984)
- AJC All Aged Stakes (1984)
- VRC Edward Manifold Stakes (1982)
- STC Canterbury Stakes (1983)
- AJC Chelmsford Stakes (1983)
- AJC Apollo Stakes (1984)
- AJC Chipping Norton Stakes (1984)

Mark Hough certainly must have felt vindicated, because Emancipation also had great success as a broodmare. She was put to Vice Regal, and Royal Pardon was the result. A Stakes winner, he was also a grey colt, and as a three-year-old, he ran second to Research in the 1989 AJC Derby.

Emancipation was also mated with Kenmare, resulting in the filly Virage; she was also teamed up with Palace Music, which resulted in another filly, La Suffragette. Both Virage and La Suffragette have gone on to produce multiple Group 1 winners in Virage De Fortune and Railings.

Another great grey for the record books.

The determined Bonecrusher
... he was the toast of Australasia

When it comes to naming a horse, we don't think there has ever been a name that so suited a horse, his career and his sheer guts and determination as much as Bonecrusher. This little colt made his way into the world on 17 September 1982. His sire was Pag-Asa, who was by the great sire Kaoru Star; while his dam was Imitation, a daughter of Oakville.

During Bonecrusher's illustrious career he was owned by Peter Mitchell and was trained by Frank Ritchie. He had 44 starts for eighteen firsts, five seconds and twelve thirds, with prize money totalling AUD$1,679,495. He was the first New Zealand thoroughbred to become a 'millionaire'.

Bonecrusher was a bargain buy for Peter Mitchell at the Waikato Yearling Sales, having been knocked down for $3250. Interestingly, maybe the stage for greatness was set unknowingly, as he was nicknamed 'Big Red' in his early days, and that just so happens to be the same nickname given to Phar Lap, Secretariat and Man o' War – great company indeed.

Sometimes great champions are defined by their accomplishments and nothing else needs to be said, but it was the race call of the 1986 WS Cox Plate that reverberates with racing enthusiasts even today. If you ever have the opportunity to look at it on YouTube and enjoy the race call again, you will certainly know what we mean.

The race was called by one of our most respected and revered race callers, Bill Collins. That year, the Cox Plate was being billed as the Match Race of the Century, as a race between the two Kiwis Bonecrusher and Our Waverley Star. Typically, it was a normal and fiercely run Cox Plate but everything changed at the 800-metre mark when Bill Collins said, 'Here come the New Zealanders – and have they gone too early?'

It was a dogged affair from the 800-metre mark, around the turn and all the way down the Moonee Valley straight. First it was Bonecrusher edging ahead, then Our Waverley Star putting the nose in front, with the rest of the field running for third-prize money. Just as Bonecrusher came again right on the line, Bill Collin's voice just echoes through the years, even today: 'It's Bonecrusher, and he races into equine immortality'.

Here are a few of Bonecrusher's victories:
- Bayer Classic (1985)
- New Zealand Derby (1985)
- Air New Zealand Stakes (1986, 1988)

- Tancred Stakes (1986)
- Australian Derby (1986)
- Caulfield Stakes (1986)
- WS Cox Plate (1986)
- Underwood Stakes (1986)
- Australian Cup (1987)

He was also declared Australian Horse of the Year in 1987.

Later in the year that he won the Cox Plate, Bonecrusher was the pre-post favourite for the Japan Cup, where he was going to run against the best racehorses in the world. Unfortunately, Bonecrusher contracted a life-threatening virus in Tokyo and had to be withdrawn. Almost as a statement from 'Big Red' and his connections, he regained his health and early in 1987 went on to win the Australian Cup – if a horse could talk, he was probably saying, 'I told you I was good'.

He continued racing up until he was seven years old, and although winning a few races, he never scaled the dizzy heights that he showed through 1985, 1986 and 1987. Bonecrusher was certainly a horse that proved to have those championship qualities when the chips were down.

Bonecrusher, Equine Immortal.

The Barb, 1860s-style racing

... he was known as the Black Demon

When the 'vault' is opened on a horse this far back, sometimes it is difficult to get all of the information that you need to do the horse justice. Even though it is more than 150 years since he was born, time has not diminished The Barb's standing among the greatest champions that Australia has seen on a racecourse.

The Barb is quite an unusual name, but when we look at the history books it appears that it was very appropriate indeed. It was a breed of horse used by the ancient Moors in the Mediterranean area and northern Africa. They were known for their speed and their ability to maintain their pace over long distances, and were not unlike the Arabian breed.

The record books will show that The Barb was by the sire Sir Hercules (1873), with his grandsire being Cap-a-Pie. Cap-a-Pie's sire was The Colonel, who won the St Leger in England in 1828, so there was some class on the sire's side. The Colonel proved to be a great sire, siring eighteen Stakes winners, who collectively won 45 Stakes races. The Barb's dam was Fair Ellen, also known as Young Gulnare, and her sire was The Doctor (GB).

He was born in 1863 near Bathurst, Australia's oldest inland settlement, just 200 km west of Sydney, New South Wales. In 1864, Honest John Tait, a well-respected trainer of thoroughbreds, bought The Barb as a yearling for 200 guineas.

The Barb was black in colour and black in temperament, and this is how he earned his nickname of the Black Demon. He was a very headstrong animal with a mind of his own. Having his very first start in a race, he showed the darker side of his nature by getting rid of the rider and just bolting out of sight.

The record books let us down a little here, but what we do know was that he contested 23 races for fifteen wins. Unfortunately there is no record that shows his placing in the remaining eight races. His prize money, in the 1860s, was listed as over £18,000. One would say, without a fear of contradiction, that if we fast forward to today's prize money and the winner's share of a couple of the races that he won then, his prize money would be approaching $5 million in today's money for just those couple of races. He certainly made his mark back in the day.

Racing first up after a spell as a three-year-old, he underlined his potential by winning the AJC Derby by two lengths. That same year he started favourite in the Melbourne Cup and won that race narrowly. In the following two years he went on and won the Sydney Cup, emphasising that he did indeed enjoy the qualities of the barb horses that roamed with the Moors centuries before – speed and endurance.

Here are some of The Barb's famous victories:

- Nursery Stakes (1865)
- AJC Derby (1866)
- Melbourne Cup (1866)

- Australasian Champion Stakes (1866)
- Launceston Town Plate (1867)
- Port Phillip Stakes (1867)
- Sydney Cup (1867, 1868)
- Craven Plate (1868)
- VRC Royal Park Stakes (1868)
- AJC Metropolitan Handicap (1868)
- Queen's Plate (1868)

In 2004, he was inducted into the Australian Racing Hall of Fame.

The Barb won both Sydney Cups of 1868 and 1869; in the latter Cup he carried 10 stone 8 lb (67 kg). As a five-year-old he won all seven starts he contested. His trainer, Honest John Tait, proved to be no slouch when it came to training distance horses, as he went on to train another three Melbourne Cup winners: Glencoe (1868), The Pearl (1871) and The Quack (1872).

The Barb retired from racing and went to a stud in the Hunter Valley region in New South Wales. As is the case with many great champions, The Barb just didn't seem to produce offspring that matched the ability of his sire. In 1888, he died at the age of 25 years, at a stud at Mitta Mitta.

A demon on the track.

The long and winding Strawberry Road
... he put Australia on the world map

What a ride this stallion gave us. Strawberry Road not only entertained all racehorse lovers in Australia, but he had a following all over the world due to what he had achieved – and what he could have achieved had a particular jockey followed instructions on the day.

Born on 28 September 1979, Strawberry Road was by the Nijinsky horse, Whiskey Road. The interest centred on his mare, Giftisa. She was a New Zealand product and her sire was Rich Gift, who just happened to be the grandson of the great sire Nasrullah. Giftisa had had just the seven starts for one win and only $1400 in prize money. Things weren't going to plan on the racetrack, and with that she had been sent to stud. That's when she was mated to the then-unknown imported stallion Whiskey Road, who was standing at Strathallan Stud just outside Canberra.

The beauty of horse racing is that this colt that had only cost $4500 went on to dominate racing in Australia and Europe. Although he had only minor success in America, he ended up with prize money then totalling US$1,713,958. He started on 45 occasions, with seventeen wins, seven seconds and seven thirds.

Strawberry Road was initially owned by media mogul Kerry Packer, Ray Stehr and John 'Singo' Singleton. Cartoonist Larry Pickering and Dr Gerry Rose, who were good friends of the group, also became small stakeholders in the colt.

During Strawberry Road's career, he was sold to Daniel Wildenstein (France) and later to Allen Paulson and Bruce McNall (United States). His training started in Queensland with Doug Bougoure, who then handed the reins to John Nicholls, who looked after the horse during the latter part of his racing in Australia and then in Germany. He was then trained by Patrick Biancone in France, and finally by Charles Whittingham in the United States.

Strawberry Road started late in his two-year-old season, and at his third start in August 1982, he won his Maiden at Eagle Farm. After a spell in Queensland he then strung together four wins in a row, so it was off to Sydney to mix it with the 'big guns' – and mix it he did. In 1983, he ended up winning ten races for the season, including three Group 1 races. During that very successful campaign, he managed to win these major Group 1 races in Australia:

- Rosehill Guineas (1983)
- AJC Derby (1983)
- Queensland Derby (1983)
- Freeway Stakes (1983)
- WS Cox Plate (1983)

At that stage, Europe and America were beckoning. Here are Strawberry Road's major wins in Europe and America:

- Grosser Preis von Baden, Germany (1984)
- Prix d'Harcourt, France (1985)
- Grand Prix de Saint-Cloud, France (1985)
- Arcadia Handicap, United States (1986)

He was also awarded the following titles in Australia and abroad:
- Australian Champion Racehorse of the Year (1983)
- German Champion Older Horse (1984)
- Australian Racing Hall of Fame inductee (2009)
- Equine Hall of Fame inductee, Queensland (2009)

Strawberry Road had many wins, but here is the story of the one that got away – The Arc, in France.

Strawberry Road's connections can remember vividly the fifth he ran in the Prix de l'Arc de Triomphe, because the race had been there for the taking. If you have the opportunity to watch footage of the great race, we are sure you would want to ask the jockey the same question that 'Singo' did immediately after the race.

After unsuccessfully trying to get Lester Piggott to ride Strawberry Road in the Arc, the connections then tried to get the great Aussie hoop Mick 'The Enforcer' Dittman over there. In the end, the talks broke down and the connections had to settle for the English jockey Greville Starkey.

The plan in the 2400-metre Arc was a simple one: Strawberry Road would sit behind the leaders and go to sleep, because he never pulled in his races. Partway down the straight, after showing him some daylight, the thoroughbred's racing style would dictate that he would then just go, go, go – after all, his runs were on the board.

There are two major issues that we should consider here. The first is Longchamp, the track. Most readers would know how long the straight is at Flemington – very long indeed. Longchamp has a very similar straight, so it was one of those tracks where the winning run came closer to the post than the turn.

The second issue is that in Europe, there are some horses that don't attract any bets in a race because the good judges perceive that they are going to be used as pacemakers for other more fancied horses.

No horse has ever led at the turn in the Arc and gone on to win. It is like leading at the turn at Flemington, competing in a 2500-metre race. As soon as they turned, Greville Starkey took off on Strawberry Road like he was a pacemaker for another horse. The rider of the eventual winner, Sagace, who had been shadowing Strawberry Road throughout the race, could not believe his luck when Greville Starkey took off on the turn; he just sat back and bided his time, and then made the run that all the connections were expecting Strawberry Road to make.

Strawberry Road ran a gallant fifth out of 22 starters. Even the French newspapers were scathing with their attack on Starkey, nicknaming him 'The Assassin'.

Is it any wonder that John Singleton nearly throttled Greville Starkey when returning to the enclosure? He explained to him, as only 'Singo' could, that his ride was against all instructions and asked him politely 'if he was deaf, dumb or just plain stupid'.

There have been lots of theories about that ride by Starkey, but for the sake of walking over a man's reputation where he cannot defend himself, we will instead leave it up to the history books. Needless to say, after Makybe Diva had won her three Melbourne Cups in Australia and there was some talk of her going to contest the Prix de l'Arc de Triomphe, John Singleton had this advice for her owner, Tony Santic: 'Make sure you go over there with your horse, take your trainer and for God's sake, take your own jockey.'

Strawberry Road was retired to stud by his American owners to Brookside Farm in Versailles, Kentucky. He went on to become a very successful sire of 368 horses, including 233 winners, some of whom won in elite company. After a short illness in 1995, the great Strawberry Road was humanely euthanised after fracturing a leg while recovering from a bout of pneumonia.

Strawberry Road, he was a true world champion of racing.

Jumping to conclusions
... and how high could they soar?

Over the decades, Australia has been privileged to see some amazing hurdlers and steeplechasers. Champion steeplechasers Karasi and Crisp have already been extensively covered in our two other books, *Off the Track* and *At the Track*.

Here are the brief resumes of some other champion hurdlers and steeplechasers.

Redleap

Foaled in 1884, by Dante, Redleap was recognised as 'the Carbine of the jumpers' by the end of his racing career. In 1889, he lined up in Australia's Grand National Hurdle at only his second race start. By race end, he had done the impossible, by winning the race at his first-ever start over hurdles. Although he faltered at the final jump, he still went on to defeat Corythus and claim the lion's share of the £1340 prize money.

However, Redleap was to suffer from recurring injury problems, and he did not appear over the jumps again until the 1892 Grand National Hurdle. In a field of 23, he ran away to win quite easily from Fire King.

His jumping ability must have been quite extraordinary, because just one week later he defeated Confidence by three lengths in the Grand National Steeplechase, carrying more than 2 stone 7 lb (15.5 kg) greater than the second place-getter, becoming the first horse to win Australia's Grand National double. He followed up one month later by winning the Caulfield Grand National Steeplechase carrying 13 stone 12 lb (88 kg). That race was the forerunner to what we know now as the Australian Steeplechase.

In 1893, Redleap was given a record 14 stone 10 lb (93 kg) in the Great Eastern Steeplechase at Warrnambool, Victoria. His owner, Septimus Miller, the Chairman of the Victorian Racing Club (VRC), decided not to run the horse, instead setting him for the Melbourne Cup even though he was a hurdler. Unfortunately, Redleap broke down, and he was immediately retired to take up stud duties at Mr Miller's property at Bacchus Marsh.

No horse in the history of major hurdle and steeplechase races has ever carried more weight to victory than Redleap. His winning distances ranged from 3 miles (4800 metres) to 3.25 miles (5200 metres). The Redleap Steeplechase is held each year at the Sandown Hillside Racecourse over 3300 metres.

Redleap raced on only seven occasions, for four wins and prize money of £5409. His wins were:

- 1889 Grand National Hurdle – 9 stone 8 lb (61 kg)
- 1892 Grand National Hurdle – 11 stone 10 lb (74.5 kg)

- 1892 Grand National Steeplechase – 13 stone 3 lb (84.5 kg)
- 1892 Australian Steeplechase – 13 stone 12 lb (87.5 kg)

There were two schools of thought on how Redleap was named. The first was that when Redleap was trialling the jumps, carrying the owner's colours of crimson, someone mentioned how high he could leap over the hurdles, hence 'Redleap'.

However, the second and more likely theory was that while travelling through the outer suburbs of Melbourne, owner Mr Miller noticed a sign, 'Redleap', over the front door of a house; with his crimson racing colours, he decided that would be the name of his horse.

And the name of the gentleman who rode Redleap in all his races? Mr William Samuel Cox. That gentleman's other claim to fame was to have the Southern Hemisphere's richest weight-for-age race named in his honour: the WS Cox Plate.

Mosstrooper

Foaled in 1921, by Kenilworth, Mosstrooper raced in the late 1920s and early 1930s. Before turning to jumps racing, Mosstrooper had an inglorious record on the racetrack, having run second only once in his first eighteen starts. Obviously Mosstrooper's owner thought that the horse was definitely not earning his keep, so the son of the French stallion Kenilworth was put up for sale. He was sold for £200 to trainer and horse dealer Gus Powell, who had all intentions of exporting him to the Indian Army.

However, while being used as a hack to round up cattle at Powell's property, Mosstrooper showed the trainer that there may be another chapter in his life – he was a natural jumper. So it was off for some intensive training, and didn't he learn his craft well?

On retirement, Mosstrooper had recorded 79 starts, with eleven wins, all over the jumps, and prize money earnings of £14,191. His record may never be surpassed.

Here are his major wins:

- 1st – 1929 Australian Hurdle – 9 stone 10 lb (61.5 kg)
- 1st – 1929 Australian Steeplechase – 10 stone 9 lb (67.5 kg)
- 1st – 1930 Australian Steeplechase – 11 stone 12 lb (75.5 kg)
- 1st – 1930 Grand National Hurdle – 10 stone 7 lb (66.5 kg)

- 1st – 1930 Grand National Steeplechase – 11 stone 10 lb (74.5 kg)
- 2nd – 1929 Grand National Steeplechase – 9 stone 6 lb (60 kg)
- 3rd – 1931 Grand National Hurdle – 12 stone 3 lb (77.5 kg)
- 3rd – 1932 Grand National Steeplechase – 12 stone 7 lb (79 kg)
- 3rd – 1933 Grand National Steeplechase – 12 stone 3 lb (77.5 kg)

Mosstrooper's record of being the only horse to ever win the Australian Hurdle / Australian Steeplechase and the Grand National Hurdle / Grand National Steeplechase doubles still stands today. Each year, Bendigo hosts the 3600-metre Mosstrooper Steeplechase.

The epitaph on Mosstrooper's tombstone says it all: 'Best Horse Ever'. It was certainly India's loss and Australia's gain!

Redditch

Foaled in 1927, by Red Dennis, Redditch was purchased as a yearling for 75 guineas, leased and then trained by William (Fred) Hoysted. He showed very little as a two- and three-year-old, although he did win one race in his first twelve starts. One thing of interest in his breeding was that his dam, Kenilworth Queen, was by the same sire as the great Mosstrooper, so the thought was that if he turned to jumps racing over much longer distances, he might just be able to put things together and turn out quite a 'breadwinner'. And that he did. He was in a league of his own.

In 1932, Redditch won five hurdle races in Australia, and finished the season with a great third in the Grand National Hurdle behind Polygonum. Now it was time to step up to the higher steeplechase fences, and this is where he made his mark. In 1933 he won the Grand National Steeplechase by eight lengths, breaking the race record by 3.75 seconds.

The race handicapper didn't miss him when weights were issued for all the main events, and in August 1933, Redditch was given an incredible 12 stone 13 lb (82 kg) in the Australian Steeplechase. He didn't disappoint and brilliantly defeated the great Mosstrooper, who placed second.

In 1934, Redditch won the Australian Steeplechase, and he then ran second to Woodlace in the Grand National Steeplechase, carrying an astonishing 2 stone 9 lb (17 kg) more than the winner.

On 13 July 1934, starting as 7/2 favourite, Redditch was struck by disaster in the Grand National Steeplechase. On the first circuit, in the home straight, Redditch hit the log fence and fractured his thigh, to the horror of the large crowd. Unfortunately he had to be euthanised. Thus ended the career of one of Australia's finest steeplechasing thoroughbreds.

Redditch had 49 starts, with fourteen wins, twelve of which were over the jumps. His stakes earnings were £7768, and he won at distances ranging from 3 miles (4800 metres) to 3.25 miles (5200 metres). Each year, the Sandown Hillside Racecourse hosts the Redditch Steeplechase, run over 3400 metres.

Here are some of his major race wins:
- 1st – 1933 Grand National Steeplechase – 12 stone 3 lb (75 kg)
- 1st – 1933 Australian Steeplechase – 12 stone 13 lb (82 kg)
- 1st – 1934 Australian Steeplechase – 12 stone 13 lb (82 kg)
- 2nd – 1934 Grand National Steeplechase – 12 stone 7 lb (79 kg)
- 3rd – 1932 Grand National Hurdle – 11 stone 9 lb (70 kg)

The death of Redditch resulted in a lengthy debate regarding the merits of solid fences on the Flemington steeplechase course. It was decided that from 1935 all solid fences would be replaced by brush steeplechase fences. Sanity prevailed. Redditch was a horse who altered history.

Pedro's Pride

Foaled in 1950, by Don Pedro, Pedro's Pride is recognised as Australia's greatest jumping mare. After being placed once from her first sixteen starts on the flat, it was thought that maybe her desire to win races was not there. It was either the breeding barn or the knackery for her.

However, through her sire, Don Pedro, the 1947 Moonee Valley Cup winner, she can be traced back to the great English stallion Gainsborough. Maybe long-distance jumps races might just bring out the best in her? Well, they did, in quite spectacular fashion.

In 1956, Pedro's Pride won three steeplechase races at Caulfield; in 1957 she won another five jumps races at the same venue. She had arrived on the jumping scene in spectacular fashion.

A huge mare, Pedro's Pride carried a massive weight to defeat Blacksmith in the 1957 Grand National Steeplechase, carrying 2 stone 7 lb (15.5 kg) more in weight. In the 1957 Australian Steeplechase, she carried a staggering 3 stone 7 lb (19.5 kg) more than runner-up Paganom.

Her ability to carry such huge weights left the Australian public in awe of her amazing steeplechase ability. The 1958 AV Hiskens Steeplechase runner-up, Greek Legend, even carried a mere 3 stone 4 lb (21 kg) less than her – a phenomenal effort by Pedro's Pride.

On retirement, Pedro's Pride had won ten of her last twelve jumps races, and had earned approximately £9000 in prize money. Here are her major wins:

- 1st – 1957 Grand National Steeplechase – 11 stone 12 lb (75.5 kg)
- 1st – 1957 Australian Steeplechase – 12 stone 6 lb (79 kg)
- 1st – 1958 AJ Hiskens Steeplechase – 12 stone 7 lb (79.5 kg)

Pedro's Pride's winning distances ranged from 2 miles (3200 metres) to 3.5 miles (5600 metres). Each year the Sandown Hillside Racecourse hosts the Pedro's Pride Steeplechase, run over 3400 metres.

She was one huge mare that carried huge weights and had a huge heart.

CHAPTER 9
Trivia Tales

Our trivia in *Off the Track* (2012) and *At the Track* (2013) highlighted the curiosities of unknown facts about thoroughbred horse racing, but in this book we have also endeavoured to tell the stories around these types of curiosities, so we are calling the chapter 'Trivia Tales'. We found many of the following trivia tales hidden within the short stories told in our books – some come from extra paragraphs throughout our original manuscripts and some take little more than one line to explain.

Berry, Berry unusual
... *which one is which?*

When jockey Nathan Berry, riding Unencumbered, won the 2014 Gold Coast Magic Millions in January 2014, he created something that may never be beaten in our lifetime, anywhere in the world.

His brother Tommy had previously won the same race in 2011, on Karuta Queen, and in 2012, on Driefontein.

This is so unusual because it makes Tommy and Nathan Berry the only identical twins to win the same million dollar race. The race is worth $2 million in prize money.

A Berry, Berry fine effort!

The Testers were Dopes

It was reported that quite a number of horses were disqualified in Queensland in 1985 for testing positive to the stimulant caffeine. There were far too many cases to not ask some big questions. There were red faces all around when the testing sticks were found to be tainted and, therefore, faulty. All fines and disqualifications were lifted.

Could the testing sticks have been already used? Perhaps stirring a coffee cup?

Run for your lives!
... unexpected, unusual and luckily unexploded!

In January 2013, contractors working at Darwin's Fanny Bay Racecourse unearthed an unexpected and unusual object – an unexploded bomb from World War II. It had been there since Japanese aircraft attacked and bombed the city in 1942.

Smile, please!
... and then there were three

Australia's first recorded triple dead-heat for first place happened on Derby Day in November 1956, when Pandie Sun (ridden by Bill Williamson), Ark Royal (ridden by Reg Heather), and Fighting Force (ridden by Jack Purtell) hit the line together in the Hotham Handicap, now known as the Lexus Quality. The judge could not separate the trio (Australia's first photo finish camera was installed at Flemington in 1946).

However, the first official triple dead-heat caught by camera was at the Aqueduct Racecourse, New York, on 10 June 1944. The judges could not split Bossuet, Wait-a-Bit and Loyal Smith.

Just split the riding fees, boys.

The 'Flasher' and his million-dollar payday

… the Tassie champ with his hoof on the till

Geegees Blackflash, a seven-year-old gelding as of February 2014, by Clangalang, from La Quita, races in the shadow of previous great thoroughbreds from the Apple Isle. Although they reached very dizzy heights indeed in Australia, this fellow currently stands alone on the Tasmanian racing scene.

Malua, the Tassie trier initially called Bagot, became a legend in the 1880s, winning the Melbourne Cup, the Grand National Hurdle and the Oakleigh Plate. Then Beer Street left Tasmania as a solid racehorse performer and went on to win the 1970 Melbourne Cup.

Piping Lane won a Hobart Cup before venturing to the mainland and was triumphant in the 1972 Melbourne Cup. Finally, last but not least, the great Sydeston, a young Tasmanian stayer, came to the Australian mainland and carried all before him. He became a weight-for-age champion in the 1990s and won many group races including the 1990 Caulfield Cup.

As a young horse, Geegees Blackflash suffered a bleeding attack and was put out for a long spell. He was owned by Paul Gerard and trained by John Luttrell, and his connections did not want to put the burden of travel on their young horse, so they decided that he would compete only in Tasmania. What a very wise decision that turned out to be.

The significance of that decision can be seen in Geegees Blackflash's record at the time of writing (up until 27 February 2014). He had just finished third in the 2014 Launceston Cup, as a seven-year-old behind the favourite, Epingle. That placing took his prize money to the very brink of the magic million: $937,150, from a total of 53 starts, with seventeen wins and 21 placings.

He is the only horse to win the 'big 3' of Tasmanian racing:
- Tasmanian Derby, 2400 metres (2010)
- Hobart Cup, 2200 metres (2012)
- Launceston Cup, 2400 metres (2013)

It seems that it is only a matter of time before the 'Flasher' salutes the judge and passes that elusive $1,000,000 mark. Who knows? He may have already achieved that milestone before you've had the chance to sit back and read *From the Track*.

Geegees Blackflash: Australia salutes the Tassie champ.

Words of wisdom and wit

...from hapless punters all over the world

I met with an accident on the way to the track; I arrived safely. *– Joe E Lewis*

Dear Lord, help me break even, I need the money. *– Jerry Smith*

A rich man is nothing but a poor man with money. *– WC Fields*

A racetrack is a place where windows clean people. *– Danny Thomas*

I backed a great horse yesterday! It took seven horses to catch him.
   – *Henny Youngman*

If you're going through hell, just keep going. – *Sir Winston Churchill*

In most betting shops, you will see three windows marked 'Bet
   Here', and only one window with the legend 'Pay Out'. – *Jeffrey
   Bernard*

A man that don't love a horse, there is something wrong with him. –
   Will Rogers

 A racehorse is an animal that can take thousands of people for a
   ride at the same time. – *anon.*

I backed a horse last week at ten to one. It came in at quarter past
   four. – *Tommy Cooper*

George said to Fred, 'I put $20 on a horse last week and he came in
   at 25 to one.' 'Wow! You must be loaded', said Fred. 'Not really',
   said George, 'the rest of the field came in at 12.30.' – *Ben A.*

The tipster said this horse would walk in. It did, but all the others
   galloped. – *anon.*

My horse came in so late the jockey was wearing pyjamas. – *anon.*

My horse was so late getting home, he tiptoed into the stable.
   – *anon.*

What's the difference between praying in church and at the track?
   At the track you really mean it! – *anon.*

Paying alimony is like feeding hay to a dead horse. – *Groucho Marx*

Nothing can make a fool of a man, like a horse. – *anon.*

The only way to end up with a small fortune on a racetrack is to
   start off with a big one. – *anon.*

I do not say that all those who go racing are rogues and vagabonds,
   but I do say that all rogues and vagabonds seem to go racing. –
   Sir Abe Bailey

The English Derby is a little like your first experience at sex – hectic,
   strenuous, and memorably pleasant and over before you know
   it. – *Bill Bryson*

Horse racing is a great equalizer. It doesn't matter if you are a
   peasant farmer, if you have a good racehorse, the Kings and
   Queens come to you. There is nothing like it. – *Jack Klugman*

A horse is dangerous at both ends and uncomfortable in the middle.
– *anon.*

I've often said there's nothing better for the inside of a man than the outside of a horse. – *Will Rogers*

I am not one of the people who believe that the main reason why a chap becomes a bookmaker is because he is too scared to steal and too heavy to become a jockey. – *Noel Whitcombe*

On being asked by Channel 4's Derek Thompson if he owned horses: 'No, son. I don't like anything that eats while I sleep.' – *Larry Hagman*

A jockey was nicknamed Sunshine, because he always came after the reins. – *anon.*

I'm lucky because I have an athlete between my legs. – *Willie Carson*

What the Best said about the best
… any wonder he had a good time while he was on top?

Legendary Irish footballer Georgie Best just stated the obvious.

'I always wanted more – more of everything.'

'I've stopped drinking, but only when I'm asleep.'

'I spent 95 per cent of my money on gambling, booze, birds and fast cars. The other 5 per cent, I squandered.'

It's 2014, not the 1940s!

It is documented in Darwin's Fanny Bay Gaol records of the 1940s and 1950s, 'prisoners are sometimes allowed to attend the races but after the last race, win or lose, they go back to their cells'.

Just imagine that today … 'Rollcall, quick!'

Two Derbies within 200 miles!
… but it was the same race and the same winner – how?

In the long history of Australian racing, we have read about and seen many colts who have been dual Derby winners and some even good enough to have been multiple Derby winners. The last dual Derby winner was Rebel Raider, who won the VRC Derby in 2008 and the South Australian Derby in 2009. The last triple Derby winner was Stormy Rex, in 1977, who won the South Australian Jockey Club (SAJC), Victorian Racing Club (VRC) and Western Australian Turf Club (WATC) Derbies.

The last and only three-year-old to win four Derbies was Dayana in 1972. He won the SAJC, VRC, WATC and Australian Derbies. The Australian Derby was last run in 1992.

But did you know that there was one horse that won a Derby, waited a few months, and won the same Derby again some 230 miles (368 km) away. It happened over 140 years ago, and it happened in Queensland, Australia.

In 1868, 1869 and 1870, the Queensland Derby was held in Gayndah, a citrus-growing region north-west of Brisbane. The winners were Hermit, Zambesi and Grafton, respectively. A few months after Grafton had won his Derby in 1870, a seemingly obscure decision was made to run the race once again, this time in Brisbane. The horses lined up again, and for the second time the Queensland Derby was won by Grafton.

At a meeting in 1871, racing authorities decided that the Queensland Derby would be a permanent fixture of the Brisbane racing calendar, so out with Gayndah and in with Brisbane.

There we have it. Two Derbies, same name, two months apart, two racetracks 230 miles apart and one winner: Grafton.

Our races, our rules.

Richard Bradfield

... trained his first Melbourne Cup winner at the age of 21

'Good day to you, gentlemen. Yes, I do know something about training racehorses, as I trained my first Melbourne Cup winner at the age of 21.'

This could well have been the opener of a very confident young racehorse trainer when meeting a client for the very first time. That young man was Richard Bradfield.

Born in 1863 in the Bendigo district of Victoria, Richard Bradfield began training around 1882; at the time of his retirement in 1940, he had numerous winners of some of Australia's major Handicap, Weight-for-Age and Cup races pass through his stable. So gifted was the young man, owners had no hesitation in placing even their expensive imported horses in his care. Bradfield had the ability to let a horse tell him when it was ready to put its best foot forward. Time, patience, and acclimatisation were key to his success.

During his illustrious career, Bradfield trained four Melbourne Cup winners: Patron (1894), The Victory (1902), Night Watch (1918) and Backwood (1924). This placed him equal third with John Tait, Walter Hickenbotham and Jim Scobie, behind the great Bart Cummings (twelve winners) and Etienne de Metre and Lee Freedman (five winners apiece).

The Caulfield Cup also provided Bradfield with rich pickings. He trained the 1918 winner King Offa and the 1919 winner Lucknow. However, it was in 1919 that the trainer wrote his name in the record books: he trained the first three place-getters of the 1919 Caulfield Cup:

- 1st: Lucknow (F. Bullock)
- 2nd: Night Watch (G. Harrison)
- 3rd: Chrome (W. Duncan)

Many trainers over the years have quinnelled the race, but none have trained first, second and third.

It wasn't until 2005 that this training feat occurred again in a Group 1 race. Sydney trainer Guy Walter trained Patezza, Court's in Session and Danni Martine to finish 1-2-3 in the Doncaster Handicap.

As stated before, Bradfield had great success with imported horses. This included Melbourne Cup winner Backwood and Caulfield Cup winners King Offa and Lucknow.

Champion jockey Harold Badger, who is remembered as the rider of the mighty Ajax, was one of many great riders to have served his apprenticeship under the master trainer.

Richard Bradfield passed away in 1944, aged 81. He was inducted into Racing's Hall of Fame in 2005.

There was another thing that Bradfield could be extremely proud of. In his 58 years of training racehorses, Mr Richard Bradfield was never once called into the stewards room. At no time during his training career did he ever have to 'please explain'.

1-2-3 ... beat that!

What are the odds of this happening?

... the tale of the till

22 October 2011: the 2040-metre Group 3 $200,000 Mitchelton Wine Vase Stakes for three-year-olds, Moonee Valley, Victoria.

Six horses faced the starter in this race, with the short-priced favourite Manawanui scaring away a lot of opposition. Here are the horses in race book order, with race starts, wins and placings, and prize money won.

1	Manawanui	7 – 5-1-1	$1,120,080
2	Collar	4 – 2-0-1	$116,793
3	Scelto	9 – 1-0-3	$32,425
4	I Feel Good	4 – 0-1-0	$19,525
5	Power Broker	2 – 1-0-0	$12,850
6	Danichi	3 – 0-0-0	$500

Saddlecloth numbers were allotted in order of winning prize money, and that is how these horses finished in the race: *1-2-3-4-5-6*. Rehearsed? Don't think so. It looks like each horse was definitely a class above the other.

The odds of this happening were 720/1. Maybe the bookies should have framed a market on that happening.

Confused? Well, so am I!

... when the old ways were not so simple

Many punters who lined up to get paid by the bookies after Tim Whiffler's win in the 1867 Melbourne Cup were told, 'Sorry, you were on the wrong Tim Whiffler.'

Well, it didn't take long for fights to break out over the confusion. Yes, there had been two Tim Whifflers in the race: 'Sydney Tim' and

'Melbourne Tim'. 'Sydney Tim' was the winner at 5/2, and 'Melbourne Tim' was the 50/1 long shot back in fifth place.

Amongst the big crowd, many of the unscrupulous punters swore that they were on 'Sydney Tim', even though their betting ticket said 'Melbourne Tim'. They claimed that they did not check their ticket after placing the bet, but had definitely wanted their wager to be on 'Sydney Tim'. How convenient.

Eventually the pandemonium settled down, and it was back to what the crowd did best – the business of drinking and punting.

After that episode at the Melbourne Cup meeting, the name Tim Whiffler on any race program may have left bookies thinking of not laying the horse at all.

Now for some further confusion, for the followers of racehorse breeding. The 'Melbourne' Tim Whiffler went on to sire a pretty handy horse in Perth, who went by the name of none other than Tim Whiffler. Not to be outdone, the 'Sydney' Tim Whiffler went on to sire the 1881 New Zealand Great Northern Derby winner by the name of, yes, Tim Whiffler.

This all probably went back to the English import that had sired Briseis, the 1876 Melbourne Cup winner. His name: Tim Whiffler.

Could you imagine it today!

Tough as teak!

... a great country veteran

Puramaka was every owner's, trainer's and jockey's delight. During his career, this tough old Makarpura gelding, trained by Ken Lafferty, won eight country Cups:

- Hamilton Cup, 2000 metres (1977, 1978, 1979, 1980)
- Warrnambool Cup, 2200 metres (1978, 1979)
- Geelong Cup, 2400 metres (1978)
- Bendigo Cup, 2200 metres (1978)

Puramaka was also very competitive on metropolitan racecourses. Amongst his wins was the 1979 Listed Bagot Handicap over 2500 metres at Flemington, defeating Gunderman.

One tough old bugger.

Lightning strikes three times
... *it was all about the finish of the race*

It is said that lightning can strike three times, and in this case never a truer word was spoken.

In *Off the Track*, we wrote that in December 2010 nine horses faced the starter and when the race had finished, number 1, Miss Reed, was the winner and they had run in race book order: *1-2-3-4-5-6-7-8-9*. The odds of that happening were 362,880/1.

In October 2011, at Moonee Valley, Manawanui led the field of six home, and they also finished in race book order: *1-2-3-4-5-6*.

Last, but not least, on 9 February 2014, the Gold Coast got into the act. Here are the horses that finished in race book order in race 4.

- 1st: No. 1 Chamandi
- 2nd: No. 2 River Spirit
- 3rd: No. 3 Albert's Choice
- 4th: No. 4 Gundy Gal
- 5th: No. 5 Platinum Lion
- 6th: No. 6 Mighty Sui
- 7th: No. 7 Etrain

That finish represented odds of 5040/1. Now, what are the odds of this happening three times in the next four years? Out with the calculator!

Poseidon and Rising Fast
... *who was the best?*

It is inevitable for people to compare horses from different eras, and this leads to the question, 'Who was the better of the two?'

In this case, was it Rising Fast, because he carried more weight in his two Caulfield Cups and three Melbourne Cups, competing as a five-, six- and seven-year-old? Or was it Poseidon, because he was only a three- and four-year-old when competing in his Caulfield and Melbourne Cups?

Poseidon and Rising Fast are the only two horses in history to win one Melbourne Cup and two Caulfield Cups. Following is a comparison of the two champions in those two great Cups. Their weights have been converted to metric.

Poseidon		Rising Fast	
1906	1st Caulfield Cup **47.5 kg**	1954	1st Caulfield Cup **55.5 kg**
1906	1st Melbourne Cup **47 kg**	1954	1st Melbourne Cup **59.5 kg**
1907	1st Caulfield Cup **58.5 kg**	1955	1st Caulfield Cup **61.5 kg**
1907	8th Melbourne Cup **65 kg**	1955	2nd Melbourne Cup **63.5 kg**
		1956	5th Melbourne Cup **64.5 kg**

As you can see, weight does stop a train. In the words of legendary trainer Bart Cummings, 'Champions should never be compared, just appreciated'.

Ah, heavy weights: a great leveller!

Can you spell that, please?

... or try to?

One of the longest named racehorses in the world was the Victorian galloper of 1889: Reverend Zacariah Stockdollinger.

However, he was clearly outdone by the Hungarian jockey who won the 6000 metre 1883 Grand Steeple-Chase de Paris on Too Good. His name? Georg Maria Gobert Graf Erdody von Monyborokerek und Monszito.

Thank God he answered to the name of Count Georg Mony.

Home in the dark!

... but at least we kept the money

The 1894 Victoria Derby provided one of the longest protest hearings on record. The winner was Haymaker, defeating Malachite by a length and a half with a further length to Bonnie Scotland in third place. On returning to scale, the connections of both Malachite and Bonnie Scotland fired in a protest.

However, the protest was so complex, the hearing was adjourned until after the last race, so as to let the rest of the races proceed in a timely manner.

After the last race, the stewards returned to interview 40 (yes, 40!) witnesses. After quite an exhausting process, both protests were dismissed and the placing stood at Haymaker first, Malachite second, Bonnie Scotland third.

What was so remarkable about that protest hearing was that it ended at 8 pm that evening. Finally the bookies could pay out.

Now, back to the cricket!
... and Warnie bowls Flintoff once again

The war was on in the Boxing Day Ashes Test at the MCG in December 2006, with Australia facing their old foe, England.

Australia made 419 in its first innings, and England only 159. Sent back in to bat by the Aussies, the Poms could only manage 161, losing by an innings and 99 runs. Shane Warne took a bag of seven wickets.

However, one must feel for the English captain, Andrew Flintoff. Back in the dressing rooms, he had just got word that back in England, the horse he co-owned and named after himself, Flintoff, had just run out of a place in a race at Haydock.

I'm sure Andrew Flintoff felt a lot sicker when he found out that later the same day at the same race meeting, a horse by the name of Warne's Way won at 9/2.

Looks like Warnie got him again!

Victoria Derby
... from an abandoned race to a place in history!

There is no doubt that the prestigious Victoria Derby held during the Spring Carnival in Melbourne each year is one of the highlights of the racing calendar. The purists regard the Derby as one of the great races of the year, a Group 1 race that carries with it great prestige and more than $1.5 million in prize money. But how did it start?

• When it was originally planned to run the first Derby in 1854, it was called the Turf Club Derby. A couple of days before the running of the race, the Derby on the race card was abandoned. Why? Because they had received just the one nomination so they had no choice but to cancel and try to promote it and gain more interest in the race for 1855. It was to be held on the first Wednesday in November and would be over 12 furlongs (2400 metres).

- The Turf Club staged the first running of the Derby in 1855. The Jockey Club, later renamed as the Victorian Racing Club, continued on the tradition.
- The first three winners of the Derby were all fillies: Rose Of May, Flying Doe and Tricolor. The last filly to win was Frances Tressady, in 1923.
- Geldings were barred from racing in the Derby between 1931 and 1956.
- Set weights for colts and fillies have changed over the years. In the first running, in 1855, the colts, geldings and fillies carried the same weight of 8 stone 5 lb (53 kg). For the running in the second year, in 1856, the colts and geldings remained at that weight, and the fillies dropped to 8 stone 3 lb (52 kg). This was changed the following year, in 1857, when the colts and geldings were asked to carry 8 stone 7 lb (54 kg), and the fillies 8 stone 4 lb (52.5 kg). Weights were increased again, in 1866, to 8 stone 10 lb (55.5 kg) for the colts and geldings and 8 stone 5 lb (53 kg) for the fillies. These are the weights they continue to be allotted today. Finally they got there!
- There have been three maiden winners in the history of the Victoria Derby. Martini-Henry won in 1888, Fire Oak in 1990 and Redding in 1992.
- Both the 1868 and 1869 Derbies were run on New Year's Day.
- Fireworks is the only horse to win the Derby twice. He first won it in November 1867, and his second win was on 1 January 1868 after a reschedule of the race date for that calendar year. He was favourite on each occasion.
- The distance of the race was increased to 2500 metres in 1973.
- The first female trainer to win the Victoria Derby was Gai Waterhouse, in 1995, with Nothin' Leica Dane.
- The first female jockey to win the Victoria Derby was Clare Lindop, in 2008, on the 50/1 outsider Rebel Raider.

- The first female owner of the Victoria Derby winner was Miss M. Gordon, in 1908, with Alawa.

Well, hope we have answered a few questions.

A world-first in Australia
... possibly!

Did you know that Patrick Payne and Michelle Payne are possibly the only brother and sister jockeys in the world to have ridden 22 Group 1 winners between them? Patrick has won eighteen Group 1 races, and up until April 2014, Michelle had won four Group 1 races.

Both siblings have won the listed 2400-metre Bendigo Cup. Patrick won it in 1994 on Ice Doctor and Michelle greeted the judge on Banana Man in 2008.

About our Cups!
... some facts behind their rich history

Here are some interesting little snippets about the Cups in each state and territory of Australia, including when they were first run and the first winner.

- Melbourne Cup – 1861, Archer
- Adelaide Cup – 1864, Falcon
- Sydney Cup – 1866, Yattendon
- Brisbane Cup – 1866, Forester
- Perth Cup – 1887, First Prince
- Hobart Cup – 1875, Ella
- Canberra Cup – 1929, Woodrow
- Darwin Cup – 1956, Satan's Son

The Adelaide Cup, first run in 1864, was not held in 1886–88, 1870–71 and 1942–43.

The Canberra Cup, first held in 1929, was not run between 1930 and 1935 due to the Great Depression. It was also not run between 1940 and 1945 due to World War ll, and it was also not run in 1947.

The strangest of all runnings of a Cup was the running of the 1885

Adelaide Cup, won by Lord Wilton. Believe it or not, it was run at Flemington Racecourse in Victoria.

Three greats
... they made us cheer year after year

Each capital city is proud of the achievements of all their Cup winners, but these three Cup winners have the edge over the others in their respective states.

- Makybe Diva, arguably one of Australia's greatest stayers of all time, won an incredible three Melbourne Cups, in 2003, 2004 and 2005.
- Lord Reims, the pride of South Australia, won three Adelaide Cups, in 1987, 1988 and 1989.
- Wood did something that in all probability will never happen again in any capital city. He won four Darwin Cups, in 1959, 1960, 1961 and 1962.

We know that Lord Reims and Wood cannot in any way compare with the mighty mare Makybe Diva, but they certainly did their capital cities proud.

puC enruobleM ehT
... where saying it backwards made sense

It makes perfectly good sense that our heading is The Melbourne Cup spelt backwards. The winner of the 1978 Melbourne Cup had something in common with the heading of our story. The winner was Arwon, and when you spell his name backwards, it spells out the town from where he came – Nowra.

The town of Nowra can also be linked to another Melbourne Cup great. It was the hometown of the very first Melbourne Cup winner, Archer.

From rocking horses to lightweight riders
... an amazing array of facts from England

The horse from which the craftsmen modelled the original rocking horse was the champion nicknamed 'The Spotted Wonder', or as we know him, The Tetrarch. He was undefeated as a two-year-old but continued to injure himself, and so was retired to the breeding barn as a two-year-old in 1913.

How did he keep injuring himself? They say that he was possibly the fastest horse of all time, and he just couldn't control the pace of his legs. His hind hoofs continually cut the fetlocks and the back of the shins of his front legs because he was just too quick for his own good.

The Grand National Steeplechase at Aintree, Liverpool, England, in 1951 was remembered for a number of reasons. The field was not ready when the starter let them go, leaving many riders at a distinct disadvantage. The race was marred by many falls and at the end only three horses stayed upright with riders. The eventual winner was a mare by the name of Nickel Coin, at 40/1. Apparently her diet consisted of 'duck eggs and stout', and she is the last mare ever to have won the great race up to and including 2013.

The 1929 Grand National at Aintree also takes pride of place in a list of trivia and facts worth noting. The race that year had an unprecedented 66 starters, a number that has never been allowed to start again for safety reasons. Of course, having 66 starters, there would have to be a good story about the winner – it certainly is a good story, because the winner was Gregalach and his price was 100/1.

One of the key factors today when judging a horse on his chances is the weight of the rider. Back in 1844 in England, the Chester Cup was run and won. While there was nothing remarkable about a horse and jockey winning, the winning horse, Red Deer, did have a bit of a 'postage stamp' on his back. His rider, Kitchner, weighed a whopping 49 lb (just over 22 kg). Thank goodness there wasn't a stiff breeze on the course that day, otherwise he could have been blown away.

Something in common
... *a reversal of fortunes!*

In 1956, Malkuri won the listed Ipswich Cup, and in 1965, Iruklam ran second in the Group 2 Tattersall's Cup. These placings were considered to be the pinnacle of their respective racing careers.

What did they have in common? It was a good case of reversals. Reverse Malkuri, and you get Iruklam. Reverse '56 and it becomes '65.

Very interesting, but a little scary!

Blame Squizzy Taylor
... *may as well!*

The day of the Coongy Handicap at Caulfield in 1922 was a day that notorious Melbourne gangster Squizzy Taylor would never forget. Former police detective, now racecourse supervisor, Mr EJ Napthine, had Taylor escorted into his office, where Napthine told him that as 'an undesirable' he was to be evicted from the Caulfield Racecourse.

Taylor protested and asked to see the VATC Racing Committee, but no, that request fell on deaf ears. With his tail between his legs, Taylor made off to his favourite watering hole and started plotting his revenge, vowing to get even. 'Someone's going to pay for this – I'm Squizzy Taylor, you can't do this to me!'

Around 4am on Caulfield Cup Day, it was later alleged that Taylor and some of his cohorts doused the old wooden grandstand with petrol and set it afire. A train driver at the nearby Caulfield Station alerted the fire brigade, but it was too late and the grandstand burnt to the ground.

Despite numerous allegations, no charges were ever made against Taylor. Maybe Squizzy had done the VATC a favour. One month prior, the Committee had decided that immediately after Caulfield Cup Day, the old wooden grandstand would be demolished to make way for a new grandstand to hold 50,000-plus patrons.

One wonders if maybe on Coongy Handicap day, Mr EJ Napthine might have had a word in Squizzy Taylor's ear and maybe a few pounds changed hands. Who knows?

Now, how do you start a flood?

The dream was right

... but the race was wrong!

In 1870, hotelier Walter Craig had a dream that his horse, Nimblefoot, won the Melbourne Cup, with the winning jockey wearing black armbands.

Well, Nimblefoot did win the Cup, but what was the reason for the jockey wearing black armbands? Unfortunately Craig took ill some days after he had that dream, and he passed away just before the Cup was run.

Seventy-six years later in May 1946, Flemington stablehand Charlie Norman had a dream that a horse with the unusual name of Spam hit the front halfway down the straight and went on to win the Melbourne Cup. Norman put the dream down to a heavy night on the grog with some of his mates. He thought nothing more of it until nominations were published for both the Caulfield and Melbourne Cups.

Lo and behold, there amongst the Melbourne Cup nominations, with a weight of 8 stone 4 lb (52.5 kg), was an Irish entry by the name of Spam, who was headed our way to run in the Cup.

The horse ran some promising races in the lead-ups to the Cup. With that, Charlie Norman and some of his mates decided to have a 'good go' at Spam, the horse with the funny name. Dreams can't be wrong – or can they?

What Norman and his mates did not do was check the horse's form back in the UK. All his wins and placings were on wet tracks, with the highlight being his 1945 Irish St Leger win on a bog track. 'No, forget that, she'll be right, mate.' The mighty plunge went on.

It was a dry spring that year in Melbourne, and on the first Tuesday in November, it was extremely hot, nudging 35 degrees, and the track was very hard. Unfortunately, Spam could not go a yard, but under the guidance of Billy Cook, he came in a creditable eighth behind Russia. Charlie and his punting mates went home stony broke. Bloody stupid dream.

The following week, the rains came. Ten days after his Melbourne Cup run and on a very soft track, Spam won a lowly Country Cup at the good odds of 10/1.

Read – your – form – guide – carefully!

Brad's been everywhere, man
... is it a world-first for Queensland?

Nowadays it is quite common for jockeys to ride at two different venues on the same day. But spare a thought for this jockey. On Saturday 18 January 2014, Brad Stewart attempted a world-first. Not only did he ride at three different venues on the same day, but he did the seemingly impossible: he rode a winner at each racecourse.

His first ride was at the Gold Coast, Queensland: at 2.05pm, he piloted home Lady De Retz at $3.60. After a quick shower, it was in the car for the 90-km trip to Brisbane to ride Motorized in the last race at Brisbane, scheduled for 5 pm. It won at $35.10. No time for a shower this time, and he left the course at 5.15 pm for the 90-minute, 130-km trip up the range to Toowoomba for the twilight meeting.

Stewart arrived on course just as they were weighing out for race 5. It was a quick change to his riding silks and around to the barrier on Ongoing Venture. The horse had an easy win and started at $2.20.

Why did he try the impossible and go to Toowoomba for that one ride? 'Well, nobody has been silly enough to ride at three different venues on the same day, but I had won on Ongoing Venture at his last start and was keen to ride him again.'

For his three winners on the day, Stewart picked up $510 in riding fees, and $2252.50 for his 5 per cent of the winning prize money.

One can bet odds-on that Brad Stewart slept very well that night.

Have saddle. Will travel.

Ten years waiting for his next win
... seemed like a lifetime!

Spare a thought for veteran jockey Lou Francis, who had been riding since 1930. Many jockeys go through a drought at some stage, where they seem to just never land a winner and the weeks and sometimes months go by.

At Caulfield Racecourse, in 1957, Lou Francis was on the outsider

Buzzie, in the Inkerman Handicap, the main race of the day. One wonders what was going through the head of poor old Lou while the jockeys were behind the barrier stalls waiting for the starter to call the horses into line. You see, the veteran jockey's last winner was ten years before, at Mentone in 1947, when he rode Lord Cavil to victory.

Surely, after all those years the drought would be broken.

On that day the racing gods must have been smiling on Lou Francis, because after a titanic struggle all the way down the straight with Beaupa and the favourite Pushover, Buzzie prevailed by a short half-head.

But there was no joy yet for the veteran jockey, because the riders of the other two horses fired in a protest for interference in the last half furlong (110 metres).

After quite a lengthy delay in the stewards room ... both protests dismissed! Lou Francis was finally a winner again. Surely there would not be another ten-year wait!

Yes, a long time between drinks for Lou Francis!

A winner to the very end
... not bad for a great Australian

Francis Joseph Hardy, better known to us as Frank Hardy, was a left-wing journalist and novelist best known for his controversial novel *Power Without Glory*. Another of his novels, *The Four-Legged Lottery*, was centred on a punter's battle with racing's insurmountable odds.

Born on 21 March 1917, Hardy was a racing devotee and punter. He passed away on 28 January 1994, and he died as many a true punter would think – honourably. He was found at his desk with a form guide in his hand.

Weight's right!

Mick O'Brien and Carbine
... where asthma took its toll on a perfect record

By 1889, the mighty Carbine already had a fearsome reputation in New Zealand and in Melbourne. The sceptics said that he couldn't continue on winning in the AJC Autumn Carnival against the Sydney champ at Randwick.

On Monday 22 April, Carbine lined up against their champion, Abercorn, in the Autumn Stakes, run over 1½ miles (2400 metres). It was a torrid affair, with Carbine failing by a neck to beat Abercorn. Carbine's jockey, Mick O'Brien, was very distressed when coming back into the yard, because he had suffered a severe asthma attack during the race and could not ride Carbine out as he was too busy gasping for breath.

They then had something to prove, and prove it they did.

- Wednesday 24 April: Carbine wins the Sydney Cup over 2 miles (3200 metres).
- Thursday 25 April: Carbine wins the All Aged Stakes over a mile (1600 metres), and the same day he wins the Cumberland Stakes over 2 miles (3200 metres).
- Saturday 26 April: Carbine wins the AJC Plate over 3 miles (4800 metres).

Four wins over six days.

And what did he do in 1890? He won all four races again, setting a record that will never been beaten. Over the six days each year, he ran a distance of 8 miles (12.8 km).

Unfortunately Mick O'Brien died a few years later from complications of asthma.

Carbine: what a champion.

Two + Two =
... speed and toughness

These four brilliant young racehorses – two fillies and two colts – did something very special, and their record may stand for a number of years. They all had the sheer speed to win the Golden Slipper in their two-year-old year, and the resolute toughness to win the Derby or the Oaks as a three-year-old.

- Skyline: Golden Slipper / AJC Derby (1958)
- Sky High: Golden Slipper / VRC Derby (1960)
- Bounding Away: Golden Slipper / AJC Oaks (1986–87)

- Miss Finland: Golden Slipper / VRC Oaks (2006)

Skyline and Sky High were both by Star Kingdom out of Flight's Daughter. The record of full brothers winning that same double in the same year can never be broken, as the AJC Derby was moved to the autumn in 1977. Miss Finland also won her two races in the same calendar year.

Between these four champion gallopers, they won a total of 27 now Group 1 races, with Sky High winning an incredible fourteen.

Who will be next?

Prize money!
... how far we have come over the years

Sometimes over a beer or three, the conversation comes around to what the dollar was worth back all those years ago and what it could buy now. We suppose it is all relevant in the scale of things, but just consider the hill that was climbed 40 years ago by a couple of very famous and much loved Australian trainers.

On 17 June 1974, TJ Smith passed the $1 million mark in stakes money for the year; at that stage he was only the second trainer to do it. Bart Cummings beat Tommy by about three hours, passing the $1 million mark earlier in the day. According to Bart, 'TJ never forgave me for it.'

We have seen how prize money has accelerated over the years since 1974, but this was a major feat by the two trainers then, considering they were only six weeks away from the end of the racing season.

The good old days!

The very last word
... that explains it all

At the end of a not-so-good day on the punt, the same thoughts probably go through a lot of punters' minds ... 'Why didn't I back that? ... I should have done this ...' etc.

Well, maybe this horse, by Refuse To Bend, says it all: Shoulda Borta Boat.

THANK YOU

Barry and I acknowledge the wonderful support of our family and friends throughout our life-changing journey. Our wives, Beth and Sandra, have been a great source of encouragement; without them, our success and our selfish application to something we love would not have been possible.

We must thank Julia Taylor and the professional and patient team at The Five Mile Press, who took a chance on our compilations and who again have extended a hand to support our journey in every way possible with the publication of the third book in the series, *From the Track*.

Our keen interests in racing history and in stories of great triumph and tragedy have left their mark on Barry and me in many ways, and the stories in this book are the product of those interests and of widespread reading and research. The content of *From the Track* was researched from the innumerable pages of books we have read, the many magazines we have leafed through and the countless number of websites and web resources that seem always to be waiting for us when we turned on our computers.

We must acknowledge the *Miller's Guide*, the *Australian Stud Book*, the 1981 *Ampol Sporting Book* and *Sports Novel*, which was one of Australia's original racing magazines. Other sources of reference and research are too numerous to mention.

Many racing facts are simply part of the public record of our global racing industry, and other stories differed in their timing, results or other facts depending on the reference we read. We have always tried to provide our reader as true a story as we could, using the references available to us. All of the stories in *From the Track* are true and told in our words, and they have not been directly extracted from any reference source.

Lastly, we are deeply indebted to those many wonderful animals and colourful racing identities for making our journey possible.

Cheers, and best wishes,

Alan and Barry Wood

ONE PARTING COMMENT

We can't end this journey without mention of our good mate Brian Doyle. He has created more than 20 cartoons for our three books and has no peer when putting pencil to sketchpad – he is definitely one of Australia's best and one of nature's gentlemen. Brian has always said, 'People like to look at pictures', and his cartoons often give a lighter view of the serious side of racing. Doyley, from the 'Ideas Man' and the 'Architect' – thanks, mate!

Baz and Al

Well, that's it, Baz.
Yeah, Al, what a journey!
Three books, Baz, what now?
Mate, how about a couple of 'malt sandwiches'?